Social Engineering and Human Hacking

Erfan Koza · Asiye Öztürk · Michael Willer

Social Engineering and Human Hacking

Strategies for the Prevention and
Defense Against Manipulation
Techniques in IT

 Springer

Erfan Koza
Hochschule Niederrhein
Krefeld, Nordrhein-Westfalen, Germany

Asiye Öztürk
Köln, Germany

Michael Willer
Bad Wildungen, Hessen, Germany

ISBN 978-3-662-72083-7   ISBN 978-3-662-72084-4   (eBook)
https://doi.org/10.1007/978-3-662-72084-4

Translation from the German language edition: "Social Engineering und Human Hacking" by Erfan Koza et al., © Der/die Herausgeber bzw. der/die Autor(en), exklusiv lizenziert an Springer-Verlag GmbH, DE, ein Teil von Springer Nature 2024. Published by Springer Berlin Heidelberg. All Rights Reserved.

This book is a translation of the original German edition "Social Engineering und Human Hacking" by Erfan Koza et al., published by Springer-Verlag GmbH, DE in 2024. The translation was done with the help of an artificial intelligence machine translation tool. A subsequent human revision was done primarily in terms of content, so that the book will read stylistically differently from a conventional translation. Springer Nature works continuously to further the development of tools for the production of books and on the related technologies to support the authors.

This Springer imprint is published by the registered company Springer-Verlag GmbH, DE, part of Springer Nature.
The registered company address is: Heidelberger Platz 3, 14197 Berlin, Germany

If disposing of this product, please recycle the paper.

Ethics of the Book

"The ethical cannot grow on selfish ground"(Albert Schweitzer).

Before we delve into the depths of the topic of social engineering, we would like to make the following clear: Our goal is not to turn you into masters of Human Hacking. This book is not intended for that purpose. Rather, this book is dedicated to the scientific and practice-oriented presentation of knowledge and techniques in the fields of social engineering, human hacking, physical penetration testing, and manipulation techniques in the context of information security.

Our goal is to support you in optimizing the holistic and complementary protection of socio-technical systems—comprising human-machine interaction—through the use of analytical and methodological investigation techniques based on the principle of causality and by embedding integrative preventive, corrective, reactive, and detective measures. You will be enabled to identify, classify, and sustainably remediate potential human and physical vulnerabilities at an early stage. The ultimate objective is to activate the human firewall in order to enhance the resilience of users and systems in line with holistic information security in the digitalized world.

Within the context of this book, the term "protection" thus encompasses two essential dimensions.

First, this involves the analytical understanding and the tactical and operational determination as well as the application of measures to secure organizations and IT systems, particularly in the field of human-centered information security. The primary objective is to ensure the confidentiality, integrity, availability, and authenticity—the so-called VIVA principle—of data and information, as well as the associated organizational, technical, and human resources. This maxim encompasses the ability to identify and assess potential human-centered threats and vulnerabilities, and to implement appropriate protective and defensive measures to minimize or eliminate them.

Secondly, "protection" refers to the development of individual skills and awareness to safeguard oneself against potential human-centered threats and attacks. We refer to this as "self-protection."

This aspect of self-protection encompasses the understanding of intrinsic and extrinsic behavior, psychological mechanisms, and the impact of targeted manipulation techniques that may be employed by attackers. The goal is to become aware of ongoing dangers and to develop the ability to protect not only oneself but also others from these dangers, whether in a digital or physical context.

To achieve this, it is essential to understand how cybercriminals, or more generally, adversaries, think, plan, and act. Only then will you be able to identify threat and behavioral patterns early on in terms of situational awareness (situational awareness)[1] and to draw on learned preventive, corrective, reactive, and detective tactics and tools accordingly.

As Sun Tzu once stated in "The Art of War" [1]:

> "If you know the enemy and know yourself, you need not fear the outcome of a hundred battles. If you know yourself but not the enemy, for every victory gained you will also suffer a defeat. If you know neither the enemy nor yourself, you will succumb in every battle."

Building on this tactical wisdom, this book is not only about learning theoretical strategies, techniques, and tools used by social engineers in the real world to cause harm. It also offers you the opportunity to explore yourself more deeply, recognize your own weaknesses, and develop a deeper understanding of the personality traits of others. This enhanced self-awareness and knowledge of human behavior are crucial elements for protecting yourself against potential and constantly evolving attacks and threats.

We therefore place particular emphasis on the paramount importance of our commitment to use these acquired skills exclusively for the benefit and protection of individuals and systems, and to consistently uphold ethical principles. We encourage you to apply your acquired knowledge in a positive and constructive manner as an "ethical hacker." Ethical hacking refers to the legitimate and responsible use of hacking techniques and skills to identify security vulnerabilities in socio-technical systems and to eliminate them before they can be exploited.

> *The sustainable protection of people and systems remains our commitment to a safer and more responsible digital world.*

In contrast to malicious hackers who act with criminal intent, as an "Ethical Human Hacker" you strive to identify vulnerabilities and strengthen security in order to prevent potential harm. It is your responsibility to apply the knowledge you acquire responsibly and to always uphold your ethical principles.

Please note that the information in this book is based on the state of the art and current knowledge up to the time of publication. However, given the constantly

---

[1]Situational awareness describes an individual's conscious perception of their environment and the associated events and threats. It is a critical skill in the military, emergency situations, aviation, and everyday life. Decisions, reactions, or rapid adaptations to changing situations are made based on this perception.

evolving nature of the subject, changes may occur. Be sure to update your knowledge regularly to keep up with the latest developments and best practices.

We wish you much success and ethical conduct in your efforts to strengthen information security and to meet the challenges of the digital age. Now that you have your ethical compass firmly in hand, we can begin...

References

1. Sun Tzu, The Art of War, Nikol, 2008.

Preface

We welcome you to a captivating journey of discovery into the world of "Social Engineering and Human Hacking." In an era where human interactions and digital communication blend seamlessly, it becomes clear that understanding the interplay between human and technical components has a decisive impact on our information security.

Thus, in the fascinating realm of information security, the mantra resonates:

'Information security can exist without people, but it remains incomplete and fragile.'

This statement is more than an insight—it is the key to a profound understanding. Here, the digital world and human relevance intersect, revealing a truth that transforms our perspective on security. For without human involvement and understanding, every protective measure remains a fragile fragment in the vast landscape of information security.

This book is therefore not only a comprehensive treatise on the techniques of social engineering, but also invites you to use this knowledge as universal tools and techniques for improved interpersonal communication. It offers a behind-the-scenes look that not only demonstrates how security systems can be outwitted, but also how these techniques can be employed to gain a deeper understanding for defending against human-centered attacks.

The authors of this book offer a new perspective, drawing from both academic research and practical fields such as human intelligence with military expertise. This combination of scholarly knowledge and hands-on experience gives the work a multifaceted and deeply practice-oriented dimension.

We not only share our insights into the methods of Social Engineering, but also discuss how the same principles can be applied positively. Discover how the very psychological mechanisms exploited in hacker attacks can also be used to build sustainable defenses, protect against such attacks, foster trust, promote teamwork, and enable effective communication. We are therefore convinced that knowledge can have a dual impact. By understanding the tactics of social engineering, you will not only be better protected against potential threats, but you can also actively contribute to improving the quality of interpersonal relationships.

This book is intended not only to raise your awareness of the pitfalls of social engineering and human hacking, but also to equip you with the tools to interact with others more consciously, openly, and securely. The techniques discussed in this book are meant not only to serve as defensive measures, but also to inspire you to optimize your own communication and strengthen your connections.

We attempt to examine the specific attack techniques in terms of the causal chain and the cause-and-effect principle using various explanatory approaches from the fields of communication and linguistics, psychology and economics, behavioral psychology, philosophy, anthropology, neurology, and security engineering. This broad perspective provides a comprehensive foundation for understanding the multifaceted aspects of social engineering.

This book is not a guide to infiltrating external networks. We believe that only those who understand the mindset of hackers can effectively protect themselves and respond appropriately in the event of an attack.

Enjoy discovering the complexity of "Social Engineering and Human Hacking." May this book not only deepen your understanding of digital security, but also enrich your interpersonal relationships.

Krefeld, Germany   Erfan Koza
Köln, Germany   Asiye Öztürk
Bad Wildungen, Germany   Michael Willer

Contents

List of Abbreviations

BaFin	Para Financial Supervisory Authority
BKA	Police Office
BSI	Para Office for Information Security
COA	Course of Action
DISC	Dominance, Influence, Steadiness, and Conscientiousness. In English: (D)ominance, (I)nfluence, (S)teadiness, and (C)onscientiousness
DKIM	DomainKeys Identified Mail
DLP	Data Loss Prevention
DMARC	Domain-based Message Authentication, Reporting, and Conformance
DNS	Domain Name System
EAC	Email Account Compromise
FBI	Para Bureau of Investigation
HUMINT	Human Intelligence
IAM	Identity Access Management
IBM	Integrated Behavior Model
IMINT	Imagery Intelligence
IT	Information Technology
KI	artificial intelligence
LLM	Large Language Model
MBTI	Myers-Briggs Type Indicator
MDM	Mobile Device Management
MFA	Multi-factor authentication
NLP	Natural Language Processing
OT	Operational Technology
OTP	One-Time Password
OODA	Observe, Orient, Decide, Act
OSINT	Open Source Intelligence
RBAC	Role-based Access Control
RFI	Request for Information
SOC	Security Operations Center
SPF	Sender Policy Framework
SCCM	System Center Configuration Manager

SOCMINT	Social Media Intelligence
SIGINT	Signal Intelligence
VISHING	Voice Phishing
VIVA	Availability, integrity, confidentiality, authenticity
VUKA	Volatility, uncertainty, complexity, ambiguity
WSUS	Windows Server Update Services

About the Authors

Erfan Koza successfully completed his doctorate in the field of information security, focusing on the mathematical modeling of decision trees and prioritization techniques in technical vulnerability management within industrial computer networks at the University of Wuppertal. As a holistic researcher, he also dedicates himself to research with an emphasis on "Human Factors in Information Security." His outstanding achievements as a doctoral candidate were recognized in 2022 with the BSI Best Student Award, particularly for his research on intrusion detection systems for stakeholders in the energy sector. Since 2019, Erfan Koza has been teaching at various German universities. His teaching activities include modules in the field of Cyber Security Management, with emphases such as "Human Aspects of Information Security" and "ISM Systems and Critical Infrastructure Protection (KRITIS)." In addition, Erfan Koza is actively engaged in combating child sexual abuse and cyber grooming, especially in his hometown of Mönchengladbach. In collaboration with various schools, he employs gamification and introduces his self-developed board game "Safe Schools." Through playful methods, digital natives are not only sensitized but also empowered to detect anomalies and proactively defend themselves. This initiative helps to raise awareness among students and the entire school community about the dangers in the digital space and to equip them with effective self-defense strategies.

Asiye Öztürk A researcher and lecturer, she is an expert in the field of preventive information security, cyber defense in operational technology, and the human factor. As a researcher and author, she contributed to the report "Preventive Information Security in the Water Sector," which was commissioned by the German Bundestag. Her outstanding research was also recognized at the 18th IT Security Congress with the BSI Best Student Award 2022. In addition to her academic work, Asiye Öztürk is actively involved in her hometown of Cologne in combating cybergrooming and child sexual abuse. Together with Dr.-Ing. Erfan Koza, she is committed to the "Safe Schools" initiative, working with children, parents, and teachers to promote greater safety in the digital space. She is also pursuing a doctorate at the Faculty of Mechanical Engineering and Safety Engineering at the University of Wuppertal, focusing on CERT-OT models. Since 2017, Asiye Öztürk has been advising critical infrastructures on integrated security issues and has served as lead auditor in numerous security projects. Her work spans various sectors, including energy and water utilities, finance, healthcare, and information and communication technology.

Michael (Mike) Willer With over 15 years of service in military intelligence for the German Armed Forces, he has specialized in intelligence gathering through human sources (HUMINT—Human Intelligence). His extensive expertise became particularly evident during various overseas deployments, especially through close cooperation with German and international military special forces. In addition to intelligence gathering, Mike spent many years as an instructor for military interrogation and interview techniques, where he was able to continually deepen his knowledge of human behavioral psychology. Alongside his primary role in military intelligence, he also trained members of NATO military special forces in behavior and survival during captivity. Since 2012, Mike has made a significant career change, moving into the private sector as an independent security consultant. Initially working as a security advisor in the private sector, he went on to found Human Risk Consulting GmbH in 2015. There, together with his team, he specializes in the human factor in security, focusing in particular on human hacking and social engineering. His primary goal is to advise and protect private individuals, companies, and public authorities against social engineering attacks stemming from industrial espionage, organized crime, and cybercrime. In addition, he is actively involved, together with friends and colleagues, in combating cyberbullying and cybergrooming. In collaboration with various schools, he employs gamification and introduces his self-developed board game "Safe Schools." Through playful methods, digital natives are not only sensitized but also empowered to recognize anomalies and proactively defend themselves. This initiative helps to raise awareness among students and the entire school community about the dangers of the digital world and to equip them with effective self-defense strategies.

Part I
White Chapter: Theory

Origins and Chronicles of Human Hacking

1

What if we told you that you are a human hacker? You would probably be surprised. The history of human hacking and social engineering is a rich tapestry, likely as old as humanity itself. Even in the earliest epochs of civilization, people not only forged tools from stone and fire, but also began to develop subtle techniques to persuade, manipulate, and influence others.

1.1 Socratic Questioning and the Trojan Horse

Our journey to the origins and chronicles of human hacking begins in ancient Greece, where we encounter the famous Greek philosopher Socrates. He was a master of "Socratic questioning," a method in which he skillfully posed questions to guide his students' thinking and led them to critically reconsider their own beliefs. Socrates was an early pioneer of social engineering, mastering the art of persuasion and inquiry long before computers and global connectivity became the focus of such discussions. Another early example of social engineering can also be found in Greek mythology, specifically in the epic *The Iliad* by Homer, written around 1184 BC. Here, the famous *Trojan Horse* (Fig. 1.1) appears as the Greek army besieges the city of Troy.

Odysseus, the main protagonist, realized that the walls of Troy were well fortified and that a direct military conquest was nearly impossible. So Odysseus chose the power of deception and ostensibly ended the battle. Together with his allies, he built a large wooden horse that looked like a "gift." Armed warriors hid inside. They left the Trojan Horse at the gates of the city and withdrew. The Trojans, believing they had won, brought the horse into the city as a trophy of victory. But that night, they lost the battle, for they had been deceived. The Trojan Horse was one of the earliest documented applications of social engineering in history—a

© The Author(s), under exclusive license to Springer-Verlag GmbH, DE, part of
Springer Nature 2025
E. Koza et al., *Social Engineering and Human Hacking*,
https://doi.org/10.1007/978-3-662-72084-4_1

Fig. 1.1 The Trojan Horse as a (primordial) symbol of deception

ruse based on manipulation and deception to gain unauthorized access to a specific critical target.

The power of deception, of pretending to be someone or something else and misleading others, is therefore older than we might have assumed. The Trojans were deceived and thus defeated. Their human emotions and feelings, such as conviction and their mental patterns[1] impaired their perception and attention [1].

This is an archetypal example showing how deception and manipulation have been successfully used for millennia. These parallels still contribute to our understanding of social engineering today.

Let us briefly examine these parallels more closely. The *power of deception* in the world of social engineering and related tactics is based on a deep understanding of human psychology and behavioral patterns. Deception works for various reasons. First, people are naturally inclined to trust others and to be benevolent. This primordial trust provides fertile ground for deception, as attackers exploit this trust to gain access to information or resources.

In deception, techniques such as flattery, sympathy, or pressure can be used to induce the victim to disclose information or perform actions they would not normally undertake.

---

[1] In "Patterns of Conflict" from 1986, U.S. Air Force officer John Boyd, America's greatest military theorist, explains that mental patterns are generally shaped by culture, inherited, and even genetically determined. Essentially, Boyd states that people approach new situations with "outdated" entrenched mental models, which may not be suitable for the new situation.

These psychological components are extremely powerful and can cause people to act against their better judgment. Deception therefore primarily aims to exploit vulnerabilities in the deeply rooted human psyche. These may include curiosity, fear, or the need for validation. These instinctive human emotions and feelings make it easier for attackers to deceive victims and prompt them to act rashly.

Another aspect in this context is the creation of surprise and distraction. Deception is often facilitated by generating distractions or surprises that confuse the victim and divert attention from the attacker's true intent.

In this way, our **perception** is deliberately manipulated and our focus is directed toward what the deceiver intends. This can result in the victim being unable to recognize the adversary's true malicious intentions and falling into the trap, leading to misguided actions and increased susceptibility to manipulation. The credibility and authority of the attacker also play a major role. Deception can make the attacker appear as a credible figure. This can happen, for example, by pretending to be an employee, a technician, or another trusted person. People are often inclined to follow instructions from apparent authorities without further questioning them. Finally, deception can trigger strong emotional reactions. These emotional responses can significantly impair the victim's ability to act rationally. This makes it easy for the attacker to steer the victim in the desired direction. The *power of deception* in the world of social engineering is therefore the result of skillful use of psychological knowledge and manipulation techniques in a highly complex and diverse environment.

In Sect. 4.2 of the White Chapter, we will examine the psychological aspects in greater detail and, in a deep dive, show how norms, roles, and values decisively influence our behavior.

> *But how can the power of deception be defined in the context of the Trojan Horse?*

Let us illustrate this with a self-experiment: The *power of deception,* as clearly demonstrated in the story of Troy, is based on several key elements.

First, **distraction** played a central role. As part of their ruse, the Greeks decided to create the impression that they were abandoning the siege and withdrawing. They left the enormous wooden Trojan Horse at the gates of Troy as an apparent peace offering or sacrifice to the gods. The Trojans, assuming that the Greeks were truly leaving, believed the horse to be a sign of peace. They opened the city gates and brought the horse inside—a classic case of a diversionary tactic. **Diversionary tactics** are strategic means designed to divert the perception, attention, and vigilance of a target from a critical point, while simultaneously pursuing another, often hidden, objective. In the story of the Trojan Horse, the impression was created that the siege was being lifted and the Greeks were retreating.

The Trojans also placed **trust** in the oversized gift due to the skillful presentation by the supposed authorities—the Greek besiegers. This trust was further reinforced by the religious dimension, as the gift was presented as an offering to the gods.

The combined effect of apparent authority and belief in divine intentions deepened the Trojans' conviction and led to their carelessness regarding the Greeks' true intentions. We call this tactical device the **concept of perceptual deception.** Our sensory organs function in accordance with their fixed and unchanging rules and show no deviations. However, our errors often arise from a misunderstanding of how these sensory impressions are interpreted [2].

The Trojans were deceived in their perception and failed to recognize that the gift was, in fact, a sophisticated ruse, beneath whose surface the hidden Greek army was concealed. This example vividly illustrates how attackers can exploit trust in supposed authorities and divine intentions through cunning deception and manipulation to achieve their goals.

From the perspective of perceptual psychology, so-called perceptual illusions are not necessarily more complex to explain than the perceptual process itself. The fascinating effect of perceptual illusions stems from our strong familiarity with everyday assumptions about the world and can prevent us from gaining deeper insights into the fundamental principles of perception. However, the effectiveness of perceptual illusions generally does not require elaborate preparations or sophisticated implementations. Often, simply creating a certain situation is sufficient, without the need for specific features, and yet perceptual illusions work flawlessly. This is mainly due to our selective perception.

Selective perception is a psychological phenomenon in which people tend to perceive and interpret information and stimuli in their environment in a *particular way* that aligns with their own **expectations, beliefs, and interests.** This means that people are inclined to pay selective attention to information that matches their existing ideas and attitudes, while giving less attention to, or even ignoring, information that contradicts them. Selective perception can manifest in various ways. Here are some examples:

Confirmation bias This is a common example of selective perception. People tend to accept information that confirms their existing beliefs and opinions, while rejecting or downplaying contradictory information.

Pattern recognition People often look for patterns and connections in information. This can lead them to see patterns even when none exist, or to interpret information in a way that fits an expected pattern.

Confirmation bias People actively seek out information that confirms their own prejudices and preferences. For example, they might choose news sources that support their political beliefs instead of consulting a variety of sources.

Neglect of counter-evidence People tend to neglect or minimize counter-evidence or information that contradicts their opinions.

Selective perception can thus lead people to perceive information and events in a distorted way and to remain within their own echo chambers. The example of the Trojan Horse provides an interesting illustration of selective perception. The Trojans were trapped in their patterns of thought and expectations, especially regarding gods and gifts. When the enormous wooden horse was offered to them, they may have ignored critical signs and information indicating a hidden threat. Their selective perception may have caused them to focus only on aspects that matched their existing beliefs and hopes. Other information pointing to the true nature of the horse may have been ignored or downplayed. This cognitive bias contributed to the people of Troy accepting the Trojan Horse as a gift, which ultimately led to their defeat.

The story of Troy thus transparently demonstrates how the **power of deception** targets human selective perception, weaknesses, and behavioral patterns. It shows how people can fall into a trap when they feel they are in a supposedly safe or familiar environment.

1.2   The Conspiracy of Catiline in Ancient Rome

Let us now continue our historical journey. Not far removed from the era of Socrates and Greek mythology, politicians and diplomats in ancient Rome also developed tactical skills in dealing with people. They recognized the power of mental and psychological influence as well as skillful manipulation. The stories of intrigue and tactical deception in the ancient Roman senates provide early examples of the application of related tactics for social engineering in political and societal contexts.

The *Conspiracy of Catiline* in 63 BC in the ancient Roman Republic is a notable example. Lucius Sergius Catilina skillfully used psychological manipulation, disinformation, and conspiracy theories to win followers and advance his political ambitions.

By promising land reforms, debt relief, and political change, he gained the support of the socially disadvantaged and discontented, while at the same time stirring up unrest to create a political crisis.

This episode illustrates how skillful social and political deception was used as a means to gain political power, and serves as a fascinating example of political intrigue in antiquity. Now that you have delved into our historical journey through the application of social engineering techniques, it is worth pausing for a moment to reflect on an important insight: The methods of manipulation techniques are **timeless.** Whether in ancient Roman politics, modern political discourse, or the digital age—the fundamental principles of influence and deception have endured for centuries. By understanding the history of the emergence and development of social engineering, we can better recognize how these methods operate in the present and future. The conspiracy of *Catiline* in 63 BC and the behavior of politicians before and during their presidency serve as outstanding examples that demonstrate the timeless nature of manipulation techniques and methods.

Both Catiline and politicians are historical figures who operated in different contexts and eras, yet share parallels in their political conduct and relationship to power. Both actors employed the art of persuasion in their political strategies to win the favor of the public and voters. Both Catiline and politicians promised change and reform in their speeches. These promises were deliberately used to address the needs and desires of their supporters.

Through skillful messaging and addressing social and political issues, they sought to win the support of their followers and strengthen their loyalty.

Another similarity was the creation of synthetic narratives, discontent, and unrest to generate a political crisis or uncertainty. Both actors presented these crises as evidence of the necessity of their political agenda.

Neither hesitated to resort to techniques of manipulation and propaganda based on empirically unsubstantiated claims, such as the ideas of the "Deep State" or the use of conspiracy theories like "QAnon." These techniques were intended to garner support and create the impression that only they held the solution to existing problems. In addition, both Catiline and politicians often concealed their true intentions and plans from the public. This indicated the use of deception and secrecy to pursue political goals.

The parallels between Catiline and politicians regarding the use of propaganda and manipulative speeches and techniques to influence the public are interesting examples of the historically timeless application of social engineering techniques in politics and society.

However, it is important to emphasize that the exact motivations and intentions of the actors are subject to scholarly debate and interpretation, as political communication is often complex, contradictory, and ambiguous.

1.3   From Court Jesters to the Printing Press

As we continue our historical journey, we now arrive in the Middle Ages, an era of knights, *courtiers and court jesters.* Even court jesters employed subtle manipulation techniques to influence the mood of their royal masters. Through humor and mockery, they steered political discussions in an entertaining and indirect manner. They demonstrated that social engineering does not always have to be serious and manipulative. It can also be used in a humorous and intelligent way to convey messages and reveal new facets of the power of deception.

Our journey now continues as we leave the early Middle Ages and arrive in the late Middle Ages of the 15th century. Here we encounter Johannes Gutenberg's groundbreaking invention: *the printing press,* which not only revolutionized the dissemination of information but also opened up new possibilities for the application of manipulation and deception techniques. Initially, this achievement led to a greater spread of knowledge and ideas, but it also enabled the distribution of religious and political literature to influence public opinion. As a result, there was a significant shift in the possibilities for information dissemination, communication, and manipulation. Earlier manipulation techniques relied heavily on direct communication and personal interactions. With the introduction of the printing press, it became possible for the first time to define manipulative content once and distribute it on a large scale, independent of the need for direct verbal communication between the parties involved. This led to widespread influence on public opinion.

The **quintessence** of this consideration is reflected in the context of the expediency of using a technology. The ability to use a technology for both positive and negative purposes is often referred to as **expediency** or **purpose-boundedness.** This means that technologies and innovations are designed to allow for a wide range of applications and interpretations.

Depending on the intentions and goals of their users, these technologies can be employed for both beneficial and harmful purposes. It is often the ethical and moral decisions of individuals or groups that determine how and for what purposes technologies are used. This quintessence highlights that new inventions and technologies must often be regarded as a double-edged sword. In our example, printing presses enabled the mass dissemination of knowledge and ideas, leading to broader education and improved information exchange.

On the other hand, they also paved the way for the spread of religious and political literature and propaganda to influence public opinion.

This universal insight persists to the present day. Modern technologies, the internet, and artificial intelligence (**AI**) offer considerable opportunities for information dissemination, but at the same time, they are vulnerable to disinformation and manipulation or can be misused as attack vectors. Above all, AI has opened up transformative possibilities in various fields [3].

In medicine, AI can be used to analyze medical images more quickly and accurately, assisting doctors in the diagnosis, treatment, and therapy of diseases. In education, AI can create personalized learning plans and help students learn individually. In the energy sector, AI can help optimize energy consumption and make renewable energy use more efficient. However, AI also carries the potential for misuse and manipulation. Deepfake technologies enable the creation of convincing fake videos or audio files that can be used for fraudulent or malicious purposes. In social media and on the internet, disinformation campaigns can be easily spread using bots and algorithms to influence public opinion. In the context of sextortion, AI can be used to transform ordinary images of real people into nude images, resulting in privacy violations and extortion. AI systems also employ the concept of prompt engineering to automatically generate program code. By specifying particular input prompts, these systems can be instructed on how code should be created and can then act programmatically. In this way, malicious code can be generated easily with little technical expertise.

The use of AI in combination with social engineering even enables individuals without specialized knowledge in this field to carry out potentially dangerous attacks. This has far-reaching implications for the entire field of cybercrime as well as for models of human and technical cyber defense, which are engaged in a direct interplay of action and reaction. The ongoing automation and intelligence

of AI systems mean that more and more tasks that previously required specialized knowledge and skills can now be performed by almost anyone. For example,
automated AI tools can be used to identify vulnerabilities in systems and applications and to generate corresponding exploit codes to take advantage of these
vulnerabilities.

This approach significantly lowers the barriers to entry and enables individuals
who previously may not have had programming skills to now carry out extensive
and dangerous attacks. **AI-powered spear phishing** also represents a particularly
threatening development, as AI can be used to create personalized and deceptively
authentic messages that are difficult for conventional security measures to detect.

With the availability of AI tools, attackers can launch mass phishing campaigns
and reach millions of potential victims simultaneously via email addresses, social
media accounts, instant messaging such as WhatsApp, or even SMS. In addition,
the phishing messages created can be tailored to specific target groups and contain personal information gathered from publicly accessible social media and other
online sources. This significantly increases the success rate of such attacks. These
examples illustrate the understanding that AI technologies can be used for both
positive and negative purposes, depending on the intentions and ethical principles
of those who deploy them.

1.4   The Birth of Global Intelligent Services

Let us take our **quintessence** with us and make a significant leap forward in our
historical journey to the 20th century. In the 20th century, the world began to experience another profound transformation in the way people collected, shared, and
protected information. The introduction of analog telephony and radio technologies revolutionized communication, enabling people to speak and exchange information with each other over even greater distances, almost in real time.

At the same time, new ideological, political, and ethnopolitical attitudes
emerged, such as imperialist, National Socialist, and racist ideologies. These ideologies also exploited the power of new communication achievements. A prominent figure who made significant use of these developments was Joseph Goebbels,
the Minister of Propaganda in Nazi Germany. He recognized the importance of
mass media such as radio, cinemas, and political advertising campaigns. These
media made it possible to disseminate ideologies and political messages on a
broad scale and to influence public opinion. Goebbels' skillful use of propaganda
and mass communication played a decisive role in spreading National Socialist
ideology and mobilizing the population for the regime's goals. This illustrates how
the power of communication technologies can be used not only for positive purposes, but also for manipulation and influencing people and societies. However,
changes in communication also led to new opportunities for information gathering.
Let us take a closer look at this development.

People and institutions, including governments, modified their ways of communicating. The modern communication options of the time made it possible to use various analog and technical means for communication.

However, this also meant that information could not only be obtained directly from individuals, but also by intercepting the data carriers used, such as letters, or by eavesdropping on analog technologies.

It was precisely during this period that various nations established official intelligence services **(Intelligence Services),** to protect their national interests both locally and globally and to guard against potential threats from within and outside the country. A notable example is the founding of the British **intelligence service MI6** (Military Intelligence, Section 6) in 1909. The British intelligence service played a crucial role during both World War I and World War II by gathering information on enemy activities and using this intelligence to support the war effort.

MI6 contributed to gaining vital insights into enemy strategies, troop movements, and planned operations, which ultimately strengthened the Allies and helped them successfully meet the challenges of World War II.

The establishment of intelligence services continued in other countries as well. During this period, many nations created similar organizations specializing in the collection and analysis of information. These developments helped to professionalize espionage techniques and tactics. This marked a significant step in the history of espionage and intelligence gathering. From then on, these intelligence services were not only focused on collecting secret information, but also on uncovering hostile activities and ensuring national security. In addition to the use of technology, spies and agents were also deployed to operate both domestically and abroad and to obtain valuable information. The term **Human Intelligence (HUMINT)** was coined during this period and refers to the acquisition of information through the use of human sources and agents. The development of HUMINT laid the foundation for many aspects of human hacking and social engineering. These disciplines also use human interactions and social manipulation mechanisms to obtain information, apply influence techniques, and bypass regular security mechanisms. In a sense, human hacking, social engineering, and HUMINT are related fields that focus on the art of interpersonal communication and manipulation to achieve specific objectives. The effective use of human sources as a means of gathering information and influencing human behavior is central to these practices.

The convergence of HUMINT, human hacking, and social engineering demonstrates how these disciplines are interconnected in various contexts and how the principles and techniques of one can be applied in the others. The connection between these fields underscores the versatility and importance of human interaction in intelligence gathering, security management, and influencing decisions and human behavior.

By the mid-20th century, human hacking and social engineering experienced a heyday closely linked to the world of espionage and the intelligence services of countries such as the USA and the USSR during the Cold War.

In this era, marked by intense geopolitical tensions and ongoing competition for strategic advantage, these manipulation and intelligence-gathering techniques were increasingly employed. Let us explore some remarkable examples and anecdotes from this period:

The Art of Deception in the Cold War During the Cold War, both the USA and the USSR invested extensive resources to gain information and advantages. Espionage and intelligence activities flourished. One of the most famous deception operations of this time was the Allies' "Operation Fortitude" during World War II. In this operation, false information about an impending invasion at Pas-de-Calais was spread to divert German troops from the actual landing in Normandy.

The Rosenholz Dossier A remarkable example of the importance of human sources and intelligence gathering is the "Rosenholz Dossier." This was a collection of documents handed over to the CIA by a Soviet defector. These documents contained valuable information about Soviet espionage activities and agents worldwide.

The Case of Kim Philby Kim Philby, a high-ranking British intelligence officer, turned out to be a double agent for the USSR. For years, he was able to pass secret information to the Soviets and was considered one of the most dangerous traitors of the Cold War.

The "Mole" Aldrich Ames Another well-known example is the case of Aldrich Ames, a senior CIA officer. He betrayed secret information to the Soviet intelligence service KGB and later to the Russian FSB (domestic intelligence service). His actions led to the exposure of several CIA agents and had serious consequences for US espionage efforts.

1.5   The Beginning of the Internet Age

With the end of the Cold War, the intensified and global adoption of **information and communication technology** simultaneously began to permeate the structures of companies and organizations. Giants such as IBM, Microsoft, and Apple gradually revolutionized the corporate landscape, which became increasingly digitalized. This digitalization not only opened up new perspectives for ideological espionage (East versus West), but also for economically motivated espionage, for example, to gain competitive advantages through the theft of know-how.

This included the theft of patents, technologies, and market strategies in order to gain an edge in the business environment. What was previously driven mainly by political or ideological motives was now expanded to include economic incentives. Ultimately, the global introduction of the **Internet** as a medium fundamentally changed the way we interact as human beings. This technological advancement brought significant benefits. Information can now be exchanged more quickly and easily, and networking between people extends across global boundaries.

The world became smaller, and human communication became more diverse and efficient.

However, the availability of the Internet also brought new challenges and concerns regarding personal privacy. The enhanced digital capability for eavesdropping and surveillance of individuals was one of the immediate consequences. The same technology that made it possible to write and speak with each other in real time also enabled these conversations to be intercepted. As a result, both individual privacy and organizational confidentiality became vulnerable. What was previously only possible through analog methods such as in-person information gathering or face-to-face manipulation was gradually revolutionized by the invention of the telephone, networked computer technology, and the Internet.

This new development also required a shift in mindset for both intelligence agencies and cybercriminals. Information can now be intercepted, manipulated, stolen, and disseminated at various points, whether in analog or digital form. In addition to HUMINT, there is now also **Signal Intelligence (SI)**, a discipline of information gathering focused on the collection and analysis of electronic signals and data from communications. This opened up new possibilities for targeted attacks on data and communications, forcing both security services and attackers to adapt and further develop their strategies and techniques. Manipulating people or gathering information became easily achievable via the Internet and telephone. Attackers could reduce their risks, as they were able to obtain information covertly without direct physical contact with their targets. This new dimension of anonymity created entirely new opportunities for attackers.

Today, such telephone attacks are known as voice phishing, or vishing for short. Voice phishing is a technique in which attackers attempt to obtain sensitive information from their targets by impersonating trusted sources or creating false emergency situations. This usually takes place via phone calls, in which attackers often pretend to be employees of banks, government agencies, or other trusted organizations. The combination of modern technology and analog manipulation techniques used in voice phishing illustrates how threats and attack methods have evolved and been revolutionized over time. Attackers exploit anonymity and the ability to overcome physical distance through global interconnectivity to pursue their objectives.

Thus, while innovations are intended to be beneficial and contribute to the good of society, they are simultaneously used as techniques for surveillance and eavesdropping. This is a form of progress that cannot be undone.

Ultimately, the technological revolution of the 20th century led to human hacking and social engineering not only entering the world of espionage and networked, global computer technology, but also the realm of professionalized and compartmentalized cybercrime.

As you can see, the possibilities for information gathering and manipulation are becoming ever more diverse and complex. From classic social engineering to espionage, motives, methods, and technologies employed vary widely. Today, technologies are primarily used in the context of cyber espionage, facial recognition,

surveillance glasses, satellite surveillance, drone surveillance, biometric identification technologies, underwater surveillance (submarines for espionage), or
encrypted channels, and these are all attributable to advances in digitalization [4].
Yet the roots and the original idea of using these techniques in their various forms
go back thousands of years and are a fascinating reflection of human nature. They
offer a glimpse into the darker, but also the more complex and diverse aspects of
our being, and describe how we think, feel, and decide to use technology.

1.6   Summary of Our Historical Journey

Our journey into the origins and chronicles of human hacking began in ancient
Greece and, for now, leads us into the 21st century, into the world of networked
computer technology. At this point, we have the opportunity to consolidate the
knowledge we have gained before proceeding. Here is a consolidated version of
the key insights from our exploration of the chronicles of human hacking and
social engineering:

UNIVERSALITY OF SOCIAL ENGINEERING
Social engineering and the art of human hacking are universal in nature, tran-
scending the boundaries of specific domains. This practice manifests in diverse
forms and can arise in various contexts, whether in information security, espionage, psychology, social interactions, or other fields [5]. The ability to influence
human behavior remains constant, regardless of the environment in which it is
applied.

MORAL AMBIGUITY AND INTRINSIC APPLICATION
Social engineering and the art of human hacking represent a skill that highlights
human communication and negotiation abilities. These techniques are initially eth-
ically neutral, as their moral orientation depends on the intended use.

The universality of this skill is evident in its everyday application by people in
a variety of situations.

For example, medical professionals and behavioral scientists use these insights
to help individuals overcome harmful habits such as quitting smoking, illustrating
the broad applicability of these techniques.

THE EVOLUTION OF SOCIAL ENGINEERING
The main insight of this examination lies in the realization that social engineering
methods are by no means static, but have evolved and been refined over the centuries. This phenomenon reflects a Darwinian aspect, in which these methods are
subject to a natural evolution. Much like in biology, the social engineering techniques that are most effective and can adapt to ever-changing human behaviors
and communication patterns survive and thrive. This ongoing optimization and
adaptation of social engineering methods demonstrates the adaptability and con-
tinual transformation within this field.

Continuity of traditional and Proven Techniques

Social engineers employ a wide range of ancient techniques and draw on proven military and intelligence procedures. These methods have been refined over centuries to increase their effectiveness. The transfer of these tried-and-tested methods into various areas of life underscores their timeless applicability.

Targeted Influence Based on Deeply Rooted Traits

The effectiveness of manipulation techniques in the realm of social engineering is based on the targeted addressing and influencing of deeply rooted human traits and behaviors. This goes beyond simple helpfulness and targets complex psychological and behavioral characteristics. These techniques are effective because they are attuned to the multifaceted nature of human psychology and communication.

Complexity of Social Engineering in the Human Psyche and Communication

The many facets of social engineering reflect the depths and nuances that exist within the human psyche and communication. The art of human hacking is not limited to superficial manipulation, but influences the deeply embedded aspects of our behavior and interactions.

It penetrates the subtle, complex layers of the human psyche to gain trust, shape beliefs, and guide actions. This depth of influence shows that social engineering is far more than mere manipulation; it is a fascinating reflection of the intrinsic complexity found in our thoughts, emotions, and social dynamics.

Like the human psyche and communication itself, social engineering is a multifaceted and rich subject that must be continually explored and understood.

Through this chronicle of human wisdom and cunning, spanning from the history books to the modern digital era, we now immerse ourselves in the world of social engineering. Here, we merge knowledge and tactics in a continuous dance to unravel the great mystery of the human psyche. On our journey, we will learn how the art of persuasion and deception has been applied across different eras and societies, and how it has continually evolved.

References

1. John Boyd, Patterns of Conflict, 1986.
2. Hermann Helmholtz (1855), Über das Sehen des Menschen. In Vorträge und Reden. 4. Aufl., Bd.1, 1896. Braunschweig: Vieweg.
3. Marc Schmitt, Ivan Flechais, Digital Deception: Generative Artificial Intelligence in Social Engineering and Phishing, 2023.
4. Pavel Y. Leonov, Alexander V. Vorobyev, Anastasia A. Ezhova, Oksana S. Kotelyanets, Aleksandra K. Zavalishina, Nikolay V. Morozov, The Main Social Engineering Techniques Aimed at Hacking Information Systems, 2021 Ural Symposium on Biomedical Engineering, Radioelectronics and Information Technology (USBEREIT), Yekaterinburg, Russland, 2021, S. 0471–0473.
5. Amy Hetro Washo, An interdisciplinary view of social engineering: A call to action for research, in: Elsevier, Computers in Human Behavior Reports,Vol. 4, 2021.

Definition: Social Engineering

Let us now continue our discussion with our postulate, "You are a Human Hacker." You are not among the malicious actors, nor are you someone who, after reading this book, will go out and pursue harmful intentions. Our intrinsic motivation is of a different nature. Yes, we are human, and yes, at one point or another, we "hack" our fellow human beings. However, this does not always involve malicious or deliberate intent.

2.1 The Four Sides of a Message

Let us immerse ourselves for a moment in an everyday situation in which Schulz von Thun's model—renowned for its theory of the four sides of a message—plays a crucial role [1]. This model (Fig. 2.1) divides a message into four aspects: appeal, self-revelation, relationship, and factual content. The appeal is the request or call to action that the sender directs to the receiver.

Imagine you are facing a technical problem that you cannot solve on your own. In a conversation with a friend or colleague, you express your problem. *Here, the appeal comes to the forefront. Your appeal is your request for help in solving this problem.*

You hope that your friend or colleague will support you with their skills and knowledge. But the appeal alone is not enough. On the relationship level, a subtle choreography unfolds. You have established a connection with your conversation partner, whether through friendship or professional collaboration.

This **relationship cue level** is the key to a successful interaction. You know that your friend or colleague is happy to help you, and you value their opinion. This strengthens the interpersonal relationship and the willingness to collaborate. On the **self-disclosure** level, you openly share your internal state and needs. You explain how *frustrated or overwhelmed* you are by this problem and how urgently

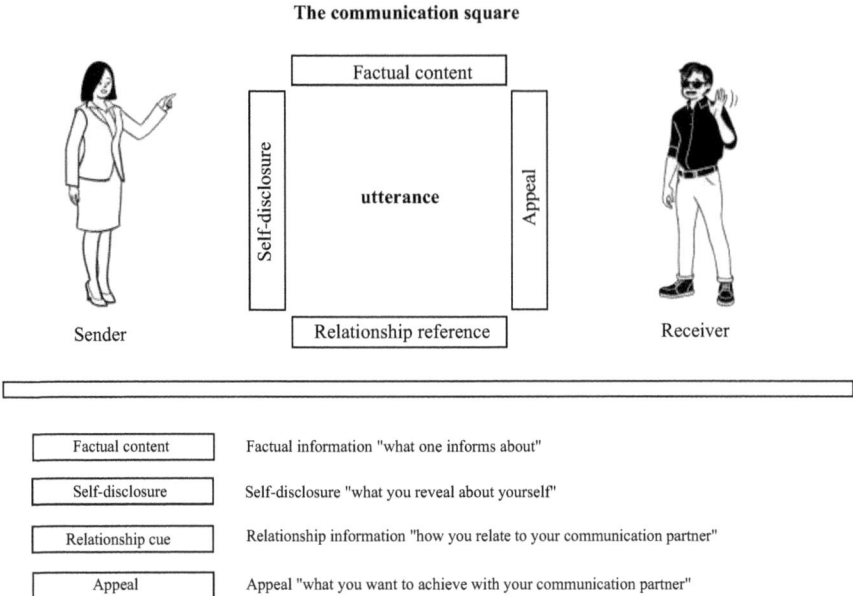

The communication square

Factual content	Factual information "what one informs about"
Self-disclosure	Self-disclosure "what you reveal about yourself"
Relationship cue	Relationship information "how you relate to your communication partner"
Appeal	Appeal "what you want to achieve with your communication partner"

Fig. 2.1 The communication square (adapted from [1])

you need support. This openness fosters understanding and empathy. Finally, the *factual content* comes into play. Here, you discuss the technical details of your problem, the various possible solutions, and the steps to resolve it.

This everyday example makes it clear that you use your interpersonal relationships and communication skills to achieve a goal—in this case, solving a technical problem. This is a common example of how we apply the principles of social engineering without harmful intent. Applying Schulz von Thun's model helps you understand and shape this dynamic communication effectively. It is further evidence that we humans are, by nature, social engineers who use social skills to shape our lives.

2.2   Anthropological Dimension of Social Engineering

With regard to the sixth point listed in Sect. 1.6 *(White Chapter),* which emphasizes the complexity of social engineering in the context of human psychology and communication, we can therefore highlight anthropological aspects in a positive light. Anthropology is a science concerned with the comprehensive study of humans in all their facets and in various cultural and historical contexts. Its aim is to deepen our understanding of humans as biological, social, and cultural beings. Anthropology examines human evolution, biological characteristics, social structures, cultural practices, languages, worldviews, and interactions in different societies [2].

In the context of social engineering, anthropological insights are of great importance, as they provide an understanding of the deeply rooted social norms, values, and behavioral patterns that social engineers recognize and manipulate. In our specific context, anthropology enables us to understand human communities and their communication patterns, including how social interactions, trust, and cooperation are established.

This understanding is crucial for exploring the effectiveness of social engineering techniques, as they are built upon the anthropological foundations of our social nature.

The anthropological perspectives and characteristics of social engineering form a direct link to the comprehensive encyclopedia of the term.

This term is considered from various contexts and perspectives, highlighting its versatility and multifaceted nature. The concept of social engineering is applied in a range of disciplines and fields, from information security to the social sciences and ethics.

This connection underscores the need for a comprehensive understanding of social engineering in order to fully grasp the numerous implications and challenges it entails. This perspective also means that the anthropological aspects and characteristics of social engineering are closely related to the comprehensive body of knowledge about the term *Social Engineering.* The encyclopedia thus contains information, descriptions, and explanations of various aspects of the term. The anthropological perspectives on social engineering provide additional insights and links to this body of knowledge.

Together, they complement each other and contribute to a comprehensive and deeper understanding of the concept of human hacking. Furthermore, anthropology can offer insights into the diversity of human cultures and the influence of cultural differences on behavior and communication. This is particularly important when social engineers operate in global contexts and must be aware of cultural sensitivities in order to be effective.

Here are some ways in which anthropological considerations may be relevant in this context:

Cultural Diversity People from different cultures have different social norms, values, and behaviors. A social engineer must take cultural differences into account to be effective. Anthropological insights help to understand cultural nuances and adapt to different environments.

Social Structures Anthropology examines the social structures and hierarchies in different societies. This knowledge can be helpful in identifying key individuals and influencers within an organization or community.

Communication and Language Linguistic anthropology contributes to the understanding of language and communication. Social engineers use communication techniques to gather or influence information. An understanding of linguistic diversity and communication styles is advantageous in this context. However, this perspective is also complemented by considering nonverbal communication.

Social Behavior Anthropology explores human behavior and social interactions. This is essential for recognizing patterns in human behavior and developing successful social engineering strategies.

Psychology and Motivation Anthropologists study human psychological motivations. A social engineer can benefit from this knowledge to understand what drives people, how they make decisions, and how they can be influenced.

Ethics and Morality Anthropological research can shed light on ethics and morality in different cultures. This is important because social engineering often raises ethical questions, especially when it involves deceiving or manipulating people.

2.3   Terminological Dimension of Social Engineering

It is becoming increasingly clear that our simple, even rudimentary, conception of social engineering is far more complex than merely imagining or assuming a straightforward vishing attack or shoulder surfing. It is a complex web of deception techniques deeply rooted in fundamental human traits and differentiated domains. This web must be carefully analyzed and understood. This is especially crucial when it comes to training security experts and defenders who must be able to:

a) recognize and understand human-centered attacks (perception),
b) protect against these threats (protection), and
c) raise awareness among employees and provide sustainable training so that they are able to put theory into practice *(behaviorist characteristic).*

This reality requires a deep understanding of the psychological and anthropological aspects of social engineering, as well as the ability to analyze and interpret complex social interactions and human behavior in order to develop effective defense strategies. Let us now transfer this idea to the here and now. In the modern digital age, the meanings, interpretations, and thought processes associated with the term "social engineering" are extremely diverse.

However, upon closer examination, it becomes evident that references to this term can also be found in philosophy. This is because philosophy has always dealt with fundamental questions of human existence, perception, and behavior. Philosophical approaches such as existential philosophy and philosophical anthropology have sought to understand the nature of humanity and its role in the universe.

These philosophical considerations have influenced discussions about "social engineering," as they provide a foundation for understanding human behavior and social interactions.

For example, in 1945, the philosopher Karl Popper mentioned the term social engineering in his book The Open Society and Its Enemies. The Spell of Plato, though not in the way we would interpret it in the present age [3]. Popper primarily addressed political and philosophical issues in order to contribute to the improvement of social structures.

He was concerned about political movements and ideologies that sought to shape society through extensive state intervention, and he criticized the notion that society could be controlled like a technical system or a machine. His reference to "social engineering" was intended to highlight that such approaches can be problematic and may endanger individual freedom and the openness of society.

The term *social engineering* has evolved over time and is now primarily used in the context of information security. In the modern context, social engineering has developed into a complex discipline that requires in-depth knowledge of human behavior, psychology, and social interactions. Even within the multifaceted world of information security, the impressive diversity of definitions and interpretations of social engineering demonstrates how complex and far-reaching this concept is in modern digital society.

For example, the *Federal Office for Information Security (BSI)* provides the following definition of social engineering [4]: *"Social engineering exploits human traits such as helpfulness, trust, fear, or respect for authority in order to skillfully manipulate individuals. In this way, cybercriminals may, for example, induce victims to disclose confidential information, bypass security features, make transfers, or install malware on their personal device or a computer within the corporate network. Social engineering itself is nothing new and has served as the basis for a wide variety of scams since time immemorial. However, in the age of digital communication, there are extremely effective new opportunities for criminals to reach millions of potential victims."*

Christopher Hadnagy, a security expert and one of the leading authorities in the field of information security, defined social engineering in his book [5] The Art of Human Hacking as *"... the act of manipulating a person to perform an action that may or may not be in the best interest of the 'target'."*

Kevin David Mitnick was an American hacker, social engineering expert, and CEO of an IT security company. Kevin Mitnick became known in the 1990s and was considered one of the most wanted hackers in the world.

After his imprisonment, he worked with various government agencies and companies to improve their IT security. Mitnick was a recognized security expert and author of several books, including *The Art of Deception,* in which he discusses social engineering and the art of deception. [6] describes social engineering as follows: *"Social engineering uses influence and persuasion to deceive people by convincing them that the social engineer is someone they are not, or through manipulation. This enables the social engineer to exploit people in order to obtain information, with or without the use of technology [own translation]."*

Verizon, which also publishes the annual Data Breach Investigations Reports (DBIR), describes social engineering as follows [7]: *"People are fundamentally social beings and tend to place excessive trust in the digital world. This makes people vulnerable to social engineering, a modern term for the oldest trick in the book: exploiting human psychology, rather than relying solely on hacking techniques, to manipulate people into disclosing confidential or personal information for fraudulent purposes [own translation]."*

2.4   Deficient Terminological Representation

In the various definitions of social engineering—whether by Christopher Hadnagy, Kevin Mitnick, Verizon, or the BSI—we find several common elements. These include the exploitation of human traits such as helpfulness, trust, fear, or respect for authority to manipulate people and induce them to perform unwanted actions or disclose confidential information.

As you may have noticed, the definitions of social engineering presented here exhibit certain shortcomings and limitations, highlighting the need for a new, more comprehensive definition. Let us examine these definitional and terminological deficits more precisely:

Limited emphasis on digital aspects: Most existing definitions of social engineering focus primarily on *analog social manipulation techniques.* However, in today's digital world, digital methods such as open source intelligence (OSINT), social media intelligence (SOCMINT), AI-based attacks, and digital technologies for information manipulation are of great importance [8]. A contemporary definition should therefore take into account both *analog and digital aspects of social engineering.*

Lack of consideration for combinatorics: Social engineering can be more effective when different techniques and channels are used in combination. For example, an attacker might create fake websites and impersonate a trusted contact to increase the success rate. Current definitions of social engineering rarely provide insight into how this *combinatorics* works or how different techniques are interwoven.

A more comprehensive definition should, however, address this aspect and *highlight the complex interactions between various digital and analog manipulation techniques.*

Lack of reference to holistic impacts: Social manipulation techniques can have significant effects on individuals and groups. A comprehensive definition should therefore *not only address financial damages,* as may occur in cases such as sextortion, but also consider the *long-term psychological harm* suffered by victims.

This includes the long-term effects on the well-being and mental health of victims, as seen, for example, in cases of cybergrooming in the context of social engineering practices such as catfishing.

2.5   Summary: A Holistic Definition of Social Engineering

A holistic perspective includes the consideration that social engineering attacks do not occur solely in organizational and enterprise-wide environments. The same principles and techniques are also applied in private settings to infiltrate personal spheres and compromise individuals.

A comprehensive definition must therefore thoroughly address the social, ethical, and psychological implications of social engineering and emphasize the need for an in-depth examination of its impact on victims. Based on these limitations, there is a need to develop a new and contemporary definition of social engineering that reflects today's complex landscape and the multidisciplinary nature of this phenomenon.

> *Social engineering is a **multidisciplinary practice** that aims to skillfully exploit human* ***social, psychological, and emotional*** *characteristics in order to induce individuals to perform actions or disclose information that are against **their own interests** or the interests of **an organization or society** . This method combines **analog and digital techniques** to* ***deceive and manipulate people*** *, and represents an ongoing challenge for information security. The **consequences** of a social engineering attack can cause both **monetary and psychological harm** , with the latter often having **long-term effects on the well-being** and* ***mental health of the victims*** *.*

Our descriptive definition of social engineering forms the foundation of this book. This definition will be central to our scientific understanding and serve as a guide for further theoretical and practical exploration.

The definition enables us to illuminate the multifaceted aspects of social engineering and to identify and describe the profound consequences of this practice in various contexts.

As the descriptive definition of social engineering makes clear, the techniques and methods of social engineering can be employed both in enterprise-related applications and in private environments. These areas each exhibit distinct characteristics, vulnerabilities, threats, and impacts. To reduce the complexity of this analysis, we will begin by presenting the corporate application domain of social engineering. Here, we focus on the fundamental principles of digital and analog manipulation techniques, which are brought together in the so-called triangulation of information security.

With this approach, we can seamlessly integrate our descriptive definition into corporate application areas and gain deeper insights into preventive, detective, reactive, and corrective measures in the fight against social engineering. In the Yellow Chapter, we broaden our perspective to consider the protection and defense against social engineering attacks in private environments.

References

1. Friedemann, Schulz von Thun, Miteinander reden 1, Rowohlt Taschenbuch, 1981.
2. Hortense Gerardo, Educational Convergence: The Anthropology, Performance, and Technology (APT) Program, in: Frontiers in Education Conference (FIE), Lincoln NE, USA, 2021.
3. Karl Raimund Popper, The open society and its enemies. The spell of Plato, London, George Routledge & Sons, ltd., 1945.
4. Bundesamt für Sicherheit in der Informationstechnik (BSI), Social Engineering – der Mensch als Schwachstelle, unter: https://www.bsi.bund.de/DE/Themen/Verbraucherinnen-und-Verbraucher/Cyber-Sicherheitslage/Methoden-der-Cyber-Kriminalitaet/Social-Engineering/social-engineering_node.html (Zugriff: 02.10.2023).
5. Christopher Hadnagy, Die Kunst des Human Hacking, mitp-Verlags GmbH & Co. KG, Frechen 2011.
6. Kevin D. Mitnick, William L. Simon, Steve Wozniak, Controlling the Human Element of Security: The Art of Deception, Wiley, 2003.
7. Verizon, Social engineering attacks to watch out for, unter: https://www.verizon.com/business/resources/articles/s/social-engineering-attacks-to-watch-out-for/ (Zugriff: 01.12.2023).
8. Isabelle Böhm, Samuel Lolagar, Open source intelligence. International Cybersecurity Law Review 2, 2021, S. 317–337.

Application Areas of Social Engineering

The domain in which analog and digital methods of social engineering are used to infiltrate and compromise organizations and companies can, understandably, be defined within the boundaries of an organization as well as at the interfaces to other organizations. In this context, we must broaden our understanding of social engineering to encompass all units, structures, and relationships that exist and are utilized within these organizational boundaries. A narrow focus solely on the "human" factor is not effective for several reasons and must be avoided in this context. In this way, the domain can be defined as a sociotechnical system in which various roles and competencies come together within a structured organizational framework and operational processes in physical spaces, in order to develop and implement profit-generating activities through strategic planning and operational execution of business processes. If we now derive the essential characteristics that enable this finely tuned interplay between different entities, objects, structures, and systems, we can state with absolute certainty that the domain of social engineering, at both the conceptual and operational levels, is defined by the declaration of

Technology, Organization, and Human

can be defined.

3.1 Triangulation of Information Security

The domain of social engineering is linked to the triangulation [1] of information security, in which the three *coherent, interactive, and complementary* units ***technical security, human security,*** and ***organizational security*** converge (Fig. 3.1).

This declaration enables a more precise examination of the specific characteristics of each area and their individual contributions to fulfilling tasks in organizational contexts. Different mechanisms, procedures, and methods are employed

E. Koza et al., *Social Engineering and Human Hacking*,
https://doi.org/10.1007/978-3-662-72084-4_3

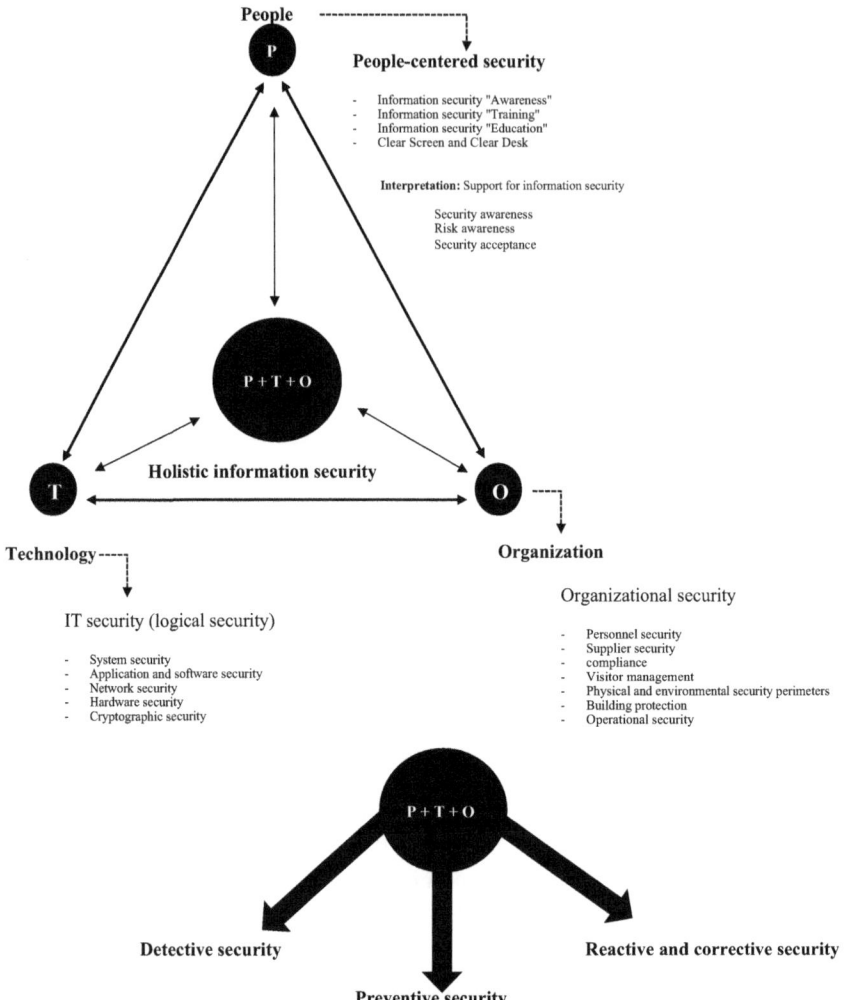

Fig. 3.1 Triangulation of information security

to achieve harmonious coordination and orchestration between technology, people, and organization, and to accomplish specific objectives. To explain this perspective, we will systematically examine the significance of each area. We will then address the properties that make this perspective unique. Each of these areas has its own distinctive specifications.

TECHNICAL SECURITY (ALSO KNOWN AS IT SECURITY)

The technical components in the triangulation of information security refer to the hardware, software, and digital infrastructure used to support and ensure information security. This includes firewall systems, antivirus software, cryptographic encryption techniques, and other technical security measures such as intrusion detection systems (IDS), security information and event management systems (SIEM), as well as other logical mechanisms in the areas of application security and network security. In organizational environments, IT security encompasses essential features of security functions that are in constant exchange and interaction with the external environment.

ORGANIZATIONAL SECURITY
The organizational security dimension of the triangulation refers to the structures, processes, and physical and environmental security perimeters within an organization. These include a wide range of complex topics such as personnel security, procurement security, supplier security, compliance, and physical security, such as property and building protection, lightning protection, fire protection, etc., and define the overall organizational security for all employees. Furthermore, organizational security also encompasses the essential processes used for organizing and managing information security.

HUMAN SECURITY (ALSO KNOWN AS HUMAN FACTOR)
The human factor is of central importance and includes employees who, from an information technology perspective, are divided into regular users and users with elevated privileges. In addition, this also includes staff from external service providers, such as cleaning personnel, as well as interns and other individuals who are each granted authorized entry, access, and use of the physical and logical units of a company. This perspective makes it clear that it applies regardless of whether these are internal, external, permanent, temporary, or contract employees.

Furthermore, the human factor in information security refers to the role and behavior of people in handling IT systems and both analog and digital information.

3.2   The Properties of the Triangulation of Information Security

Let us now examine the properties that link these three areas together.

Coherence means that the areas of IT security, organizational security, and human security are directly related to each other and form a unified system.

This system is capable of determining the interactions among people, technology, and organization, and ensuring that they are well coordinated.

Coherence thus means that these three areas together form a functioning security system, in which the relationships between people, technology, and organization are clearly defined and orchestrated according to specific objectives.

Interactivity refers to the way in which these three areas relate to and influence each other. It emphasizes that decisions and actions in one area have an impact on the others. An effective security system therefore takes these interactions into account and ensures that technical, human, and organizational aspects are aligned.

Complementarity means that the different aspects of information security complement and work together to create a comprehensive security system. This prevents redundant or contradictory security measures. Instead, technical, human, and organizational security measures should work together harmoniously to effectively ensure the security of data and systems. In this context, complementarity also means that an adequate level of information security is achieved when all these areas are finely tuned, coordinated, tactically anchored, and operationally executed. Only then, and only then, can holistic protection in information security be achieved.

In the triangulation of information security, coherence, interactivity, and complementarity play a decisive role in creating a holistic and effective security system that equally ensures the security of people, technology, and organization.

3.3   Summary: Holistic Nature of Information Security

In summary, the triangulation of information security yields a crucial guiding principle for understanding and securing the domain of social engineering, which we would like to propose as the key takeaway from this section.

> The **triangulation of information security,** comprising the interlocking properties of **technology, people, and organization,** forms the central concept for comprehensively capturing and securing the domain of social engineering. It underscores the necessity of a holistic and closely coordinated approach, in which these three areas are aligned to ensure an optimal level of security. By understanding this triangulation, organizations can better grasp the complex interactions among technology, people, and organizational structures within their domain to defend against social engineering attacks, and can implement targeted measures for prevention, detection, and response to potential threats. This holistic approach is essential to ensure an effective and comprehensive level of protection against the diverse deception and manipulation techniques of social engineering.

With this summary, we emphasize the fundamental importance of the triangulation of information security for a comprehensive understanding and successful defense against social engineering threats. In the next chapter, we will examine the psychological background of social engineering in greater detail and finally address the characteristics that explain why social engineering attacks are so successful.

References

1. Erfan Koza, Eine empirische Kontentanalyse zur Ermittlung von praxisorientierten Optimierungsfeldern zur Resilienz-Erhöhung der IT-Systeme im Sinne der ganzheitlichen Betrachtung der Informationssicherheit. Hemmnisse und Erfolgsfaktoren eines nachhaltigen und effizienten Informationssicherheitsmanagementsystems, in: Informatik 2021 Computer Science & Sustainability, Gesellschaft für Informatik, Lecture Notes in Informatics, S. 819–831.

Psychological Backgrounds of Social Engineering

In social engineering, the human hacker targets the emotions of their victim. Rational thinking often takes a back seat in this context. The victim's decisions are guided by their feelings. *But is it really that simple?* The psychology of social engineering is highly diverse and complex, as it draws on multiple scientific disciplines. To fully understand the psychological foundations of social engineering, we must consider the following scientific aspects in their entirety:

Social Psychology Social psychology examines how people think, feel, and act in social situations. Social engineers leverage these insights to understand and influence people's thinking and behavior in various social contexts. They exploit human needs for belonging, recognition, and social influence to develop manipulation techniques.

Behavioral Economics Behavioral economics analyzes how people act in economic decision-making processes. Social engineers use findings from behavioral economics to identify psychological pressure points and prompt individuals to perform certain actions. This can even lead people to act against their own economic interests.

Neuroscience Neuroscience provides insights into how the brain functions and processes information. Social engineers draw on neuroscience to develop deception techniques based on brain processes. They understand how information is processed in the brain in order to craft convincing stories and manipulative messages.

Communication Science Communication science studies how messages are transmitted and interpreted. Social engineers use techniques from communication science to create persuasive narratives and develop manipulative communication

E. Koza et al., *Social Engineering and Human Hacking*, https://doi.org/10.1007/978-3-662-72084-4_4

strategies. They understand how messages can be conveyed most effectively to influence the desired behavior.

Personality Psychology Personality psychology deals with individual differences in behavior and personality traits. Social engineers tailor their approach to individual personalities in order to specifically target a person's psychological vulnerabilities. They exploit personality traits to mislead and manipulate people.

Emotion Psychology Emotion psychology investigates the role of emotions in human behavior. Social engineers exploit emotions such as fear, curiosity, and empathy to influence people. They understand how emotions affect decision-making and use this knowledge to lure people into fabricated scenarios and deceive them.

Perception Psychology Perception psychology analyzes how people absorb, interpret, and process information from their environment. Social engineers use insights from perception psychology to specifically influence the victim's perception and manipulate their sensory experience.

These various scientific fields help to illustrate the diversity and complexity of the psychological foundations of social engineering. To provide an adequate and scientifically sound answer to the initial question, a comprehensive series of books on this topic would likely be required.

Our aim, however, is to provide you with a scientifically grounded foundation of knowledge that enables you to understand the interrelationships of specific human-centered attack techniques, mechanisms, and methods by independently acquiring the necessary knowledge through the comprehension and integration of individual arguments. This will enable you to incorporate the various elements into the required context of analysis and thus establish an evidential basis for your understanding, making it easier for you to apply defense strategies effectively in practice.

To meet this scientific and empirical standard, we will begin with a fundamental understanding of the complexity of the subject before addressing the individual levels of influence. In this scientific context, it is crucial to emphasize that our discussion represents only a limited excerpt from this multifaceted world. It is important to recognize and take into account that statements and explanations regarding the psychological foundations of social engineering, due to their inherent complexity and depth, can inevitably provide only a limited explanation. Nevertheless, this limited explanation offers valuable insights into an extremely challenging topic.

So, let go of the notion that a human hacker **merely and simply** exploits human traits. The way we are socialized is shaped by various factors, including culture, environment, friendships, upbringing, and numerous other influences. These fundamental elements are crucial to our identity and affect our perception and behavior. As human beings, we have a deep need for group belonging and acceptance within society. Praise and recognition affirm that our contributions and behavior are valued by others.

4.1   Helpfulness, Praise, and Recognition

Praise and recognition motivate us to continue striving. They reinforce our actions and make our efforts feel worthwhile. Recognition also triggers positive emotions such as joy, pride, and satisfaction. This contributes to our emotional well-being and mental health. While our personal traits are generally positive and socially oriented, they also carry certain risks for ourselves and our information security.

When we receive recognition from others, it strengthens our interpersonal relationships. It shows that we are attentive and value the achievements and efforts of others. Praise and recognition affirm our abilities and help us develop our self-image and self-confidence. In addition, positive feedback can help reduce stress and improve our well-being. **Helpfulness**—the willingness to assist others—is regarded by many as a positive human trait. Some people value help not only as conscious support, but also see the gratitude they receive in return as a significant reward.

Often, after providing assistance, we simply receive a "thank you" in return. Although this small word holds immense meaning for all of us, for some people it takes on an additional dimension. In such cases, the focus is not only on helpfulness, but rather on the underlying motivation: the pursuit of **praise and recognition.** There are many ways to receive praise and recognition, including volunteer work, membership in clubs or associations, or by publishing videos, images, and posts on social media [1].

People who receive little praise and recognition in their private or professional lives seek it elsewhere.

Human hackers deliberately exploit our need for affirmation and appreciation. Victims may feel flattered and perceive the apparent appreciation as genuine, without realizing they may be being manipulated. Defending against a cleverly orchestrated vishing attack is extremely challenging for those called. This is due in part to the fact that attackers possess not only technical skills, but can also use appropriate tools to manipulate the caller ID so that it matches the selected target. As a result, it becomes difficult to obtain information based on the number, since the true identity of the caller remains concealed.

Unlike in the physical world, where we can perceive clothing and body language, on the phone only our sense of hearing is active. The lack of visual cues prompts our brain to create corresponding images through communication, so that ongoing mental images of the caller are formed.

Because facial expressions and gestures cannot be perceived, the brain tries to fill in the gaps with words and descriptions. This creates an impression based solely on the subjective and selective perception and background of the person being called.

The telephone is a fascinating technology, but also a dangerous means of communication, as the mental images it creates can influence people's behavior and reactions. When an attacker deliberately uses dialect, intonation, volume, and background noises, the impression of a "real and genuine" conversation can quickly arise.

By purposefully employing various vocal and linguistic techniques, the attacker can manipulate their target and steer them toward a desired perspective. Manipulating speech style allows the attacker, for example, to appear convincing or trustworthy.

Emphasis and volume can be used to evoke emotions or influence the victim [1]. A specific dialect or manner of speaking can be manipulated so that the attacker appears to be a familiar person or someone with legitimate authority, in order to gain the victim's trust.

Skillful integration of background noises enhances the credibility of the call and creates the illusion that the caller is in an authentic location. All of these sophisticated techniques contribute to making the victim less suspicious and foster the illusion of trustworthy communication. This makes it easier for the human hacker to obtain sensitive information or persuade the victim to take actions that serve the attacker's objectives.

This illustrates that the behavior of human hackers in the context of social engineering is far more complex than simply exploiting human traits by definition. It involves deliberately addressing fundamental human needs for recognition, affirmation, and belonging, as well as skillfully manipulating the psychological mechanisms that govern these needs. Various communicative means are employed to place victims in an illusory situation in which they willingly disclose information or perform actions they would not undertake in a rational state. These techniques, based on psychological principles, enable human hackers to establish a connection and gain the trust of their victims.

Consequently, we should be aware that social engineering in the context of information security is based on a deep understanding of human psychology and social interaction. It is not merely the willingness to help, but a complex interplay of emotions, needs, and social mechanisms that is exploited by skilled hackers.

Having now examined the complexity behind the psychological background of social engineering, we will systematically introduce some fundamental scientific theories of a general nature that can help you better understand the psychological underpinnings of social engineering.

4.2   Roles, Norms, and Values

We begin with perceptual psychology. A multitude of factors directly influence our perception, and in many cases, this influence occurs almost automatically, intuitively, and instinctively. *In this context, phylogenetic factors such as* **roles, norms, and values** *as well as ontogenetic factors such as individual* **personal development and maturation** *play an essential role in perception. In addition, current* **genetic and cognitive factors** *also contribute to how we perceive the world around us* (Fig. 4.1).

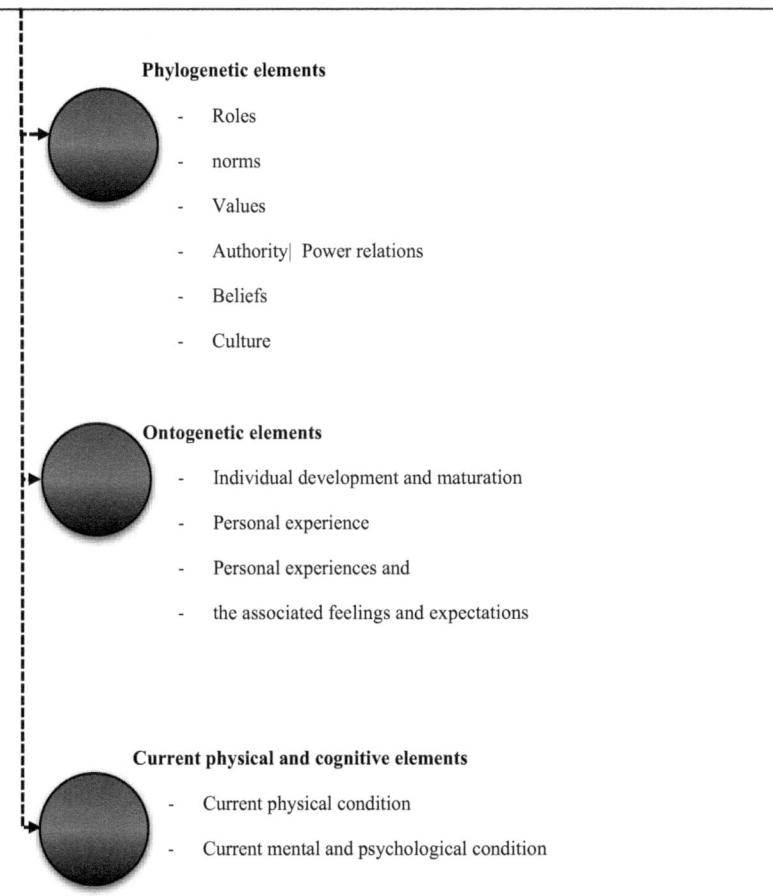

Fig. 4.1 Factors influencing perception

Let us now take a closer look at these aspects. Phylogenetic influences play an important role, as they encompass characteristics that have a direct impact on our perception and, consequently, on our behavior.

Phylogenetic influences refer to biological and evolutionary factors that have played a role throughout human development and continue to do so. These factors have shaped our ability to develop social structures and to act within groups. These social groups, in turn, have produced roles, norms, and values that guide the behavior of individuals within these groups. Human perception and behavior are directly influenced by these phylogenetic factors. An example of this is the innate human ability to recognize faces and interpret social signals from the facial expressions and gestures of others. These are abilities that have evolved to promote interpersonal social interaction and cooperation.

Human hackers understand these phylogenetic influences and deliberately exploit them in their manipulation strategies. They can leverage human empathy, the desire for belonging, and the ability to identify with others to build trust and influence their targets. A deep understanding of these evolutionary factors enables social engineers to pull subtle psychological levers to achieve their objectives.

Within social groups, people assume **roles** that define expectations for their behavior in certain positions or functions. These roles—whether as a father, mother, grandmother, professor, supervisor, or IT helpdesk employee—are the result of phylogenetic influences that foster the need for cooperation and specialization in social groups. Human hackers deliberately exploit these expectations to manipulate the emotional state and mindset of their targets and to gain trust. By pretending to hold a particular role or by imitating the expected behavior of a role, they create an emotional and personal connection and increase their chances of achieving their goal.

Norms that develop within social groups are also a product of phylogenetic influences rooted in the need for cooperation and social cohesion. These norms include patterns of behavior and protocols, or so-called social conventions, that are accepted within a group, community, or society and define expectations for behavior in various situations. They serve as a kind of social manual and influence how people act in specific contexts. Human hackers use their understanding of these norms to influence the actions, reactions, and decisions of their targets. By deliberately appealing to or even breaking social norms of politeness, respect, or discretion in interactions, they can steer their victims in the desired direction and set the stage for their scenario.

Values are deeply rooted beliefs that are considered desirable within a society. On this basis, people make decisions and derive their behavior. Every individual possesses personal values that are strongly shaped by personal experiences and social influences.

Human hackers recognize the importance of these individual as well as collective values in interactions and deliberately use them to instill confidence in their targets and apply manipulative strategies.

4.3   Honesty

Another example is **honesty.** Honesty is regarded as a fundamental value in many cultures and societies. People are encouraged to tell the truth and act honestly in order to foster trust in interpersonal relationships. This value is reflected in social norms and expectations that aim to promote honesty. A positive example of the importance of this universal value can be seen in a professional context. Suppose an employee of a company becomes aware of a potential business problem that needs to be identified and resolved to prevent possible negative consequences.

Because of the universal value of honesty, the employee feels obliged to inform their supervisors or colleagues about the situation, even if it may be uncomfortable. In this case, the universal value of honesty helps to promote ethical behavior and address potential issues before they escalate into more serious problems.

However, honesty can also be exploited by a human hacker, who deliberately leverages a person's reliability and honesty as part of a manipulation strategy. Here is an example of how this can happen:

Suppose a human hacker learns that a person is honest and trustworthy and tends to share information unfiltered when asked. The attacker could use this knowledge to create an apparently trustworthy situation:

Pretending an Emergency The attacker could pretend to be in an urgent emergency, claiming that a total network outage is imminent. *"Nothing is working anymore."* They might approach the honest person and ask them to disclose confidential information or grant access to protected resources in order to resolve the supposed emergency.

Emphasizing Ethics and Trust The attacker could refer to the importance of honesty and trust, claiming that only an honest person can be trusted to resolve the situation. They might pressure the honest person not to share information with other employees or supervisors in order to maintain the supposed confidentiality.

Creating Pressure The attacker could apply pressure by claiming that time is running out and a complete "blackout" can no longer be ruled out. This can prompt the victim to make quick decisions without sufficient consideration.

In this scenario, the human hacker exploits the person's honesty to persuade them to disclose confidential information or resources that are in fact used for malicious purposes. The attacker appeals to the value of honesty and trust to induce the victim to violate their own security measures.

4.4   Integrated Behavior Model in the Context of Social Engineering

The scientific explanation of how values, norms, and roles influence our perception and, consequently, our behavior can be detailed using the **Integrated Behavior Model** (IBM) by Montaño and Kasprzyk (2008). The IBM [2] is a significant theoretical model developed to understand and explain human behavior in various contexts. It adapts and unifies key concepts from different social and behavioral psychology theories into a single descriptive model.

The IBM (Fig. 4.2) considers human behavior as dependent on five central factors:

- Knowledge and skills,
- Habit,

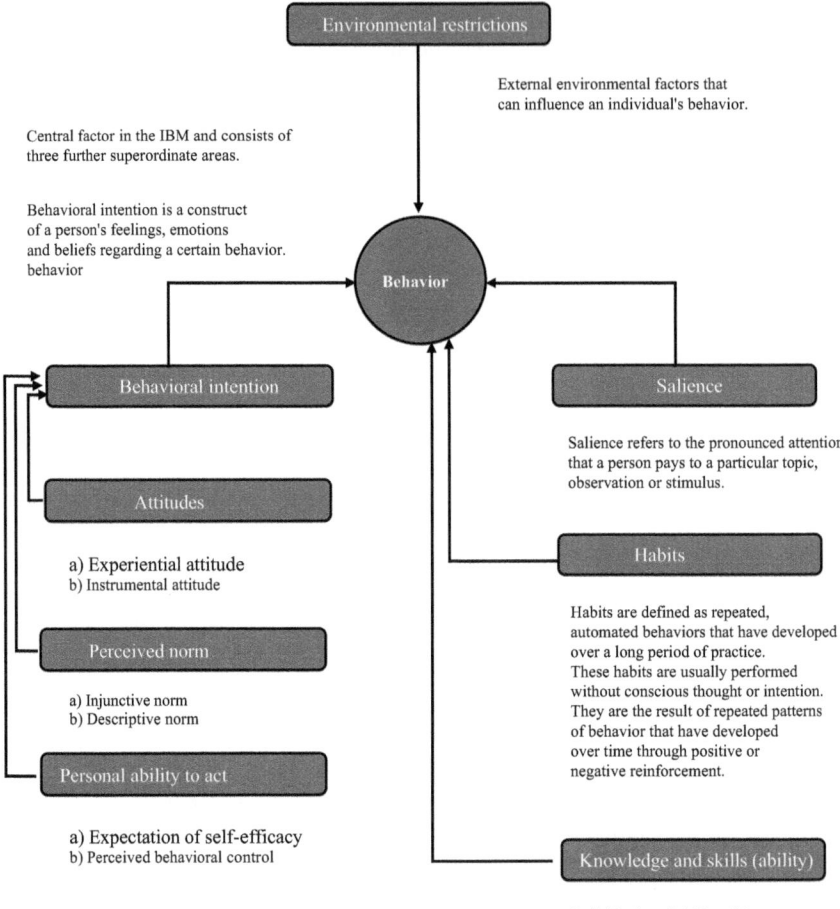

Fig. 4.2 IBM

- Salience,
- Environmental restrictions, and
- Behavioral intention.

Knowledge and Skills This factor refers to a person's knowledge and skills required to perform a specific action. An individual must possess the necessary knowledge and required skills to successfully carry out an action.

Habit Habits play an important role in behavior. When an action becomes a habit, it is often performed automatically and without conscious thought.

Salience Salience refers to the importance or relevance of an action for an individual. The more salient an action is, the more likely it is to be performed.

Environmental Restrictions This factor encompasses external influences and obstacles that can affect a person's behavior. These constraints can make it more difficult or easier to implement an action.

Behavioral Intention Behavioral intention is a **central** factor in the IBM and has the greatest influence on a person's behavior. It refers to a person's feelings, emotions, and beliefs about performing a specific action. However, behavioral intention—meaning a person's willingness to perform a particular action—is a complex construct that itself encompasses various aspects. In particular, the individual's beliefs play an important role, as they represent cognitive information about a specific issue or entity, often linked to an emotional component. For example, a belief might be that sharing information over the phone does not constitute a "security risk." If a person with this belief shares information, no negative emotions are triggered. On the contrary, emotions remain within the normal range or are even experienced positively, since the communication was open and clear. This belief can be traced back to childhood and thus leads to a deeply rooted attitude in those affected. From a scientific perspective, the formation of beliefs and trust is based on cognitive and social processes whose influence can extend back to early childhood. For instance, children learn and internalize beliefs and convictions in their early years, based on their interactions with parents, teachers, and their environment. These beliefs can become deeply ingrained and influence how people interpret and respond to the world.

Trust in the security of telephone communication may be based on previous experiences, individual differences, and available information. Strong trust in this means of communication leads to positive emotions and promotes effective and open interaction. This demonstrates how our past and beliefs can shape our psychological and social responses. Another concrete example from the field of information security is when someone believes that opening email attachments and enabling file macros poses no danger, because their father, who works as an IT specialist, has always said that one can safely trust the security of electronic email communication within the secured corporate network.

The father's belief that the IT department only allows verified emails suggests that opening and enabling a macro-based Word file within the corporate network poses no risk or cannot pose a risk. A person who has acquired this individual belief from their father is, in practice, more susceptible to falling into security traps and more likely to become a victim of phishing attacks with hidden execution codes in attached files.

Behavioral intention is thus the result of several differentiated and interwoven events that can be traced on a timeline from childhood to the present adult age.

In detail, it represents a complex structure that can be summarized by three essential areas, each based on individual origin factors:

- **Attitude:**
  - Experiential attitude, and
  - Instrumental attitude,
- **Perceived norm**:
  - Injunctive norm,
  - Descriptive norm,
- **Personal agency**:
  - Self-efficacy expectation,
  - Perceived behavioral control.

The individual **attitude** can be traced back to two origin factors: experiential attitude and instrumental attitude. **Experiential attitude** refers to a person's emotions and feelings regarding a specific behavior. For example, people experience positive feelings when they are able to help others or reliably identify spam emails. **Instrumental attitude** defines a person's beliefs about a particular behavior.

For instance, employees may be convinced that visitor management is a valuable organizational tool for providing visitors with name badges. As a result, there is a high likelihood that strangers without name badges will be proactively approached and stopped by end users.

The **perceived norm** also consists of two further aspects: the injunctive norm and the descriptive norm. The **injunctive norm** describes the expectations of the social environment regarding accepted and rejected behaviors. It indicates which behaviors, norms, and values are accepted by others in the environment and which are rejected. This perspective is significantly influenced by the beliefs of the social environment.

A concrete example of this could be found in the context of a "clear desk" policy, where, for instance, a community places great importance on ensuring that the office door is locked when leaving the office, even if only temporarily, to prevent potential on-site sabotage. The community's expectation is that every member follows this measure and implements it appropriately. The **descriptive norm** describes an individual's perception of how people in their social environment actually behave, regardless of others' approval or disapproval.

In addition to the characteristics listed above, personal agency also plays a significant role, which can be defined by **self-efficacy expectation** and **perceived behavioral control. Self-efficacy expectation** refers to an individual's level of confidence or trust in their own ability to successfully perform a specific action. In other words, it is the belief that one is capable of carrying out a particular task or behavioral change. This factor considers how strongly a person believes they are able to take the necessary steps to change their behavior. High self-efficacy expectation can increase motivation and willingness to implement behavioral change.

For example, this could mean that a person, due to their high self-efficacy expectation, feels capable of approaching individuals in the company who are not wearing the appropriate identification, whether it be a badge, visitor pass, or employee ID.

Perceived behavioral control refers to an individual's assessment or estimated likelihood of how easy or difficult it is to perform a specific behavior or to implement a behavioral change. It considers the perceived ability to overcome external obstacles or barriers and to actually put the desired behavior into practice. People may have varying degrees of perceived behavioral control for different behaviors or situations. If someone feels that the behavioral change is within their control and that there are no insurmountable obstacles, perceived behavioral control is high.

According to the integrated behavioral model, the two factors of self-efficacy and perceived behavioral control are important determinants of behavior. They influence a person's willingness and ability to successfully implement an intended behavioral change.

4.5   Practical Understanding of IBM

We would now like to familiarize you with the practical application and understanding of the previously introduced integrated behavioral model [2] using an example. The topic we will use is phishing. The main focus is to demonstrate how the integrated behavioral model (IBM) can descriptively explain why a person clicks or does not click on a link.

It becomes apparent that several different factors interact in a dynamic way and influence each other to varying degrees.

This enables us to develop a deeper understanding of how individual behavior is determined and influenced. External and internal influences are in a reciprocal relationship, allowing external influences to affect internal beliefs and vice versa. Moreover, there are additional dependencies between the individual determinants that are not immediately obvious. For example, the factor "knowledge" can influence both the injunctive norm and the descriptive norm. However, it becomes even more interesting when we replace the side-by-side comparison of the two IBM applications "clicking or not clicking" with a separate analysis of each scenario.

It is immediately noticeable that security-compliant behavior is a product of both individual and collective behavior and, as a result, is highly dependent on the interpretation of the individual as well as the community.

This supports our postulate that companies with a mature security and error culture, as well as an appropriate mindset regarding information security, are predestined to create a collaborative environment in which both collective and individual security are promoted and demanded. The comparison of the IBM applications thus allows us not only to identify the individual factors that foster and generate security-compliant behavior, but also to see how a sense for the harmonization and orchestration of information security can be developed (Fig. 4.3).

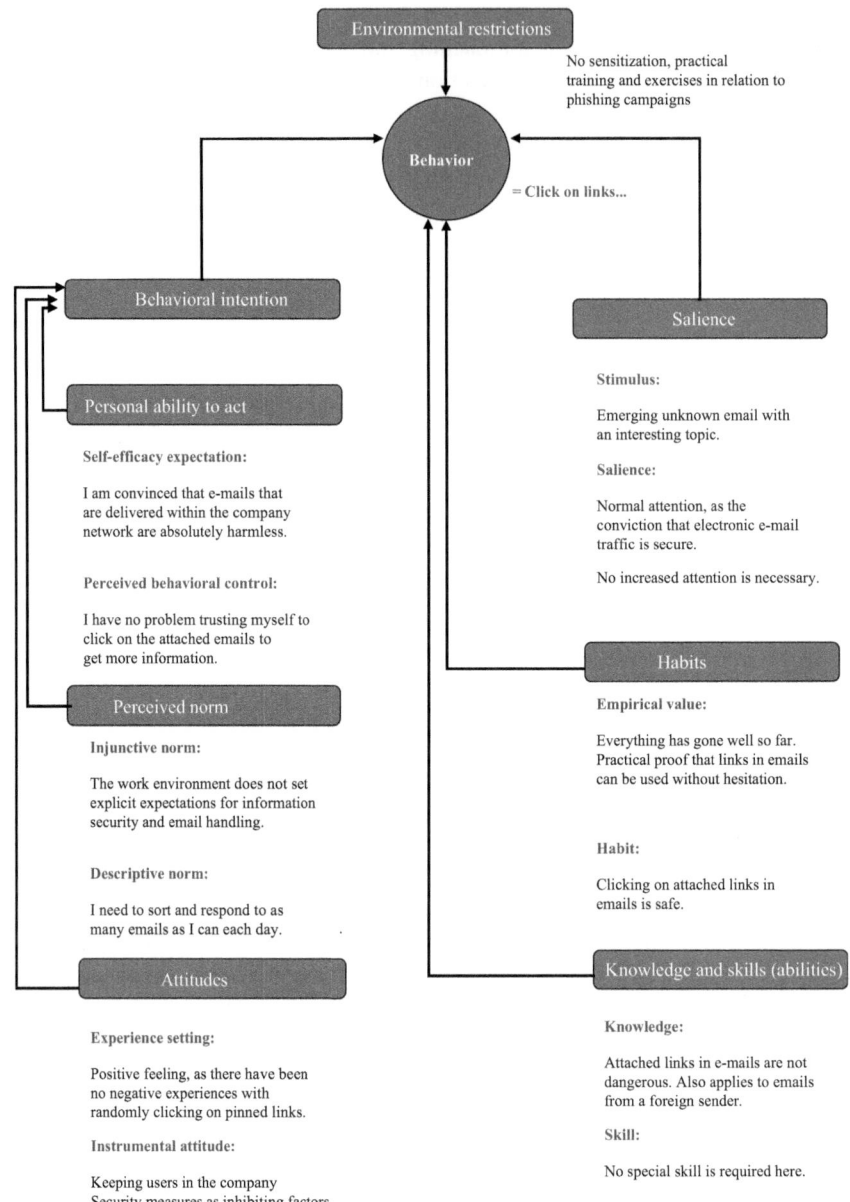

Fig. 4.3 Application of IBM in the context of information security (negative)

A closer look at the two IBM scenarios also reveals that IBM takes into account all three previously defined influencing elements on perception and integrates them into its environment, even if they are named differently (Fig. 4.4).

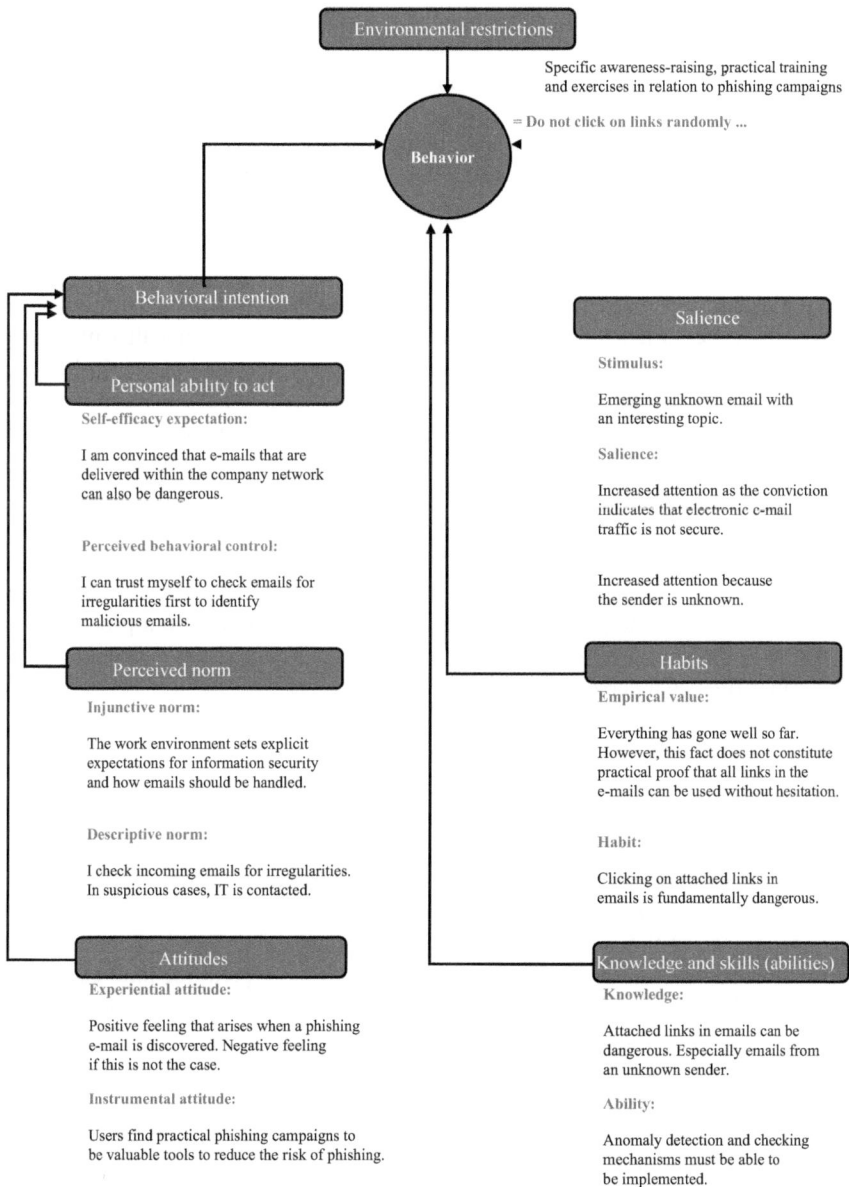

Fig. 4.4 Application of IBM in the context of information security (positive)

In doing so, not only phylogenetic elements are considered, but also ontogenetic elements such as experiential attitude, instrumental attitude, as well as current cognitive abilities like knowledge and skills, to explain behavior.

Let us now return to our main explanatory objective, using IBM to explain the influencing elements on perception and behavior. In IBM, as illustrated in our examples, the influence of norms and values is primarily defined by the injunctive norm, which represents the expectations within a particular social environment. For instance, in a professional community, values such as helpfulness and politeness, along with associated norms, may be perceived as expectations from other members of the organization. These perceived injunctive norms create certain expectations regarding an individual's behavior. The crucial aspect, however, is that there is an important bridge between perception and behavior. Roles, norms, and values influence perception and activate behavioral intention by triggering the injunctive norm. This injunctive norm generates expectations. In response, the person compares these expectations with their own personal memories and feelings. This process leads to a specific interpretation and a feeling that ultimately manifests in observable behavior. When a social engineer or human hacker pretends to represent certain norms and values, they deliberately manipulate these expectations in the victim. The victim then adjusts their behavioral intention to act in accordance with the fabricated norms and values, assuming that their behavior meets the expectations.

If we now consider experiential attitude, we see that the emotions and emotional state of the victim regarding this particular behavior can indeed be positive, as the person is adhering to common social conventions and behavioral rules, which generally evoke positive feelings. This targeted manipulation process illustrates how norms and values, through the injunctive norm, shape expectations and thus can influence a person's behavior.

4.6 Mail Carrier and Kahneman's Systems

Let us now continue our explanatory approach with the following example.

Imagine you are in a business setting and are expecting the arrival of a mail carrier who is supposed to deliver a package for your company. You are familiar with the appearance of the supposed mail carrier, as they wear a standard uniform that is easily recognizable by its distinctive color and logo, typical for mail carriers of this particular organization. In this situation, you suddenly notice a person wearing the expected attire, matching the image stored in your mind.

Your brain automatically responds to this visual information by drawing on familiar patterns and expectations.

You judge the person solely based on their specific outward appearance as an authoritative individual, authorized to reliably and confidentially deliver packages from sender to recipient.

This assessment is based solely on the fact that the striking external visual features of the supposed mail carrier align with your expectations. You feel that the mail carrier is a trustworthy person delivering packages for your organization. This generates a positive and familiar feeling. At this moment, you do not necessarily consider that, in principle, anyone could order and wear the same clothing at low cost via online platforms. Moreover, someone could carry an empty package as a prop to fake an identity, potentially misleading you and indicating an attacker.

Why is this the case? Why does our brain decide in a matter of nanoseconds, without carefully verifying the person, that this is a trustworthy individual who poses no immediate threat?

We will now explain this using behavioral economics and Daniel Kahneman's "systems" [3]. Together with his research partner Amos Tversky, he published numerous studies and works that explain the understanding of human decision-making processes. A key work based on his research is the book **Thinking, Fast and Slow,** in which he describes the two main systems of thinking, known in cognitive psychology as **System 1 and System 2** (Fig. 4.5).

According to Kahneman, there are two fundamental thinking systems in the human brain. The first system, known as System 1, is an intuitive and automatic mode of thinking. It enables quick, instinctive responses based on experience and pattern recognition. System 1 operates effortlessly and requires no conscious effort. It is activated for everyday tasks such as recognizing faces, assessing

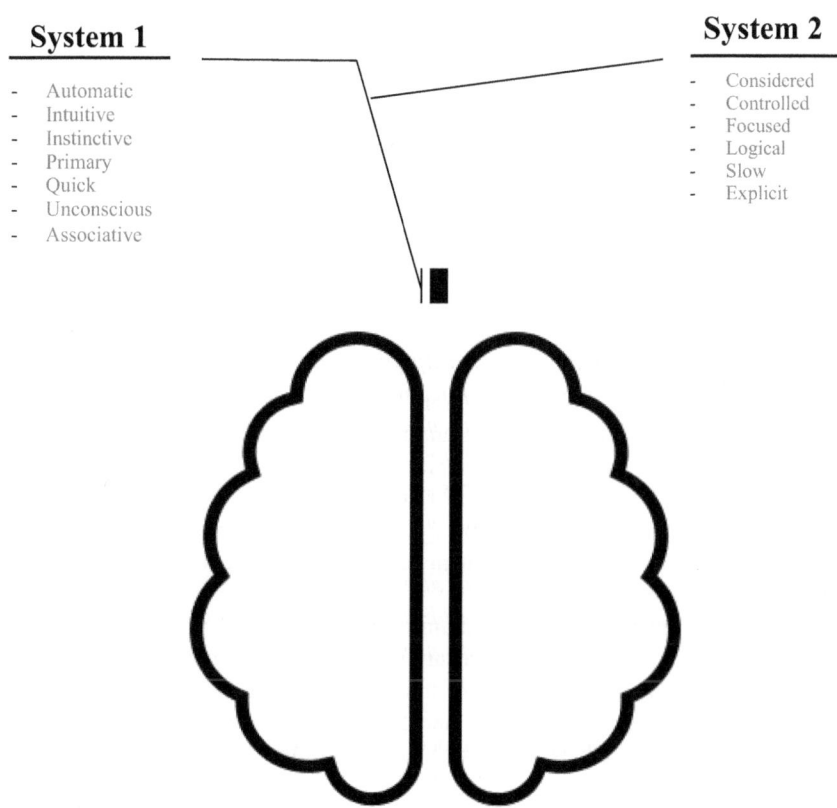

Fig. 4.5   Kahneman's systems, D. (2016) [3]

dangers, and reading simple words. However, **System 1** is prone to errors and can lead to biases and misjudgments.

System 2, on the other hand, is deliberate, effortful, and requires mental exertion. It is activated when complex problems need to be solved, mathematical calculations performed, or uncertain decisions made. System 2 encompasses logical thinking, analysis, and reflection. It serves to monitor and, if necessary, correct the impulsive reactions of System 1. For better illustration, let us briefly consider the following two questions.

Question 1: Did you lock the front door?

Question 2: Have you finished the audit report for Safety GmbH?
For many people, the first question triggers a certain uncertainty. The uncertainty that arises with the question, "Did you lock the front door?" stems from the fact that this action has become a habit or automatic routine for many. It is so deeply integrated into their daily lives that they often no longer consciously think about whether they locked the door or not. System 1, the fast and automatic thinking system, has developed this habit over time to speed up decision-making, avoid unnecessary strain on System 2, and make everyday life more efficient. When you stand in front of your door and ask yourself this question, System 1 is active and tends to provide the answer based on habit and experience. However, this can lead to uncertainty, as System 1 operates automatically, intuitively, quickly, and without conscious deliberation. There is always the possibility that an action was accidentally forgotten. On the other hand, the question, "Have you finished the audit report for Safety GmbH?" requires a different type of response, one based on more conscious reflection and current knowledge. System 2, the slow and deliberate thinking system, is activated to answer this question. People are aware that they need to recall the completion of the report, and they think about it consciously before responding. This leads to a different kind of answer, which is generally less uncertain. The immediate and almost automatic decision of our brain to identify the supposed person as a trustworthy mail carrier, without careful verification, can be explained using Kahneman's System 1 and System 2.

In the scenario described, "System 1" is activated first. This intuitive and automatic thinking system enables spontaneous conclusions to be drawn based on experience and pattern recognition.

The person is wearing the expected uniform, which, due to your experience and pattern recognition, is identified as a familiar image. System 1 works lightning-fast and effortlessly, allowing for the immediate identification of the person as a harmless mail carrier. The positive and familiar feeling that arises is a typical result of System 1. It enables us to make quick judgments based on rapid associations and past experiences. In this case, it creates the impression that this is a trustworthy and legitimate person who delivers packages securely and confidentially.

Now, please briefly put on your **pessimistic glasses** by actively integrating the knowledge you have gained into your cognitive assessment and interpretation of your perception: "The mail carrier could also be an attacker!" This is where

System 2 comes into play, as we examine the situation more closely. System 2 is a conscious and deliberate thinking system that requires mental effort. It can serve to correct impulsive reactions from System 1. In the context of our example with the supposed mail carrier, System 2 might be activated if the person suddenly has doubts about the mail carrier's identity, especially when considering possible human-centered threats. This is also where the connection to the IBM factor "Knowledge and Skills" comes in.

If the target individuals are informed about such attack vectors and types, they are more likely not to take such scenarios for granted, but instead to display a suspicious and healthy preventive defensive behavior. At this point, their mind recalls the old adage: "Better safe than sorry." In such cases, System 2 is activated first to recognize the situation and conduct further investigation.

4.7 Emotional Stimulus-Response Chain

How do we move from perception to behavior? Let us take a closer look at the emotional stimulus-response chain. The emotional stimulus-response chain is a concept in psychological research that describes the sequence of steps by which emotional stimuli lead to emotional reactions and ultimately to behaviors. This concept highlights the close interplay between perception, interpretation, emotion, and response. To answer the question of how the transition from perception to behavior occurs, a detailed examination of the emotional stimulus-response chain is essential (Fig. 4.6). Therefore, in order to answer how perception leads to behavior, it is first important to understand the emotional stimulus-response chain.

The first step in this chain is the **perception** of a stimulus. This stimulus can be either internal (e.g., thoughts or memories) or external (e.g., external events or situations). Perception occurs through the senses and sensory organs. After perception comes the **cognitive interpretation** of the emotional stimulus. At this stage, the stimulus is interpreted and evaluated. The individual interpretation influences how the stimulus is perceived and what impact it has on emotional responses.

The connection between perception and interpretation in psychology can be described as a complex cognitive process in which external perceptions interact with internal expectations, stored memories, and general experiences. This process is central to the interpretation and evaluation of environmental stimuli and influences how we respond to these stimuli.

The cognition of perception and interpretation is an essential part of the cognitive process in which external sensory information interacts with internal expectations and already stored memories. This process enables the interpretation of environmental stimuli and influences the emergence of sensations and the resulting actions.

The process begins with the **perception** of environmental stimuli, which are captured by the sensory organs. This sensory information is raw and unprocessed. In parallel with perception, existing **expectations** are activated. These expectations may be based on individual assumptions, cultural influences, and context.

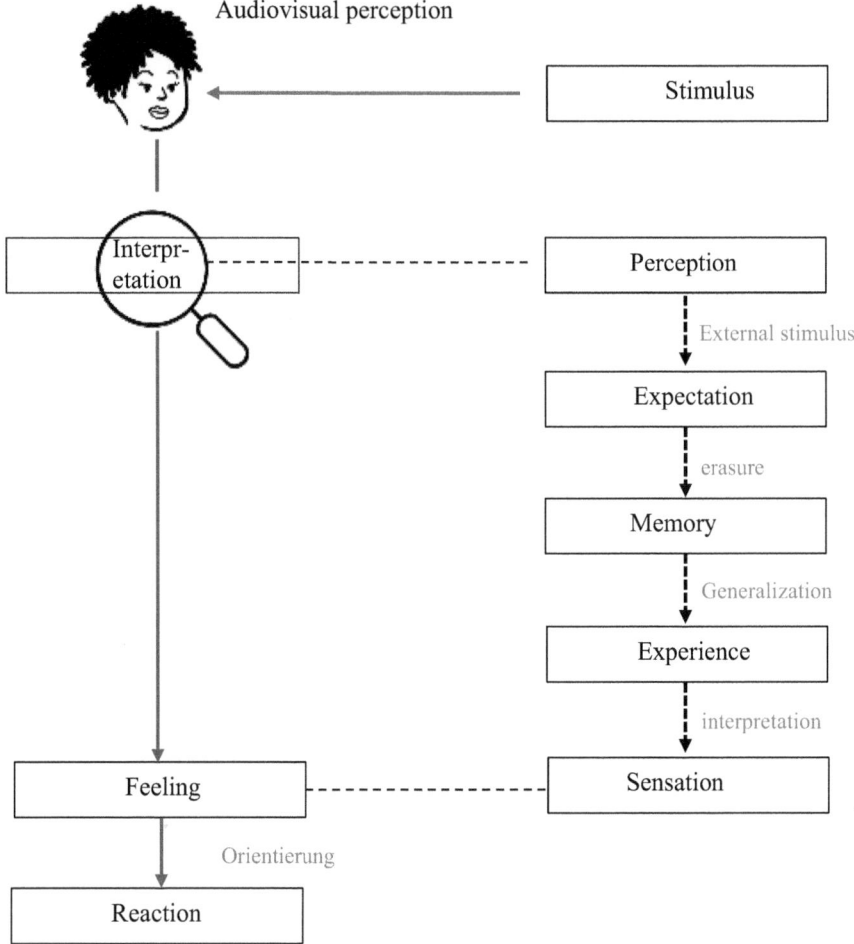

Fig. 4.6 Emotional stimulus-response chain with additional explanation

The expectations are linked to relevant stored **memories and experiences.** This step allows the perception to be embedded in an existing cognitive context. The combination of perception, expectation, and memory leads to the interpretation and evaluation of the stimulus. At this stage, the **interpretation** of the stimulus as significant or insignificant, safe or threatening, pleasant or unpleasant takes place. As a result of the cognitive interpretation of the stimulus, emotions arise. These emotions can cover a wide spectrum, including joy, fear, anger, sadness, and much more. The type and intensity of these emotions are largely influenced by the cognitive interpretation of the stimulus. Finally, the interpreted emotions lead to the selection of a behavioral response. This response can range from simple motor actions to complex cognitive decisions. It is influenced by the emotions and the individual interpretation of the stimulus.

What is the relevance of the emotional stimulus-response chain for our human behavior?

So far, we have explained what the emotional stimulus-response chain is, and now we will discuss the significance of this concept for our analysis.

A human hacker can deliberately trigger our conditioned reflexes by presenting targeted stimuli linked to certain memories, thereby influencing our individual behavioral patterns. A vivid example illustrates this: When we see a saber-toothed tiger (stimulus), the expectation is immediately triggered that it might attack us, based on the memory that it has already eaten someone in our environment (negative experience). As a result, the emotion of fear arises and our automatic reaction is to flee.

If a human hacker skillfully presents a stimulus associated with a specific negative memory, it can cause us to revert to pre-programmed behavioral patterns. In this state, we act less analytically and logically, and instead respond more intuitively. This makes us vulnerable to manipulation during this phase, and a skilled hacker can exploit this to their advantage. The mechanism is similar to a conditioned reflex, in which the stimulus triggers an automatic response without conscious analysis (Fig. 4.7).

You can see, therefore, that the emotional stimulus-response chain, just like IBM and Kahneman's systems, each provide partial answers to our questions, which we must then piece together to arrive at a unified and reasonably robust answer. Thus, the psychological backgrounds of social engineering are diverse and complex in nature.

However, the individual partial levels of this analysis make it clear that the art of human hacking is inextricably linked to human emotions and our very existence.

It is precisely those qualities that make us social beings—such as our fears, worries, familiarity, affection, love, sense of duty, honesty, helpfulness, praise and recognition, and much more—that are exploited here.

To make the explanation of the psychological backgrounds regarding the types of social engineering attacks even simpler and more understandable, we will now describe our explanations in terms of specific feelings and emotions.

4.8   Power Dynamics and Authority

Let us now take a closer look at how power dynamics can influence our decisions. The "Milgram Experiment," conducted in the 1960s by psychologist Stanley Milgram, clearly demonstrates that people often tend to comply with the demands of authority figures, even when doing so raises moral concerns or goes against their own beliefs. In this experiment, participants were assigned the roles of "teacher" and "learner." However, the "learners" were actually actors, a fact unknown to the "teachers." For every incorrect answer given by the "learners," the "teachers" were instructed to administer an electric shock. As the experiment progressed, the "learners" gave clear indications that they were in pain. Although the

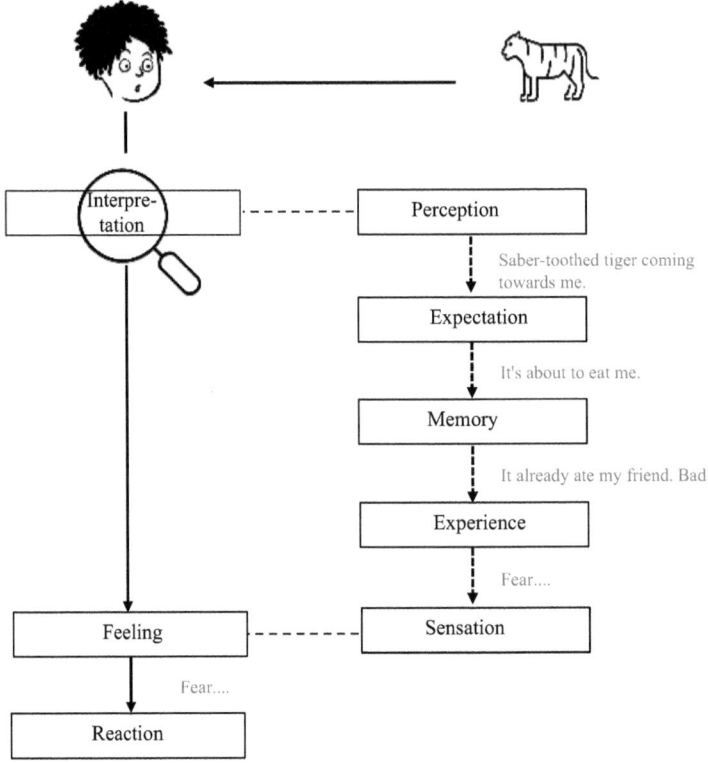

Escape = conditioned reflex (system 1)

Fig. 4.7 Emotional stimulus-response chain with explanation of the conditioned reflex

"teachers" increasingly expressed concerns about the electric shocks, they continued with the experiment because the authority figure, the experimenter, verbally instructed them to do so. Numerous studies have shown that **authority** plays a significant role in influencing people.[1] In the 2013 study [4] "A study of social engineering fraud," it was shown that 100% (n = 100) of participants dropped their guard against threats and risks when *authority* was used in phishing emails.

---

[1] In [5] "On the anatomy of social engineering attacks—A literature-based dissection of successful attacks," the authors Bullé et al. (2017, p. 14) examine principles used in social engineering attacks. The persuasion principle of authority is the most frequently used (see Chap. 3—Results).

In [6] "Breaching the human firewall: social engineering in phishing and spear-phishing emails," the authors Butavicus et al. (2016) identify authority as the most effective persuasion strategy.

Halevi et al. (2015) also found in their study [7] "Spear-phishing in the wild: a real-world study of personality, phishing self-efficacy and vulnerability to spear-phishing attacks" that authority is the most effective strategy in phishing scams.

Authority also proved to be the greatest success factor in advance-fee fraud attempts, convincing 84% of participants. What does authority refer to? In the Milgram experiment, we clearly saw that the experimenter, who exercises delegation in his role, represents an authority figure. However, authority is not limited to a person's role.

An authority figure can be a law enforcement officer, CEO, professor (title), a celebrity (status), or even a well-known functional role such as a mail carrier or cleaning staff.

4.9 Pressure and Urgency

In addition to authority, the aspects of **urgency and pressure** also play a crucial role in keeping the victim's rational judgment as far in the background as possible. While the social engineer creates a scenario in which they, as an authority figure, urgently need something—such as a password or access—they demand quick action from their target. The target feels pressured to act immediately. Stress here acts as a perception inhibitor. The victim reacts without pausing to think. Rational judgment stands no chance. In the aforementioned study [4], *urgency* was shown to be the second most enticing tactic in phishing emails at 71%, and in advance-fee fraud at 70%. Urgency does not always have to come from an authority figure. Perhaps you have also encountered the "grandchild scam 2.0" attempt via the WhatsApp messenger service (Fig. 4.8):

The message is clearly spam. We recognize that—or do we? You have to put yourself in the situation: as a parent, which is exactly what the social engineer does. They set up a scenario and deliberately target emotions they want to influence. Every feeling triggers a reaction. This is precisely where the social engineer wants to elicit the reaction of a concerned parent.

On closer inspection (which is difficult in the moment, as our selective perception is impaired), we notice the following:

Mobile and SIM are broken. The old number should be deleted.
Why? So that it is immediately overwritten and contacting the actual child is not possible.

Can you help me? I have a problem. – The self-disclosure here means: I am dependent on you. I need you.

I urgently need to pay a bill, but I can't log in with this phone.
This statement serves as a perception deception and provides a "logical" explanation for why mom or dad has to take care of it.

Can you transfer it? I have to pay it today.
Another indication that it has to be done quickly. The social engineer thus ensures that rational thinking remains suppressed. They now build up pressure. The emotions

Fig. 4.8 Grandchild scam
2.0

associated with immediately helping one's own child—being "needed" as a parent—take over.

4.10   Ego and Our Favorite Sin: "Vanity"

However, we have saved one essential psychological background—at the same time, the number one source of danger—for the conclusion.

The **ego**…

The interplay of perhaps the three most unpredictable letters in the world. "Ego," from the Latin for "I," describes the individual, their personality, self-awareness, and identity, as well as their self-perception. When we talk about ego, the basics of Freudian theory, such as the **id, ego, and superego,** immediately come to mind.

The "id" represents the deeply rooted, instinctive drives and desires of an individual, while the "ego" is concerned with ethics, morality, and the internalized values of society.

And the "superego" brings our environment and its influences on us into focus. However, we do not intend to delve too deeply into the complex theory of Sigmund Freud here.

Rather, the ego of a person plays a special role for us when we talk about social engineering. But what is the connection? The "ego" of a person serves as a mediator between the demands of the reality of the "superego" and the needs of the "id." Our "ego," or self, is a component of our psyche and personality.

When we talk about ego, the term often carries a negative connotation. However, a healthy ego is essential for understanding how the world works and for our self-concept. It can help us boost our self-confidence and self-esteem, understand our needs, and establish the goals and boundaries of our identity.

Nevertheless, an unbalanced or inflated ego can also be self-destructive. If our ego is too pronounced, it can lead to selfishness, arrogance, excessive pride, or a lack of empathy. The key point is that the term itself is not inherently negative; rather, it is the lack of balance that becomes problematic.

In the context of social engineering, we are dealing with psychological and social core aspects when it comes to manipulating and deceiving people. This is precisely where the victim's ego plays an important role. The social engineer, who is highly skilled in the tactics of human psychology, knows how to influence this psyche. An inflated ego causes people to become overconfident, unable to properly assess themselves or the situation they are in. It becomes especially dangerous when the attacker realizes that their target has an excessive ego. Then, the game becomes easy. Through flattery or affirmation of their opinions, the attacker deliberately appeals to the ego, builds trust, offers approval, and positively influences the person's self-image. It is a skillful game. The more critically the victim questions the situation and their own actions, the harder it becomes for the social engineer.

A well-trained, healthy ego that is aware of the risks, on the other hand, can be used as a strength—and this brings us back to the point where the human factor is seen as an asset. If a person assesses the situation based on facts rather than on emotions that have been triggered within them, they are more reflective. This is a sign of a balanced ego.

An example in a corporate context might be the following: An employee regularly shares updates about their project results with their network via social media channels. In a recently published post, Mr. Anton Meier writes:

Numerous members congratulate him. A few days after his post, he receives a private inquiry. A manager from another company, who saw the post, contacts him and says he is very interested in the project that Mr. Meier successfully completed. What Anton Meier does not know is that the manager is actually a social engineer.

He showers his target with praise and recognition, emphasizes shared goals and interests, and affirms his approach. In doing so, he builds trust, which leads the employee to be open to a conversation in which he discloses further internal information about his project.

The social engineer manipulates and deceives his target by satisfying the need for approval and recognition for their hard work in order to achieve his own goals.

He deliberately targets the ego. By boosting the victim's ego, he engages in what is known in the field as ***ego-hacking or ego-baiting.*** In this way, he achieves his goal of obtaining information. The victim saves him as a friendly contact and thinks nothing more of it (Fig. 4.9).

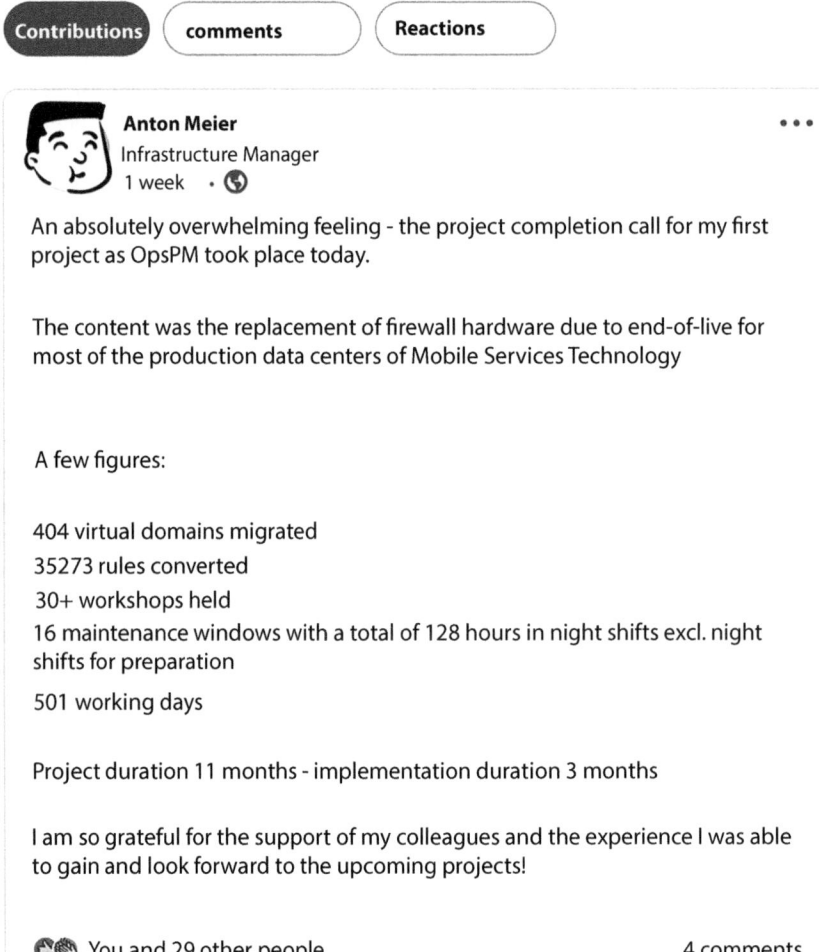

All activities

Contributions   comments   Reactions

Anton Meier
Infrastructure Manager
1 week   · 🌐   • • •

An absolutely overwhelming feeling - the project completion call for my first project as OpsPM took place today.

The content was the replacement of firewall hardware due to end-of-live for most of the production data centers of Mobile Services Technology

A few figures:

404 virtual domains migrated
35273 rules converted
30+ workshops held
16 maintenance windows with a total of 128 hours in night shifts excl. night shifts for preparation
501 working days

Project duration 11 months - implementation duration 3 months

I am so grateful for the support of my colleagues and the experience I was able to gain and look forward to the upcoming projects!

👍❤️ You and 29 other people   4 comments

Fig. 4.9 Example: Ego-hacking

4.11 Fear

Fear is also a powerful emotion that each of us experiences. Every emotion triggers a reaction, but the nature of that reaction depends greatly on the individual. While behavioral psychology works to help people overcome their fears, social engineers exploit this emotion for their own purposes. In social engineering, exploiting the emotion of fear is a powerful tool for the human hacker. For example, the human hacker can use fear as leverage. They may issue a threat of consequences to force the victim to act. The fear of consequences triggers a reaction that may be either considered or automatically impulsive.

Let's look at a scenario:

It is 5:30 p.m. on a Friday afternoon, just before Christmas. Most colleagues are already on their way home. A colleague from the IT department calls and claims that after the firewall replacement, a security vulnerability was discovered that requires immediate action, as systems are already infected with viruses and data loss is imminent. A classic false alarm to create a distraction. The attacker appears to have information about the systems used in the company, making him seem credible at first glance.

IT colleague: Unfortunately, Mr. Meier, who was responsible for the hardware replacement, is already on his way home. It's urgent, otherwise serious damage could occur.

Here, the pressure card is played after the distraction. The question we now have to ask is: how did he get this information?

It's simple. He bases his story on a recently published post by a certain Mr. Anton Meier. With a quick search, he knows that a project was recently completed in which firewall hardware was replaced. He now exploits exactly this scenario to pose as an internal IT colleague.

The attacker gives instructions over the phone, which the victim is to follow step by step. After downloading a file, the victim is told to visit a website. The victim complies, because time is of the essence. Here, the attacker deliberately exploits the victim's fear and uncertainty. The victim has no chance to evade, consult others, or question the person on the phone, because they have not been sufficiently sensitized.

The attacker senses the fear and uncertainty, as he is a professional in exploiting emotions. He knows how to wrap up the conversation so that his victim does not feel uneasy in the days that follow.

IT colleague: "Thank you so much, you're a lifesaver. I don't even want to imagine what would have happened if you hadn't picked up. I'll take care of the last updates, then I'll also head off for my well-deserved holidays. Ms. Lanze, thank you, that's what I call good teamwork. I wish you a restful holiday season. I'll be on vacation after Christmas, so we'll probably speak again next year, when Mr. Meier is back as well. Happy New Year in advance!"

In this way, he ensures that the end of the conversation is steered in a different direction. He gives her further recognition. He is *friendly* and thanks her for her active support, thereby alleviating her *fear* and sense of uncertainty. He then shifts the conversation to another topic. Instead of dealing with her uneasy feeling, Ms. Lanze now focuses on her upcoming holidays. She shuts down her computer and finishes her work.

4.12 Curiosity

Curiosity is the source of knowledge. It describes the interest in and motivation for new information, experiences, or ideas. Through *curiosity,* we develop ourselves further and look beyond our own horizons. We acquire new skills and gain a better understanding of the world. This illustrates the positive effects of curiosity on people.

However, in the wrong context, curiosity can also have negative consequences. Social engineers exploit human curiosity and create incentives to arouse interest.

They lure their victims into traps by enticing them to click on certain links, for example, to claim prizes, vouchers, or secret information. They promise special offers and *exclusive* opportunities for certain products or services. Receiving unusual messages can also spark our curiosity and prompt us to interact. Once a basis for interaction has been established—such as clicking a link or replying to a message—the social engineer can ensnare the victim. This may lead the victim to log in to a website or disclose sensitive information, such as an address for prize delivery or account details.

An example of exploiting curiosity could be an email with an attachment and a subject line such as "Register today," "Your data on the dark web," "Your photo," "Annual report," "Your invoice," "Layoff list," "Graduation gift," or similar. The targeted manipulation of curiosity is therefore a common tactic used by social engineers.

4.13 Gullibility

Gullibility is closely linked to the need for harmony, which is also relevant in the context of social engineering. Even when a situation or person seems odd, people tend to find explanations that justify the behavior. Gullible individuals firmly believe that, fundamentally, people are good, and are reluctant to be convinced otherwise.

A practical example illustrates how gullibility can lead to problematic situations in the context of social engineering. Consider the case of an agitated man named Reiner Reus. After greeting the administrator, Reiner addresses her informally and explains that he is one of the many field staff in the company. He says he is preparing for a pitch with a potential client and asks his "colleague" to send him the previous correspondence and related offers, or to briefly summarize the key points over the phone. Due to the high workload this week, he claims he has not been able to prepare adequately for this important meeting. In this scenario, the administrator's gullibility is exploited to obtain sensitive information.

The psychological manipulation is carried out through the deliberate use of linguistic and verbal elements. By using informal language, the human hacker attempts to quickly build rapport and establish a sense of camaraderie. Speaking rapidly serves to create pressure and heighten the target's attention. At the same time, by staging an apparent emergency, the attacker exploits the victim's willingness to help. In this manipulative context, key information can easily fall into the wrong hands.

4.14   Reciprocity Principle—Tit for Tat

The **reciprocity principle** is a social-psychological concept based on the idea of mutual exchange. It states that people tend to respond to a positive action with a corresponding positive action, and to a negative action with a corresponding negative action. This social exchange mechanism forms the basis for the development and maintenance of interpersonal relationships. As a social-psychological concept, the reciprocity principle manifests itself in numerous everyday situations.

A clear example of this is the free sample offer in supermarkets. By giving customers free product samples, the provider creates an obligation for a reciprocal gesture—namely, considering a purchase. The initial free action generates a psychological expectation of reciprocity.

Another example can be found in the world of online marketing. Companies often offer free resources, such as white papers or e-books. By providing this information free of charge, a sense of obligation is created in the reader. In many cases, this obligation is fulfilled through positive actions such as subscribing to a newsletter or purchasing additional paid offers.

In the context of social engineering, the reciprocity principle (Fig. 4.10) is deliberately used to manipulate the victim. For example, an attacker can create a sense of obligation or guilt in the victim through a small favor or act of kindness. The victim then feels more inclined to reciprocate by performing a desired action or disclosing information. This technique is based on the psychological drive to fulfill social obligations and return positive actions. The targeted use of

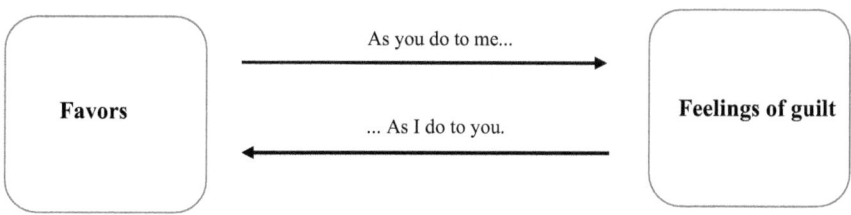

Fig. 4.10 Schematic illustration of the reciprocity principle

the reciprocity principle is an effective method in the social engineering toolkit to gain trust and influence the victim's behavior.

However, in social interactions, the subtle impact of manipulation techniques such as the reciprocity principle in everyday situations is often underestimated. An experimental approach could be to deliberately initiate a social situation during a train journey. For example, at the usual moment of sitting down, one might start a brief small talk, which could lead either to a continued conversation or a one-off exchange.

In the first phase of this experiment, the initiator takes the floor and delivers a one-minute monologue on a specific topic, such as switching from driving to taking the train, or doing light office work during the journey. After the monologue, a deliberate silence is maintained to observe how the other person reacts. The aim is to test the natural urge to reciprocate.

This experimental approach not only enables the analysis of reciprocity in social interactions, but also provides insight into possible manipulation techniques. In a similar situation, a human hacker could consciously steer the conversation, build trust, and guide the discussion toward the desired topic.

Through active listening, skillful questioning, and leveraging commonalities, the human hacker can manipulate the victim and steer the conversation in the desired direction, whether in a professional context or on personal topics. This demonstrates how subtle social mechanisms can be deliberately used to influence interpersonal behavior.

References

1. Asiye Öztürk, Michael Willer, Vishing: Die unsichtbare Gefahr am Telefon, unter: https://www.it-daily.net/it-sicherheit/cybercrime/vishing-die-unsichtbare-gefahr-am-telefon (Zugriff: 01.12.2023).
2. Daniel Montaño, Danuta, Kasprzyk, Theory of Reasoned Action, Theory of Planned Behavior, and the Integrated Behavioral Model, im Buch: Health Behavior: Theory, Research, and Practice, 2008.
3. Daniel Kahneman, Schnelles Denken, Langsames Denken, Penguin Verlag, 2016.
4. Brandon Atkins, Wilson Huang, A Study of Social Engineering in Online Frauds, Open Journal of Sciences, 2013.
5. Jan-Willem Hendrik Bullée, Lorena Montoya, Wolter Pieters, Marianne Junger, Pieter Hartel, On the anatomy of social engineering attacks—A literature-based dissection of successful attacks, in: Journal of Investigative Psychology and Offender Profiling, Vol. 15, Issue 1, 2017.
6. Marcus Butavicius, Kathryn Parsons, Malcolm Pattinson, Agata McCormac, Breaching the Human Firewall: Social engineering in Phishing and Spear-Phishing Emails, in: Australasian Conference on Information Systems, 2015.
7. Tzipora Halevi, Nasir D. Memon, Oded Nov, Spear-Phishing in the Wild: A Real-World Study of Personality, Phishing Self-Efficacy and Vulnerability to Spear-Phishing Attacks, in: SSRN Electronic Journal, 2015.

Types of Social Engineering

5

The human factor occupies a central position in the context of social engineering, both directly (immediately) and indirectly (mediately). In cases of direct involvement, individuals are actively engaged in intentional actions, as can be the case with insider threats [1]. These actors, motivated by various reasons including revenge, financial gain, or ideological motives, carry out attacks ranging from the theft of analog and digital data sets, the deliberate disclosure of classified information, to the theft of hardware. To counter these threats, preventive, reactive, and detective security models and mechanisms are required. Their strategic and tactical composition must be defined and implemented differently from the measures used to address human-centered threats, such as those that can arise in the realm of social engineering. Countermeasures range from personnel-related security precautions and process design, to the application of principles such as the principle of least privilege [2] and the needs-based allocation of physical and logical rights, up to security principles like the four-eyes principle. In addition, technical measures such as screen recording and real-time monitoring of download rates can be implemented to, for example, monitor unauthorized downloading of data sets. The challenge in defending against insider threats actually lies with the insiders themselves [3]. Internal actors often possess detailed knowledge of monitoring technologies, software and hardware configuration characteristics, integrated default values, and alarm system thresholds, among other things. Moreover, they are often well acquainted with organizational processes, such as shift changes. This frequently enables them to easily circumvent preventive and detective mechanisms.

In the context of social engineering, by contrast, the involvement of the human factor is indirect. Here, individuals become victims without being consciously and intentionally involved in acts of sabotage. Examples of indirect involvement include phishing attacks, in which people are tricked into clicking on malicious links or disclosing confidential information without being aware of the potential danger.

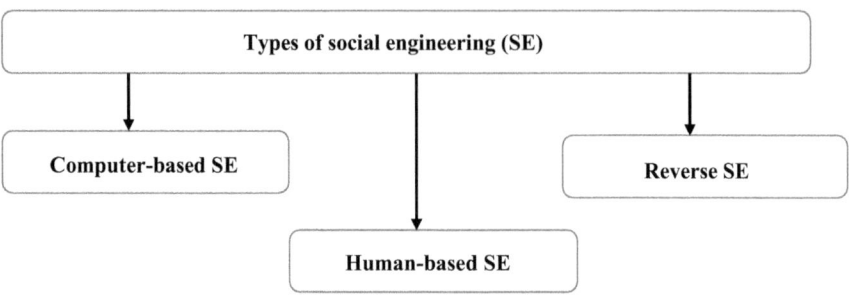

Fig. 5.1 Types of Social Engineering

In such scenarios, the challenge lies in raising employee awareness to improve their ability to recognize and defend against social engineering attacks. Countermeasures span various levels such as "knowledge," "motivation," and "ability," which affect not only individual employees within a company but also the community and the collective level of an organization. This extends from executive management to all other operational roles, both internal and external, permanent and temporary.

Let us now recall our definition of social engineering:

Social engineering is a multidisciplinary practice aimed at skillfully exploiting human social, psychological, and emotional characteristics to induce individuals to perform actions or disclose information that are against their own interests or those of an organization or society. This method combines analog and digital techniques to deceive and manipulate people, and represents an ongoing challenge for information security. The consequences of a social engineering attack can cause both monetary and psychological harm, with the latter often having long-term effects on the well-being and mental health of the victims.

Based on our definition, we can see that social engineering is often conceptualized and operationalized in various forms. In the scientific literature, these forms are described as ***human-based, computer-based,*** and ***reverse*** social engineering ([4]; Fig. 5.1).

5.1 Human-based Social Engineering

Human-based social engineering focuses on manipulating human behavior to obtain information [5]. One example is "pretexting," in which the human hacker invents a false identity or story to build emotional bridges or trust with the victim. Through skillful deception, human hackers can thus gain access to sensitive information. Another tool in the repertoire [6] of human-based social engineering is ***quizzes.*** These are used under the guise of entertainment to collect personal information. Victims are enticed to answer seemingly harmless questions without recognizing the attacker's true intentions. This approach demonstrates how adeptly social engineers exploit human emotions and social interactions to obtain confidential data.

A real-world attack that used the technique of *quizzes* became known in connection with the social media platform Facebook. This was the well-known "Cambridge Analytica" scandal in 2018. Cambridge Analytica, a data analytics company, developed an app called *"thisisyourdigitallife,"* which was disguised as a personality test.

Users were invited to participate in this quiz, and in the process, personal data was collected not only from the participant but also from their Facebook friends. What users did not realize was that the collected information was used for political purposes, to create personalized political advertising. This incident illustrates how seemingly harmless quizzes can be used to extract extensive personal data and misuse it for various purposes.

The ongoing digitalization has therefore not only changed the way we exchange and access information, but also influenced the dynamics of social interactions.

5.2 Computer-based Social Engineering

Computer-based Social Engineering reflects this evolutionary fusion of human behavior and technological elements. The "social" in "computer-based social engineering" refers to the use of psychological tactics to exploit human weaknesses and behavioral patterns. The term emphasizes that social interactions are increasingly influenced by digital technologies. In a connected world, many social interactions take place online. The use of social media, email, and other digital communication platforms creates new attack vectors [7] for social engineers. They rely on these digital channels to contact and influence their victims. Computer-based social engineering highlights how closely human behavior and digital technologies are intertwined. This fusion is evident not only in the use of digital platforms, but also in the integration of AI and machine learning into attack methods. Social engineers can use technologies to develop personalized attacks and simulate human-like interactions.

The term thus makes it clear that these attacks are not just about the use of technology, but about a complex combination of social and psychological strategies with digital tools.

Computer-based social engineering refers to attacks that are carried out at the technological level using social and psychological strategies. This includes malware, spear phishing, and "watering hole attacks." For example, watering hole attacks are targeted attacks in which social engineers compromise a website that is regularly visited by potential victims. The name is derived from the analogy of attackers lying in wait at a place frequently visited by their targets, like a predator at a watering hole waiting for its prey.

The attackers identify websites that members of the target group often visit or are required to visit, and infiltrate them with malicious software.

In doing so, vulnerabilities in the website itself or in the underlying systems can be exploited to inject malware or logical keyloggers to capture account names and passwords. This malicious software is then installed unnoticed on the devices of website visitors, where it can ultimately be used to conduct spying activities.

The human hackers select specific target groups they wish to attack and employ so-called hunting strategies to find suitable victims. The selection is often based on the interests or professional activities of potential victims, such as those in a particular industry or professional group. Watering hole attacks also rely on psychological manipulation to lure victims into visiting an infected website. The human hackers may use fake content or notifications that are attractive to the target group. An example of this could be a fake advertisement for the sale of kittens on eBay. The trick is that only a few blurry pictures are uploaded. The supposed seller refers to their Facebook profile, where numerous pictures of their cute kittens have already been posted. They encourage potential buyers to access their Facebook account and even provide a link that leads directly to their Facebook page. When redirected via the provided link, the victim is taken to a manipulated website through a type of attack known as "pharming." Pharming is an evolution of the phishing scam, in which human hackers attempt to obtain personal information by creating fake websites. They assign a legitimate website a false IP address to redirect users to a fraudulent server. These fake websites are hosted on the attackers' servers. Pharming involves the targeted manipulation of DNS requests, using the Domain Name System (DNS) to translate web addresses into IP addresses. Once the victim arrives at the fake Facebook page, they are prompted to enter their username and password to access their account. If the victim provides this information, the human hacker reads the data via the integrated keylogger and subsequently gains full access to all of the victim's records and information.

5.3 Reverse Social Engineering

Reverse Social Engineering in the context of social engineering occurs when the victim is manipulated into contacting the attacker directly [8]. This approach is based on the victim taking the first step and actively reaching out to the attacker, whether by phone call, email, or another form of communication. The attacker skillfully crafts bait to prompt the victim to make contact.

This can take various forms, including:

Fake Warnings and Security Concerns The attacker may create fake security warnings or threats that suggest to the victim that their personal data is at risk. The victim is then prompted to contact the supposed security service or support hotline.

Pretend Technical Support The victim may receive a call or email from someone claiming to be a member of a technical support team. The attacker asserts that there are issues with the account or its security and convinces the victim to call back or take further action.

Prize Notifications or Rewards The victim is informed that they have won a fantastic prize or reward. To claim the prize, the victim is asked to contact the sender or provide personal information.

In *reverse social engineering,* the victim receives a fake email purporting to be from the customer support of a large company. The email warns of alleged unauthorized access to the victim's account and urges them to immediately call a provided phone number. The attacker, posing as a support representative on the other end, instructs the victim to take certain actions to resolve supposed security issues. In reality, however, the victim is opening a channel for the attacker to obtain further information or install malware. These examples illustrate how reverse engineering in the context of social engineering aims to prompt the victim to proactively make contact, thereby paving the way for further manipulation.

References

1. Kristin Weber, Andreas E. Schütz, Tobias Fertig, Insider Threats – Der Feind in den eigenen Reihen, in: Weber, K., Reinheimer, S. (eds) Faktor Mensch. Edition HMD. Springer Vieweg, Wiesbaden, 2022.
2. Samuel Jero, Juliana Furgala, Runya Pan, Phani Kishore epalli, Alexandra Clifford, Bite Ye, Roger Khazan, Bryan C. Ward, Gabriel Parmer, Richard Skowyra, Practical Principle of Least Privilege for Secure Embedded Systems, in: IEEE 27th Real-Time and Embedded Technology and Applications Symposium (RTAS), Nashville, TN, USA, 2021, S. 1–13.
3. Jason R. C. Nurse, Oliver Buckley, Philip A. Legg, Michael Goldsmith, Sadie Creese, Gordon R. T. Wright, Monica Whitty, Understanding Insider Threat: A Framework for Characterising Attacks, in: IEEE Security and Privacy Workshops, San Jose, CA, USA, 2014, S. 214–228.
4. Ayush Bishnoi, Garv, Saar Bishnoi, Neha Gupta, Comprehensive Assessment of Reverse Social Engineering to Understand Social Engineering Attacks, in: 5th International Conference on Smart Systems and Inventive Technology (ICSSIT), Tirunelveli, Indien, 2023, S. 681–685.
5. R. O. Oveh, G. O. Aziken, Mitigating Social Engineering Attack: A Focus on the Weak Human Link, 2022 5th Information Technology for Education and Development (ITED), Abuja, Nigerien, 2022, S. 1–4.
6. Nikola Pavković, Luka Perkov, Social Engineering Toolkit — A systematic approach to social engineering, in: Proceedings of the 34th International Convention MIPRO, Opatija, Kroatien, 2011, S. 1485–1489.
7. Wasim Alexan, Eyad Mamdouh, Mohamed ElBeltagy, Ahmed Ashraf, M. Moustafa, Hashem Al-Qurashi, Social Engineering and Technical Security Fusion, in: International Telecommunications Conference (ITC-Egypt), Alexandria, Ägypten, 2022, S. 1–5.
8. Danesh Irani, Marco Balduzzi, Davide Balzarotti Engin Kirda, Calton Pu, Reverse Social Engineering Attacks in Online Social Networks in: Holz, T., Bos, H. (eds) Detection of Intrusions and Malware, and Vulnerability Assessment. DIMVA. Lecture Notes in Computer Science, Vol. 6739. Springer, Berlin, Heidelberg, 2011.

6.1   Mitnick/Simon Attack Cycle Model

The phases of the **social engineering attack cycle,** as classified by Mitnick and Simon [1], primarily focus on the general steps and developmental stages of a social engineering attack. These phases serve as a framework for understanding the psychological mechanisms and the progression of a successful attack. The specific attack tactics and techniques employed during a social engineering attack are highly diverse and context-dependent. They depend heavily on the individual goals of the attacker, the characteristics of the target, and the particular situation. Since there are virtually infinite variations of attack scenarios, it is difficult to provide a comprehensive list of specific tactics and techniques that covers all possible contexts. Instead, Mitnick and Simon [1] offer an abstract model that focuses on the fundamental steps and principles that are effective in the various phases of a social engineering attack (Fig. 6.1). Understanding these fundamental principles enables one to grasp the dynamics and psychological aspects of social engineering, regardless of the specific tactics an attacker may employ.

Phase 1: Information Gathering
The core idea of this phase is to build a comprehensive knowledge base about the target. Through extensive information gathering, the attacker can identify specific vulnerabilities and points of attack. This phase serves as the foundation for the subsequent steps and enables the attacker to develop personalized and convincing attacks.

Phase 2: Relationship Building
Establishing a relationship in social engineering is crucial, as it relies on social bonds and psychological mechanisms. This step allows the attacker to build trust

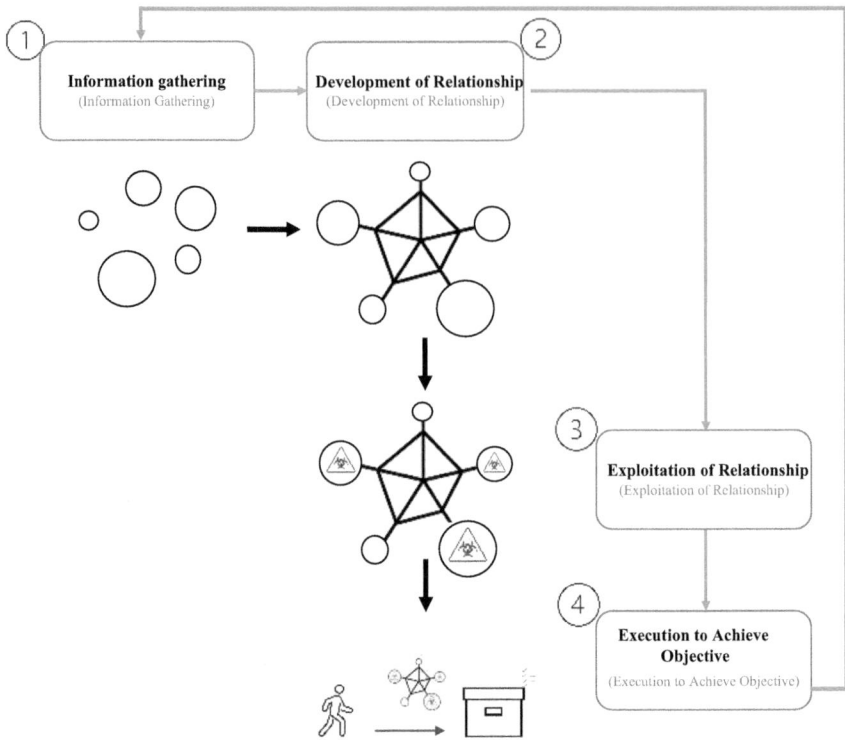

Fig. 6.1 Social engineering attack cycles [adapted from 1]

with the victim and persuade them to disclose personal information or grant access to protected resources. Relationship building serves as the basis for the next phase.

Phase 3: Exploitation of the Relationship
The skillful exploitation of the established relationship enables the attacker to achieve their objective. Through targeted manipulation, the attacker can induce the victim to perform actions that serve the attacker's interests.

Exploitation of the relationship is subtle and designed to bypass the victim's vigilance, prompting them to act against their own interests.

Phase 4: Execution of the Attack Objective
The actual attack objective is carried out in this phase. The attacker leverages the information gathered in the previous steps and the established relationship to achieve their goal. This may include data theft, system access, or other manipulative actions.

The phases of the attack are not strictly linear and may vary depending on the context. The cycle allows the attacker to flexibly adapt to the victim's responses and continuously refine the attack. This cyclical nature makes the model particularly effective and allows it to accommodate the dynamics of human interaction.

6.2 Limitations of the Mitnick/Simon Attack Cycle Model

However, the conceptual structure of the social engineering attack cycle also presents several critical considerations that should be taken into account from a scientific perspective:

Static Structure of the Information Gathering Phase and Lack of Overlap and Feedback
The model emphasizes a linear sequence of phases, which appears too rigid given the dynamic and context-dependent nature of social interactions. In reality, the phases may overlap or occur in a different order, depending on the specific circumstances of an attack.

Lack of Reference to Teamwork and Task Distribution
The model tends to attribute all tasks to a single individual, which does not reflect the realities of social engineering attacks. In practice, human hackers often work in teams, with different members taking on various tasks and acting in a coordinated manner.

Missing Phase of Explicit Attack Planning
A crucial phase in which the attack is planned in advance, alternative strategies are developed, and an exit strategy is defined, appears to be missing from the model. This planning phase is essential for responding to unforeseen events and maximizing the effectiveness of the attack.

Continuous Information Gathering
The example of a tailgating attack illustrates that the **information gathering** phase does not occur only at the beginning and cannot be considered complete before the start of the second phase. Continuous information gathering remains crucial throughout the entire attack cycle to obtain up-to-date information and planning data.

Suppose an attacker gains unauthorized access to a critical security area of a building through tailgating. After entering, the attacker discovers that the interior layout has changed and the current floor plan is outdated. In this case, a so-called **Request for Information (RFI)** is generated. The attacker contacts specific team members responsible for information gathering during the attack and who are in real-time communication with the attacker. These team members use OSINT and SOCMINT to search for information in real time that is needed on site. In this scenario, the team could coordinate and navigate on site by continuously gathering information via OSINT and SOCMINT, providing additional details about the current state of the interior. For example, by identifying the service providers responsible for interior design and obtaining publicly available information about corridors and escape routes.

The identified critical aspects highlight the need for an **adaptive, interactive, and incrementalmodeling** approach in the context of the social engineering attack cycle. Revising the existing model to take these aspects into account could lead to a more precise and realistic representation that better meets the actual dynamic requirements of social engineering attack cycles.

6.3   Social Engineering Attack Cycle Model

In the following section, we present our new model of the social engineering attack cycle, which is based on five iterative and incremental phases. This updated model distinguishes itself through its adaptive, interactive, and incremental approach, reflecting the need for a more precise and realistic depiction of attack cycles in the context of social engineering.

Compared to the traditional model, which features a static structure, our new model addresses several critical aspects, including the lack of overlap and feedback in the information gathering phase, the absence of teamwork and task distribution, the omission of an explicit attack planning phase and exit strategy, as well as the necessity for continuous information gathering throughout the entire attack cycle. The following diagram illustrates our five-stage model of the social engineering attack cycle.

We will now examine each phase of our new model (Fig. 6.2) in detail, beginning with the first phase, **Phase 1 Information Gathering.** Phase 1, defined as "Information Gathering," serves as an omnipresent and fundamental phase that continuously extends through all other phases. It is considered complete when the exit strategy is activated and the operational attack action is thus concluded. The essential importance of this phase is underscored by its key role both before and during the attack. The feedback and parallel progression of this phase highlight its foundational role in the overall attack structure.

Phase 2, Preparation, involves the consolidation, networking, and analysis of the information collected in the first phase. The focus here is on verifying the completeness, validity, and accuracy of the information.

If deficiencies or inaccuracies are identified, the task of further information gathering is delegated back to Phase 1. If the information is usable, strategic and tactical attack planning begins.

Phase 3, Attack Planning, encompasses team formation, task assignment, concretization of attack plans, and prioritization of primary and alternative attack paths. A central outcome of this phase is the definition of exit strategies, which are essential for professional human hackers to ensure a successful and low-risk attack.

Phase 4, Infiltration, refers to the invasive part of the attack, which is carried out on the previously determined **Action Day** in accordance with the attack planning phase. This step carries the highest risk and sometimes requires tactical

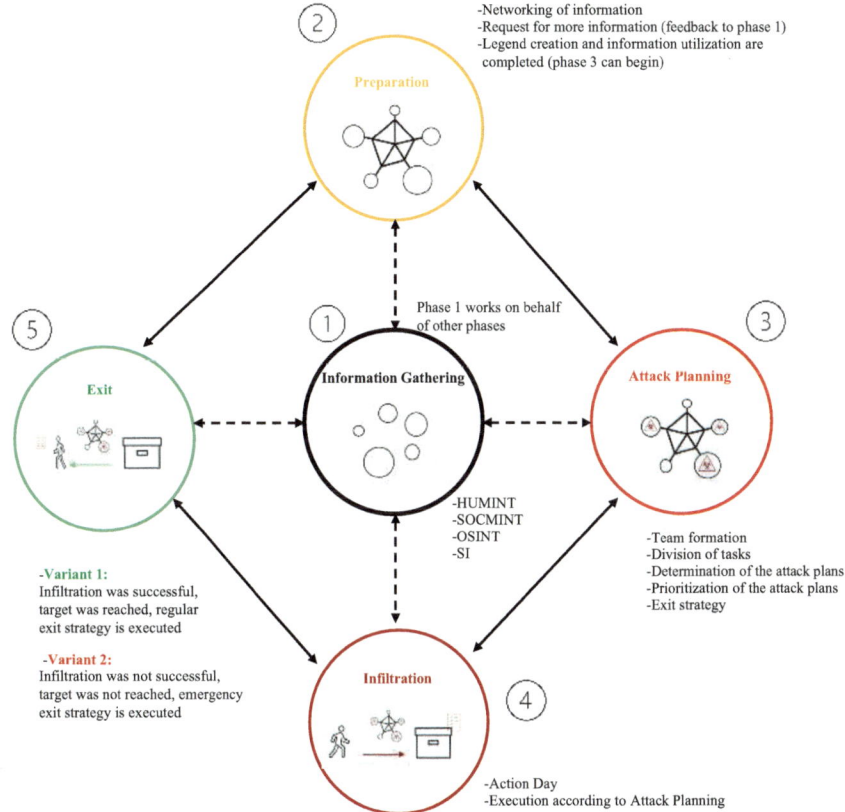

Fig. 6.2 Social Engineering Attack Model

execution on site. If successful and the objective is achieved, the regular exit strategy is activated.

This regular exit strategy in **Phase 5, Exit,** is executed calmly, orderly, and systematically to minimize attention and traceability. Hybrid-simultaneous attacks, in which not only the on-site attackers must execute the exit strategy, but also other human hackers, for example those performing technical manipulations of the communication system, are not uncommon. Here, too, it must be ensured that all attackers leave the organization as inconspicuously as possible, without arousing interest. During the real-time attack, feedback in the form of RFIs can be sent to Phase 1. In the event of failure, the emergency exit strategy must be activated.

6.4 HUMINT

"It is better to overestimate a threat twice than to underestimate it once." (Andreas Maier).

In the following sections, before we provide a deeper insight into the world of human hacking, we would like to clarify the two terms **HUMINT** and **OSINT** in more detail.

HUMINT, short for Human Intelligence, refers to the collection of information from human sources. Within the family of intelligence disciplines, which also includes SIGINT (Signal Intelligence), IMINT (Imagery Intelligence), and OSINT (Open Source Intelligence), HUMINT is situated in the military context [2].

This form of intelligence gathering is used by intelligence agencies, military intelligence, government investigative authorities, as well as in civilian sectors such as competitive intelligence.

The origins of HUMINT go back a long way and are inextricably linked to the history of intelligence services and military operations, as already discussed in Chap. 1 of the White Chapter. Even in ancient times, human sources were used to gather information about enemies, strategies, or plans, long before the term HUMINT was coined. In the modern context, HUMINT gained particular significance during the 20th century, especially during the Cold War. The collection of information by undercover agents and human sources played a decisive role in espionage and in gathering secret information about hostile states.

The techniques and methods of HUMINT have evolved over time and have been continuously refined by intelligence agencies, the military, and law enforcement authorities. This was done to remain relevant in the face of changing technologies, political landscapes, and global threats.

Today, HUMINT plays a role in various fields, not only in the military context. Police, security services, companies, and even criminal actors use the basic principles of HUMINT to collect information. This can be for security purposes, strategic planning, or, in the context of social engineering, to exploit human weaknesses and carry out attacks on individuals and organizations.

In the context of social engineering, however, HUMINT plays a crucial role, especially in analog attacks in real life—whether on the street, during lunch breaks, at the hotel bar, or at industry conferences.

The likelihood of becoming the target of a HUMINT attack or approach depends on various factors. Analog attacks offer the attacker immediate control, as they can directly observe the target's reactions. The attacker can adapt to the environment, intensify the attack, or withdraw subtly. The disadvantages are that the attacker must at least partially reveal their identity and must make the physical effort to approach the target in person. Compared to digital attacks, this requires greater physical proximity.

Assessing whether one could become the target of a HUMINT operation requires considering whom one is dealing with and whether, from the attacker's perspective, the use of HUMINT is justified.

HUMINT operators require a broad skill set, specific abilities, personality traits, and a pronounced psychological disposition to obtain information through direct interaction with people.

An effective HUMINT operator or agent should possess the following ten key qualifications:

Empathy and Social Competence The ability to adopt the perspective of others, recognize emotions, and build interpersonal relationships.

Trustworthiness and Integrity The competence to gain and maintain trust without crossing ethical boundaries.

Communication Skills The ability to communicate precisely, ask targeted questions, and gather information without arousing suspicion.

Discretion and Confidentiality The competence to handle information confidentially and deal carefully with sensitive data.

Observational Skills and Analytical Thinking The ability to detect subtle cues and nonverbal signals, as well as to analyze and interpret information.

Adaptability and Flexibility The ability to adapt to different situations and personalities in order to obtain the desired information.

Perseverance and Patience The ability to remain persistent even when information is not immediately available, and to maintain patience in order to build long-term relationships.

Psychological Insight and Understanding of People The ability to understand people's motives, behaviors, and needs.

Risk Assessment and Management Skills The competence to assess risks and take appropriate measures to ensure one's own safety as well as the integrity of the mission.

Ability to Work in a Team In many situations, HUMINT operators work in teams, making cooperation and teamwork skills advantageous.

These qualities are crucial for success in the field of HUMINT. Individuals working in this area often have to deal with complex and unpredictable situations and must rely on their interpersonal skills to gather information while adhering to ethical standards.

Before delving into HUMINT techniques, it is important to note that the use of surveillance devices or direct eavesdropping can also yield information from people. However, this is more accurately classified as information gathering and is not considered a classic HUMINT technique. Therefore, this is less about information acquisition (illegal means and methods) and more about information elicitation, as all information is disclosed voluntarily—though it cannot be ruled out that the victims were previously subjected to psychological manipulation.

In addition to the qualities listed above, the successful use of HUMINT requires various techniques to unobtrusively obtain information from people.

Psychological Profiling and Personality Analysis: This technique uses psychological methods to analyze and understand a target person's behavior, personality, and motivation.

Observation and Surveillance: Observation techniques are employed here to collect behavioral patterns, interactions, and other important information about a person or group.

Interest Analysisand Profiling: This method involves studying and analyzing a target person's interests, personality traits, and motivations to predict actions and influence them.

Undercover Operations and Disguise: The HUMINT operator immerses themselves in a group or environment to collect first-hand information without being recognized as an outsider or spy.

Source Recruitment: This involves actively attempting to recruit informants or agents in order to establish long-term sources of information.

Active Listening: This skill involves listening attentively, picking up on details, and reading between the lines to obtain important information.

Building Trust and Relationships: The goal is to deliberately establish a foundation of trust to increase the target person's willingness to share information. This can be achieved through shared interests or by generating sympathy.

Manipulation Techniques: Various methods to influence a person's behavior or mindset and obtain information, for example through praise, recognition, bribery, threats, reciprocity, flattery, and more.

Body Language and Nonverbal Cues: This involves understanding and exploiting nonverbal signals to recognize emotions, discomfort, or goodwill and to respond accordingly in order to build trust.

Framing and Questioning: The art of asking questions in such a way that the desired information is obtained without arousing suspicion or distrust.

Rapport Building: The ability to quickly establish a relationship in order to create an atmosphere of trust and openness.

Exploiting Authority: Leveraging authority or hierarchies to induce the target person to disclose information they would not normally reveal.

Cross-Referencing and Validation: The ability to collect and verify information from various sources to confirm credibility and accuracy.

Dealing with Resistance and Distrust: Strategies to overcome resistance or distrust on the part of the target, for example through negotiation, distraction, or patience.

Information Sharing and Debriefing: This involves the systematic collection of information through conversations with sources and debriefing after operations or meetings to extract relevant information.

HUMINT should be regarded as a potentially highly effective attack technique, even though the likelihood of being targeted and attacked by a person using HUMINT techniques is lower than by a phishing email.

Nevertheless, the question arises as to what options are available to an attacker, even if the probability is lower, when a human hacker possesses the comprehensive skill set of a HUMINT operator. What would it say about the quality of social engineering attacks if even an email correspondence or a vishing call were conducted by a HUMINT operator? As defenders, we do not know in advance exactly which attacker we are dealing with.

Nonetheless, it is advisable to always assume that potential attackers are better trained than we are. This assumption underscores the need to prepare for a wide range of attack scenarios, including those that could be carried out by highly skilled HUMINT operators.

6.5 OSINT

Open Source Intelligence (**OSINT**) refers to the systematic collection, analysis, and use of information from publicly accessible sources. These include the internet, including social media, online mapping tools, news articles, public records, and other freely available information sources. The goal of OSINT is to gain insights into various types of data, ranging from personal information and organizational data to geographic and financial data. OSINT methods include searching public databases, tracking social media posts, analyzing online images, and other techniques.

By compiling and analyzing this information, OSINT practitioners can create comprehensive profiles of individuals, organizations, or events.

6.5.1 Importance of OSINT in the Context of Social Engineering

OSINT plays a crucial role in the context of social engineering [3]. The importance of OSINT in the field of social engineering arises from several key factors. OSINT enables social engineers to collect highly relevant and personalized information about their targets. By understanding individual preferences, activities, and networks, social engineers can develop more convincing attacks.

Success requires building trust. OSINT can help establish trust by creating the impression that the attacker possesses detailed information about the victim. This can be achieved by citing personal details or referencing past events. OSINT also enables social engineers to identify suitable attack vectors. By understanding a target's social structure and hierarchy, attackers can specifically exploit weaknesses in the human line of defense and personalize their approach to blend into the social context and appear authentic. Understanding social norms, behaviors, and relationships is essential for carrying out effective social attacks. This makes the attacks more credible and increases the likelihood that victims will respond to manipulation. Overall, OSINT is a powerful tool in the arsenal of a social engineer, as it is the key to information gathering and social manipulation.

6.5.2   Origin and Development of OSINT

The origins of OSINT can be traced back to the earliest days of human information gathering. In military contexts, collecting intelligence about the enemy has always been of critical importance. Historically, in addition to HUMINT—gathering information through human sources—publicly available sources such as newspapers, maps, and official documents were also utilized.

During the Cold War, the development of OSINT reached a turning point, particularly due to the activities of intelligence agencies. The East-West conflict led to intensified efforts to collect information from publicly accessible sources. Not only traditional sources like newspapers played a role, but also the systematic analysis of radio and television broadcasts.

With the advent of the Internet in the 1990s, OSINT underwent a revolutionary transformation. Digitization enabled rapid and comprehensive access to an almost limitless amount of information. Search engines, online archives, social media, and companies specializing in the processing and provision of information became valuable sources for OSINT practitioners.

The past decades have seen an explosive increase in the technologies available for OSINT. Advances in machine learning, data analysis, and AI have significantly improved the efficiency and accuracy of OSINT tools.

Automated scans, image recognition, and speech analysis are examples of modern technologies that have been integrated into OSINT and are continuously being developed further.

The widespread use of social media has greatly expanded the digital footprint of individuals and organizations. OSINT can now create detailed profiles that include not only personal information but also behavioral patterns and social connections. Globalization has turned OSINT into an international tool, enabling information to be accessed from anywhere in the world in near real time. The increasing interconnection of databases and public information across national borders has made OSINT a global discipline.

The increased availability of information has also brought challenges in the areas of data protection and ethics. The protection of personal data and respect for privacy have become major concerns, as reflected in legislation such as the General Data Protection Regulation (GDPR) in the European Union.

The origins and development of OSINT highlight the revolutionary impact of gathering information from publicly accessible sources. From the beginnings of human espionage to the era of digital technologies, OSINT has undergone a fascinating evolution.

6.5.3   OSINT Fundamentals

The social engineer is primarily interested in personal information about their target, including real names, aliases, dates of birth, addresses, phone numbers, professional backgrounds, education, as well as other biographical details, interests, friends, and social media interactions [4].

Social media often serve as rich sources of personal information, as users voluntarily disclose many details about themselves or others.

Organizational data refers to information about companies, institutions, or other organizations. This includes company names, industries, organizational charts, locations, business models, partnerships, and legal structures. Such information can be extracted from public business registers, official websites, and other published sources.

With the increase in visual and audio content on the Internet, images, audio files, and video data have also become important sources of information. Image analysis tools, for example, enable facial recognition or the identification of locations. OSINT can also be used to examine publicly available audio or video files for clues and relevant information.

Geographic data includes information about places, locations, and geographic features, ranging from GPS coordinates in social media posts to cartographic data of public spaces. Financial data encompasses information about budgets, financial transactions, public financial reports of companies, and more.

A fundamental and widespread OSINT method is the use of search engines.

Through skillful search queries, for example using Google operators, specific information about individuals, companies, or topics can be found. Although Google has established itself as the most widely used search engine, it can sometimes be useful to use more than one search engine. Metasearch engines offer the advantage of aggregating results from multiple search engines, which increases the number of hits but does not necessarily make it easier to analyze the displayed data.

The analysis of social media platforms enables the extraction of personal information, social connections, and activities. OSINT practitioners can gain important insights by monitoring profiles and analyzing posts and interactions. Various OSINT tools [5], such as Maltego and SpiderFoot for visualizing connections, Shodan for searching for networked devices in the Internet of Things, and Recon-ng for gathering information across different platforms, are available.

The combination of different data types and the analysis of data sets can yield profound insights. Linking information from various sources enables OSINT practitioners to create comprehensive profiles and understand complex relationships.

By analyzing OSINT data, an attacker can create convincing attack scenarios based on the collected information. This may involve using familiar names, topics, or events to increase the likelihood of successful manipulation. OSINT enables attacks to be tailored so that they seamlessly fit into the victim's environment.

The connection between OSINT and social engineering lies in building trust and credibility.

OSINT provides information that enables an attacker to present themselves as a trustworthy source. This may include knowledge of personal preferences, professional backgrounds, or mutual contacts. Building trust is therefore crucial to persuade the victim to comply with requests or disclose sensitive information.

OSINT enables the personalization of attack vectors. Instead of sending generic phishing emails, an attacker can use OSINT to craft personalized messages (spear phishing). These can target specific professional challenges, interests, or even personal relationships. The integration of OSINT into social engineering thus makes attacks more targeted and convincing.

Technical (IT) security solutions can also be identified or analyzed using OSINT. In the reconnaissance phase of a penetration test, OSINT can be used to identify images of the target object and provide insights into access control systems and video surveillance systems [6]. Even in promotional videos of the target company, OSINT can reveal sensitive information, such as readable documents on walls or visible PC workstations with identifiable operating systems and applications.

The value of OSINT depends heavily on the ability to gather information in a targeted manner. It is essential to define clear objectives for information gathering and to search specifically for relevant data without getting lost on the Internet. A solid understanding of the specific information needed for a successful social engineering attack is crucial.

Successful OSINT requires not only the collection of data but also the contextual analysis of this information. The ability to establish connections between different pieces of information and to conduct a holistic analysis significantly improves the chances of success.

The diversity of available information and the wide range of OSINT methods and techniques underscore the complexity and power of this discipline. The success of OSINT often lies in the skillful application of a combination of these elements to achieve precise and relevant results.

The identification and use of trustworthy sources are key factors for the success of OSINT. Reliable information comes from credible sources, and the ability to identify such sources minimizes the risk of misinformation. OSINT practitioners should learn to distinguish between reliable and potentially misleading sources and further assess the information obtained in terms of its likelihood.

The speed and timeliness of information gathering are additional critical success factors. OSINT data quickly becomes outdated, especially in the dynamic online world. An effective OSINT practitioner must be able to ensure the currency of the collected information and make rapid decisions based on this data.

The OSINT landscape is constantly evolving, and successful practitioners must be flexible and adaptable.

Creativity plays a central role in the development of new methods for information gathering and in adapting to changing platforms and technologies. Analytical skills are also crucial for extracting meaningful insights from the collected data. OSINT in the context of social engineering requires the ability to recognize patterns, establish connections, and prioritize relevant information. Analytical skills contribute to the creation of precise profiles of target individuals or organizations. Continuous professional development should be standard for every OSINT practitioner. Participation in training, keeping up with technological developments, and adapting to new tools and methods are essential components of ongoing education for OSINT practitioners in the context of social engineering [7].

A significant evolution in the field of OSINT is the increased automation of information acquisition processes. By leveraging AI and machine learning, OSINT tools and platforms can search large volumes of data more efficiently, extract relevant information, and identify relationships. This automation enables faster and more accurate information gathering in real time.

In light of the growing threats posed by cybercrime and activities on the darknet, OSINT practitioners are increasingly integrating monitoring tools to observe activities in these hidden online spaces.

The identification of potential risks and attack vectors originating from the darknet is becoming a significant component of OSINT investigations and research.

With the increasing use of images, videos, and audio content on online platforms, multimedia analysis is emerging as an important development in the OSINT field. Tools that enable the processing and analysis of multimedia content expand the possibilities for information gathering and help create a more comprehensive picture of target individuals or organizations.

The availability of OSINT sources from various parts of the world is increasing as more information is shared online. OSINT practitioners must therefore be able to access globally distributed data sources and take cultural differences into account. The globalization of OSINT opens up new opportunities but also brings challenges regarding data protection and legal considerations. In particular, the proliferation of deepfake technologies could significantly impact the OSINT landscape in the area of social engineering. The ability to create deceptively realistic fake content increases the risk of manipulation and deception. OSINT practitioners must be able to detect such technologies and consider their impact on the credibility of information.

The growing sensitivity to data protection and the introduction of stricter data privacy laws worldwide are expected to influence the way OSINT is conducted. Future trends may include increased requirements for compliance with data protection regulations and ethical standards for OSINT practitioners.

Companies may increasingly use OSINT to monitor their own online presence, detect threats at an early stage, and identify vulnerabilities in their security architecture. The integration of OSINT into internal corporate security strategies could lead to closer collaboration between OSINT experts and security teams. This would also be an important step for companies toward active rather than reactive cyber defense. The integration of OSINT into cyber threat intelligence is expected to increase as companies need to strengthen their early detection capabilities for cyber threats. Linking OSINT with other sources of threat data enables more comprehensive threat analysis and helps improve preventive measures.

Developments in the field of OSINT and the associated trends in social engineering are influenced by technological advances, legal requirements, and the evolving threat landscape. Proactive adaptation to these trends is essential to ensure the effective use of OSINT in the context of social engineering.

OSINT is undoubtedly to be regarded as one of the most important assets for a social engineer. A social engineering attack is based on knowledge about the target individual and the motives, intentions, attitudes, and emotions that can be derived from it.

The social engineer uses this individual knowledge, together with general, culture-specific knowledge, to predict the behavior of the target and exploit it for their own purposes. In the next chapter, we will address the ongoing development of social engineering.

References

1. Kevin D. Mitnick, William L. Simon, Steve Wozniak, Controlling the Human Element of Security: The Art of Deception, Wiley, 2003.
2. Gabriel Traian Ungureanu, Open Source Intelligence (OSINT). The way ahead, in: Journal of Defense Resources Management, Vol. 12, Issue 1, 2021, S. 177–200.
3. Fahimeh Tabatabaei, Douglas Wells, Open Source Intelligence Investigation – OSINT in the Context of Cyber-Security, Heidelberg: Springer International Publishing AG, 2016, S. 215–221.
4. Takayuki Sasaki, Katsunari Yoshioka, Tsutomu Matsumoto, Who are you? OSINT-based Profiling of Infrastructure Honeypot Visitors, in: 11th International Symposium on Digital Forensics and Security (ISDFS), Chattanooga, TN, USA, 2023, S. 1–6.
5. Marcus Walkow, Daniela Pöhn, Systematically Searching for Identity-Related Information in the Internet with OSINT Tools, in: 9th International Conference on Information Systems Security and Privacy (ICISSP 2023), Neubiberg, Deutschland, 2023, S. 402–409.
6. Anton O. Bryushinin, Alexandr. V. Dushkin, Maxim A. Melshiyan, Automation of the Information Collection Process by Osint Methods for Penetration Testing During Information Security Audit, in: Conference of Russian Young Researchers in Electrical and Electronic Engineering (ElConRus), Saint Petersburg, Russland, 2022, S. 242–246.
7. Leslie Ball, Gavin Ewan, Natalie Coull, Undermining Social Engineering using Open Source Intelligence Gathering, in: Proceedings of the International Conference on Knowledge Discovery and Information Retrieval (KDIR), 2012 S. 275–280.

Evolution of Social Engineering

7

Evolution, as a continuous process of adaptation and change, exhibits clear parallels to the dynamics found in social engineering. In both contexts, successful adaptation to the environment is crucial for the survival and propagation of certain traits or techniques. In the field of social engineering, not only is the historical testing of methods relevant, but also their ongoing adaptation to a changing environment. Much like in evolution, where the most effective adaptations survive and dominate, social engineering methods must be continuously optimized to remain effective in an evolving threat landscape. It is essential to emphasize that the current manifestations of social engineering attacks are only temporary. While we remain static in our defenses, hackers and cybercriminals employ creativity and agility to constantly develop new, modified attacks.

In a perpetual contest against a dynamic adversary, static defense strategies will inevitably be inferior. Therefore, it is necessary not only to understand existing methods but also to keep pace with the continuously evolving techniques of social engineering and adapt flexibly. This insight enables a proactive defense and empowers us to effectively meet the challenges of an ever-changing threat landscape.

In this context, our discussion begins with AI and its significance for information security, particularly in the realm of social engineering. AI is based on algorithms and models that enable machines to perform human-like tasks, learn, and solve problems. A learning system in AI refers to a machine's ability to learn from experience and adapt to improve its performance. This learning process is driven by algorithms trained on data to recognize patterns and make predictions. Interaction with users occurs via so-called prompts [1].

Prompt engineering involves designing the formulation of input prompts so that the model generates the desired information or responses precisely and effectively.

This experimental process can yield various outcomes, and skillful prompt engineering enhances the performance of the AI model.

A user enters a text prompt, and the model then generates a response. This interaction can be iterative, with the user reacting to the generated responses and thereby influencing the progress or direction of the conversation. This iterative interaction allows the model to adjust to the user's specific requirements and context.

The input is processed by a large language model (LLM), which converts natural language into a machine-readable format. These models are characterized by their ability to process large volumes of text data, learn from it, and perform complex linguistic tasks. Models such as GPT-3 (Generative Pre-trained Transformer 3) are examples of LLMs [2, 3].

Overall, the flexibility and versatility of LLMs enable them to handle a variety of tasks, from text generation and translation to question-answering, based on the provided prompts. The introduction of AI into the world of cybercrime and social engineering has undoubtedly ushered in a new era of cyber defense strategies and models. The ability for any user to interact with AI models through simple text input, regardless of programming knowledge, not only creates opportunities but also poses significant risks [4, 5]. Intuitive communication with AI models allows individuals without deep technical expertise to design and execute advanced attack scenarios. This includes, for example, generating malicious code and personalized phishing attacks. The easy access to such techniques significantly increases the threat landscape.

AI-powered social engineering tools enable the automation of attacks [6]. By leveraging AI models, attackers can develop and execute complex attack scenarios without a deep understanding of the underlying technology. This leads to an increase in attacks and broader vulnerability. AI enables precise personalization of phishing attacks, as models can learn from interactions with users and develop targeted attacks. This means that phishing emails or messages become more personalized and convincing, increasing the likelihood of a successful attack.

We must also consider the role of publicly available code in AI-driven attacks. It is undeniable that publicly accessible code, especially on platforms like GitHub, plays a significant role in the development of AI-powered attacks. This development presents a major challenge for information security and increases the complexity of defense mechanisms.

GitHub and similar platforms serve as resources for a wide range of AI code, including algorithms for scraping and other potentially harmful activities. Public availability makes it easier for attackers to access existing code and adapt it for their own purposes.

In the following, we present how AI, as a driving force, has initiated an evolutionary development in the context of cybercrime and social engineering. The techniques and methods presented are based on research findings developed and analyzed from moral and ethical perspectives. As emphasized at the beginning of our journey, you can only effectively protect your IT systems, your involved employees, and yourself if you adhere to the principle of *Situational Awareness* [7]:

"Get to know your potential attackers and the environment of your digital landscape in 360 degrees."

Comprehensive knowledge of the mindset and behavior of potential attackers is crucial for developing and implementing targeted preventive, reactive, and detective security measures. In this context, it becomes clear that a deep understanding of the motivations, tactics, and objectives of potential attackers is essential for optimally aligning your security architecture and addressing vulnerabilities in a targeted manner. This foundation enables effective defense that continuously adapts to the changing threat landscape—situational awareness at its best. Numerous insights can thus be gained from observation, which can then be integrated into preventive, detective, and reactive models to protect your information security. Therefore, the following section aims to illustrate these application areas of AI without disclosing detailed attack steps or content.

As part of our research initiative entitled *"AI for and against Information Security",* an experimental approach was taken to investigate the effectiveness of AI in the context of social engineering, particularly with regard to the phenomenon of catfishing on business- and entertainment-focused social media platforms. Only legal and approved AI tools were used in strict compliance with moral and ethical principles.

7.1   Modified Catfishing in the Context of Social Engineering

Catfishing is a form of identity fraud in which an individual adopts a fake online persona to deceive others. This deception can involve creating a false identity using fabricated information, images, and social profiles.

The term "catfishing" originates from the metaphor of fishing with live bait, where the fraudster, like an angler, lays out bait to attract unsuspecting individuals [8].

In the context of catfishing, fake profiles are often created on social networks, dating platforms, or other online communities.

The motivations for catfishing can be diverse, ranging from personal amusement and interpersonal relationships to fraudulent intentions. The process of catfishing often involves deliberately crafting an identity that aligns with the expectations and interests of potential victims. This may include using fake photos, inventing personal stories, and pretending to have certain characteristics or interests [9].

Within this research initiative, the catfisher was generated using AI, with detailed prompts defined to specify and refine gender, age, ethnicity, residential address, professional fields, and skills. Based on these specifications, the AI created a profile summarizing the catfisher's attributes. Additionally, the AI was instructed to generate a fictitious affiliation for the catfisher.

In this scenario, the catfisher was positioned as a female recruiter working for a fictitious staffing company.

The generated information was then transferred into a professionally crafted LinkedIn profile, including physical characteristics, personal traits, background information, preferences, skills, and hobbies. This profile was further used as a prompt for an AI image generation tool to give the catfisher an authentic face.

The time required to develop the catfisher was only one day, while establishing credibility through activities and comments on LinkedIn was more time-consuming. AI was used to comment on posts, write its own comments, and communicate with other members. These interactions took place over several months, with AI employed to create a convincing and authentic virtual persona.

The deliberate decision to design the catfisher as a female recruiter made it possible to quickly gain a considerable number of followers on the selected platforms, especially LinkedIn (over 1,000 contacts).

Bitter insights from our research highlight that AI significantly facilitates the work of a catfisher in terms of time investment, precision, and content generation. This increase in efficiency is remarkable. It should be emphasized that only legal AI tools were used, which should be subject to strict moral and ethical standards. Nevertheless, this very AI is not capable of truly recognizing and determining the intent of a request. Therefore, we repeatedly resort to backdoors in our prompts to circumvent the moral and ethical guidelines of the AI. This underscores the fact that even an attacker can easily bypass these ethical barriers of AI tools.

After successfully establishing our catfisher as an authentic person who actively communicates with other members, shares posts, writes comments, and has built an extremely convincing network, we can begin to execute targeted attack types.

7.2   AI-based OSINT and Phishing

Scraping, the extraction of data from websites, is an example of a technique whose code is publicly available, for instance, via online services for the development and version control of programming projects. Integrating scraping code into AI models enables attackers to develop automated mechanisms for large-scale data collection, which can then serve as the basis for personalized attacks. The use of public code increases the complexity of attacks, as attackers can access a wide range of tools without having to develop the program code themselves. The variability of attacks increases, as different techniques can be combined and adapted. This method particularly facilitates work in the field of SOCMINT by collecting information about a target through data available on social media platforms.

This information can then be cross-referenced to define attacks or make the necessary preparations.

At this stage of our research initiative, we explored another approach to refine the effectiveness of AI-modified attack techniques. The selected scraper collects basic information about the chosen target individual from the selected business network, which serves as the basis for a subsequent phishing attack. The goal is to enable the automated collection and processing of this data in a purposefully crafted email.

Simultaneously, program code is generated based on prompt specifications. This program code should be able to use the embedded information from our scraper to compose an automated and authentic email.

After generating our scraper and email generation tool, we can now merge both programs into a single source code. This allows the information collected by the scraper, organized into specific categories and classes, to be immediately transferred to the email generation function. This function retrieves the information from the buffer, incorporates it into the desired content, and generates the appropriate phishing email. Next, our AI-generated code calls the provider function [10]. This function invokes and embeds the email provider. The email text (body) is formatted and, through integration, can finally be sent to the sender and recipient.

7.3   AI-based Cross-Site Scripting and Keylogger

At this stage, we employ various attack techniques and scenarios to infiltrate the target individual. Here, we again rely on AI to generate the corresponding source codes. These codes are compiled exclusively based on our own and expert-verified prompt specifications, as well as by embedding freely available code. Once again, we observe that with just a few methodological approaches, it is possible to generate malicious code that violates the moral and ethical guidelines of AI.

In this phase, we tested the feasibility and execution of two attacks—cross-site scripting (XSS) and a logical keylogger [11, 12].

XSS is a security vulnerability that allows an attacker to inject malicious code (usually in the form of JavaScript) into web pages viewed by other users. The attack is carried out by embedding malicious code into input fields or URLs, which is then executed by other users of the affected website. A logical keylogger is a specific type of keylogger designed to track a user's keystrokes and activities without inserting physical hardware into the affected system. Unlike hardware keyloggers, which are physically connected to the keyboard or computer, logical keyloggers are software programs.

This type of keylogger is often implemented as malicious software that is secretly installed on a computer to monitor the user's keystrokes. The collected data, such as usernames, passwords, and other confidential information, is then sent to a remote server or directly to the attacker.

As soon as the target individual opens our attached link, an XSS attack is executed to activate malicious code, including spyware, on the victim's computer. By exploiting XSS vulnerabilities in our prepared website, we can inject JavaScript code that is executed in the context of the target individual. This code enables the theft of user data such as online banking information, session hijacking, or the execution of further malicious activities. In addition, we employ a logical keylogger method, which was also fully generated by AI. The target individual is prompted to create a new account to complete the information for their talent profile. While the target is creating a new account, our keylogger runs in the background, capturing all keystrokes in plain text. In both cases, the results demonstrate how alarmingly easy it is to use AI for attack planning and execution.

7.4   AI-based Cybergrooming and Sextortion

In a parallel line of research, we are also continuing our catfishing experiment, this time leveraging the capabilities available to us on the entertainment-focused social media platform.

Our catfisher is also very well connected here and now has access to a wide range of images that can be stolen and misused in various contexts, depending on the attacker's imagination. To continue our scientific investigation, we generate another fictitious account with several AI-generated images. These images resemble a real person but are entirely generated by AI. None of these images depict a minor.

The creation of this fake account enabled us to continue our research activities without violating legal obligations or moral and ethical guidelines.

Our attack scenario is as follows: The originally defined catfisher automatically collects images belonging to our second fictitious, generated person. These AI-generated images are extracted. Essentially, these images depict ordinary scenes showing everyday situations, vacations, and leisure activities of the fictitious person. In all images, the person is more than appropriately dressed. Special care is taken to ensure that the AI-generated fake images present plain and simple depictions. After the automated extraction of these images, the stolen images from the fake account are passed on to other AI image generation tools. These images now serve as the basis for the AI image generation tool to create nude images of the fake person from the ordinary pictures using a precise prompt.

Sextortion, a portmanteau of "sex" and "extortion," refers to a form of blackmail in which the perpetrator threatens to publish sexual images, videos, or information about the victim unless certain demands are met. In the context of sextortion, AI-generated nude images can also be used.

Perpetrators often obtain secretly recorded material of the victim in advance, either through fraudulent means or by exploiting trust. They then use this content to blackmail the victim, demanding financial payments or further images and actions.

However, the use of AI has also revolutionized this area. In the context of sextortion, attackers now use AI to generate aesthetic and realistic nude images. These manipulated images are sent to the target person, accompanied by the misleading claim that they are authentic images of the individual.

Through the skillful use of manipulation and intimidation techniques, attackers succeed in convincing the target that these are indeed their own images. In this way, they are able to continue their extortion successfully. This development demonstrates that AI is used not only to exploit real images but also to create fictional yet deceptively realistic depictions to blackmail victims in the context of sextortion.

Publicly accessible Instagram accounts thus represent potential sources of images that could be misused for sextortion purposes. These accounts provide public access to images, stories, and highlights that can be viewed by anyone, even without having an Instagram account.

The images can then be edited using AI tools, similar to deepfakes. There are thus AI tools available on the clearnet that enable such manipulations.

The use of our original catfish account opens up additional possibilities, especially in the area of cybergrooming [13]. *Cybergrooming* refers to a form of abuse in the digital space in which adults, often under a false identity, attempt to make online contact with minors for sexual or manipulative purposes. These actions can take place on various online platforms, social networks, or chatrooms. The term is composed of "cyber" (referring to the digital world) and "grooming" (in the context of manipulative approaches). Typically, cybergrooming begins with the deliberate building of trust between the adult and the minor through friendly communication, gifts, or sharing common interests. The perpetrator tries to establish an emotional bond in order to later exploit the victim for sexual or manipulative purposes. The use of fake identities, images, and information is a common tactic to deceive the victim. The digital nature of cybergrooming allows perpetrators to remain anonymous more easily and to conceal their identity.

In this particularly concerning scenario, catfishing and AI could also play a threatening role.

In the context of cybergrooming, the catfisher, supported by AI, could assume a fake identity to deliberately contact minors. AI could assist in creating realistic profiles that match the interests and preferences of the target group. Through skillful communication tailored to the individual needs of minors, the catfisher could build trust and potentially initiate harmful interactions.

The use of AI in pedosexual contexts highlights a disturbing increase in vulnerability and fragility in the use of modern communication tools. This development illustrates how disastrous the use of digital media can be without adequate media literacy and information security. The associated dangers are not only monetary in nature but also extend to psychological aspects that can affect victims for many years. The use of AI in pedosexual contacts represents one of the most serious developments in this area.

This development requires a highly sophisticated solution in which all parties involved—from children and parents to teachers—must be trained both preventively and reactively. Awareness and training should not only focus on technological aspects but also address psychological and social skills in order to establish effective measures against these threatening developments.

7.5   AI-based Disinformation Campaigns and Deepfakes

In recent days, AI has had significant impacts on various areas of society, particularly in the context of deepfakes and disinformation campaigns.

These developments also have direct implications for the field of social engineering. In the realm of deepfakes, advancing AI technology enables the creation of deceptively realistic fake content, such as videos or audio files, which are difficult to distinguish from genuine recordings. This has the potential to seriously affect the credibility of information, as fake content can be used fraudulently.

Disinformation campaigns also benefit from AI, as algorithms can be used to spread personalized and targeted false information. Social engineering techniques are employed to trick people into clicking on fake news or links, leading to further dissemination of disinformation. An illustrative scenario would be the creation of a fake social media profile for an internet troll using AI, which is then used to spread false information. These techniques can be used to specifically influence individuals or groups, whether for political, economic, or other motives. An internet troll is a person who deliberately posts provocative, offensive, or disruptive comments or actions online to elicit emotional reactions and create unrest in online communities. This behavior can take various forms, including insults, intentional misinformation, incitement, and the aim of derailing discussions.

The challenge here often lies in the fact that constantly evolving AI technology makes it increasingly difficult to distinguish authentic from fake content. This increases people's susceptibility to manipulation and can undermine trust in digital information. The ongoing digitalization has ushered in an era in which information has become a powerful tool in political conflicts.

The integration of AI into this sphere has far-reaching effects on how disinformation campaigns are designed and how hybrid warfare is conducted. The dissemination of false information and the manipulation of public opinion are becoming more efficient and sophisticated through AI technologies. Algorithms analyze vast amounts of data to develop and amplify tailored, emotionally appealing narratives. This development has dramatically expanded the ability to influence opinions.

AI makes it possible to introduce and reinforce targeted narratives. By analyzing behavioral data, the technology can identify specific messages that can be effectively embedded into existing beliefs. This contributes to the creation of narratives that can have a destabilizing effect on societies.

In the context of hybrid warfare, states and non-state actors use AI to orchestrate political instability. This can include the spread of disinformation, sabotage of critical infrastructure, and targeted cyberattacks. The use of AI often makes such attacks difficult to detect and increases their effectiveness. The deployment of AI in disinformation campaigns and hybrid warfare has profound effects on society. Misinformation can influence political decisions, undermine trust in institutions, and exacerbate social tensions. This necessitates enhanced media literacy and preventive measures at the political level.

The integration of AI into disinformation campaigns marks a significant development in hybrid warfare. The international community must take action to address this challenge and build more resilient societies that are resistant to AI-driven manipulation.

7.6   Virtual HUMINT

HUMINT refers to information collected through human sources. In the context of social engineering, this approach can be virtualized. *Virtual HUMINT* involves the use of simulated human-like entities, whether in the form of chatbots, virtual assistants, or advanced AI-driven personas. These virtual HUMINT agents can gather information by interacting with users and building trust. By leveraging natural language processing (NLP), they can conduct realistic conversations and extract targeted information. The challenge here lies in distinguishing between genuine and virtual interactions, as the latter are becoming increasingly difficult to differentiate from human interactions.

The evolution of social engineering through the integration of AI and virtual HUMINT opens up new dimensions of deception.

The ability to conduct personalized attacks and blur the boundaries between real and virtual interactions requires continuous adaptation of security measures.

7.7   Summary

The rapid development of AI has not only led to positive applications but also has a dark side through the modification of application tools. These modifications enable the use of AI tools without ethical constraints, posing a significant challenge in the field of information security.

Users who program and deploy such tools exploit the flexibility of AI systems to adapt them to their own needs. This means that ethical principles and security precautions implemented in standard AI applications can be bypassed. As a result, AI tools are created that operate without moral restrictions and can be immediately used for criminal purposes.

This development opens up a new dimension of cybercrime, in which modified AI tools can be used not only autonomously but also in a targeted and efficient manner. The consequences range from intensified attacks on security systems to a potential escalation of cybercrime. It is therefore increasingly urgent not only to promote the positive applications of AI but also to develop robust ethical standards and security mechanisms to curb the misuse of modified AI tools.

In detail, we can arrive at the following key points:

a) *The use of standard AI with fixed ethical guidelines can be circumvented through targeted prompting, making AI accessible for illegitimate purposes. The flexibility of AI allows moral restrictions to be bypassed and enables its use for various irregular purposes.*
b) *By using AI, especially prompt engineering with large language models (LLMs), attackers with rudimentary knowledge of programming and social engineering can carry out successful automated attacks. This leads to a significant increase in efficiency and success while minimizing the time required.*

c) *The application areas of AI in the context* of cybercrime *are diverse and largely depend on the imagination of the attackers. This ranges from data theft to serious attacks such as sextortion or activities related to child exploitation.*

d) *AI can also be used for political destabilization, disinformation campaigns, and the creation of deepfakes. The manipulation of information, public opinion, and narrative content through AI poses a significant threat.*

e) *The use of AI in conjunction with communication applications and social media requires comprehensive training in media literacy and information security. Our research shows that many online participants handle their data, images, and privacy carelessly, which poses a profound risk. Exploiting these weaknesses does not necessarily require the use of AI to cause harm in today's environment.*

f) *In addition, it can be observed that alternative AI models lacking clear moral and ethical guidelines present an additional challenge. These models could be used without restrictions for illegal purposes, further increasing the risks and misuse of AI.*

The ongoing evolution of social engineering requires continuous adaptation to new threats, including those posed by AI. The next chapter will present strategic and tactical measures against social engineering, providing you with the means to effectively defend against these sophisticated attack methods. These measures range from awareness campaigns and tactical solutions to comprehensive strategies aimed at strengthening resilience to social engineering attacks at both the individual and organizational levels.

References

1. Aleksandar J. Spasić and Dragan S. Janković, Using ChatGPT Standard Prompt Engineering Techniques in Lesson Preparation: Role, Instructions and Seed-Word Prompts, in: 58th International Scientific Conference on Information, Communication and Energy Systems and Technologies (ICEST), Nis, Serbien, 2023, S. 47–50.
2. Hendrik Strobelt, Albert Webson, Victor Sanh, Benjamin Hoover, Johanna Beyer, Hanspeter Pfister, Alexander M. Rush, Interactive and Visual Prompt Engineering for Ad-hoc Task Adaptation with Large Language Models, in IEEE Transactions on Visualization and Computer Graphics, Vol. 29, No. 1, 2023, S. 1146–1156.
3. Nazif Aydin, O. Ayhan Erdem, A Research On The New Generation Artificial Intelligence Technology Generative Pretraining Transformer 3, 2022 in: 3rd International Informatics and Software Engineering Conference (IISEC), Ankara, Türkei, 2022, pp. 1–6.
4. Liudmila Azarova, Maria Kudryavtseva, Larisa Sharakhina, Key Advantages and Risks of Implementing Artificial Intelligence in the Activities of Professional Communicators, in: IEEE Communication Strategies in Digital Society Seminar (ComSDS), St. Petersburg, Russland, 2020, S. 82–86.
5. P. S. Lozhnikov and S. S. Zhumazhanova, Potenzial Information Security Risks in The Implementation of AI—Based Systems, in: Dynamics of Systems, Mechanisms and Machines (Dynamics), Omsk, Russland, 2022, S. 1–4.

6. Zhou Yang, Chenyu Wang, Jieke Shi, Thong Hoang, Pavneet Kochhar, Qinghua Lu, Zhenchang Xing, David Lo, What Do Users Ask in Open-Source AI Repositories? An Empirical Study of GitHub Issues, in: IEEE/ACM 20th International Conference on Mining Software Repositories (MSR), Melbourne, Australien, 2023, S. 79–91.
7. Kjonath Kwizera and Liu Zhaohui, Improving Cyber security Situational Awareness and Cyber-Attack Detection Based on Analytic Data Mining Techniques, in: 6th International Symposium on Computer and Information Processing Technology (ISCIPT), Changsha, China, 2021, S. 596–599.
8. Walid Magdy, Yehia Elkhatib, Gareth Tyson, Sagar Joglekar and Nishanth Sastry, Fake it till you make it: Fishing for Catfishes, in: IEEE/ACM International Conference on Advances in Social Networks Analysis and Mining (ASONAM), Sydney, NSW, Australien, 2017, S. 497–504.
9. Vijay Tiwari, Analysis and detection of fake profile over social network, in: International Conference on Computing, Communication and Automation (ICCCA), Greater Noida, Indien, 2017, S. 175–179.
10. Meraj Farheen Ansari, Amrutanshu Panigrahi, Geethamanikanta Jakka, Abhilash Pati and Krutikanta Bhattacharya, Prevention of Phishing attacks using AI Algorithm, in: 2nd Odisha International Conference on Electrical Power Engineering, Communication and Computing Technology (ODICON), Bhubaneswar, Indien, 2022, S. 1–5.
11. Martin Kappes, Netzwerk- und Datensicherheit. Eine praktische Einführung, Springer Vieweg Wiesbaden. 2. Auflage, 2013.
12. Jörg Schwenk, Sicherheit und Kryptographie im Internet. Theorie und Praxiss, Springer Vieweg Wiesbaden, 4. Auflage, 2014.
13. Cindy Ehlert, Thomas-Gabriel Rüdiger, Defensible Digital Space. Die Übertragbarkeit der Defensible Space Theory auf den digitalen Raum, Kriminologie für das digitale Zeitalter, Springer VS Wiesbaden, 2020, S. 151–171.

Global Defense Concepts

8

In this chapter, we present global defense concepts and approaches for organizations in the areas of preventive, reactive, and detective information security. Our focus is on providing a holistic overview of these defense concepts to explain our approaches in a differentiated and comprehensible manner. A fundamental understanding is that preventive, reactive, and detective concepts cannot exist in isolation. Rather, they must be viewed as interwoven security concepts whose methods and approaches interact to create a coordinated defense context.

With a preventive emphasis, we draw on the core principle of risk management, which specifies how to deal with uncertainties regarding the **probability** or **frequency** and the actual "impact" of an event or risk. When considering these dimensions, mental security models are required in order to identify threats relevant to the specific reality of the organization under consideration, rather than abstract or general threat scenarios, in the sense of situational awareness.

Knowledge of which areas of an organization are exposed to which social engineering threats constitutes valuable information. With this insight, targeted, sustainable, and cost-efficient measures can be defined, ultimately enabling better resource allocation.

The so-called targeting process involves identifying soft targets within an organization that could easily fall victim to social engineering methods and attack techniques. This highlights that not all areas of an organization are equally exposed to the risks of social engineering.

In our context, targeting refers to the process of selecting and identifying targets that may be attacked by social engineering attack types and techniques. The objective is to locate soft targets, facilities, or resources in order to protect them using strategic, tactical, or operational measures.

Targeting involves a thorough analysis of information to determine precise and relevant targets. This includes information about roles and responsibilities, physical facilities, and other relevant factors generated as part of threat intelligence.

E. Koza et al., *Social Engineering and Human Hacking*, https://doi.org/10.1007/978-3-662-72084-4_8

Our first solution approach, the **Observation Matrix**, therefore focuses on targeting and the identification and analysis of role- and topic-based interactivity, dynamics, and diversity of human-centered attacks. It enables efficient mapping of existing individual human and physical vulnerabilities to potential social engineering threats. The first solution approach thus comprises a tactical and operational tool for identifying and monitoring human and physical vulnerabilities and threats, as well as communicating this information to relevant stakeholders. The threat matrix thus serves to make the threat landscape transparent, traceable, and visible to all parties involved.

This enables a clear definition of the objective threat situation and allows for comprehensive planning, tracking, and evaluation of subsequent post-activities. However, a preventive defense concept is not completely decoupled from reactive and detective paradigms and capabilities. In our specific context, we particularly combine preventive and detective methods of threat intelligence with the principles of situational awareness to conduct a targeted threat analysis.

The second solution approach thus builds on the insights gained from the observation matrix. This approach uses the information obtained to determine the topics and focus areas of upcoming information awareness programs and campaigns.

The goal is to enable targeted and efficient training. For this purpose, we employ our **resilience plan**.

The third solution approach introduces the assessment tool **Social Engineering Pentest**. This tool makes it possible, for example, to subject specific areas to a social engineering pentest based on the results of the threat matrix. The primary purpose of the social engineering pentest is to assess the effectiveness of the already defined defense concepts, including physical security concepts and implemented resilience measures.

Secondarily, the social engineering pentest, analogous to logical pentests and red teaming, is conducted to actually identify security breaches and gaps in defense concepts by exploiting a real physical or human security vulnerability. The analysis of the social engineering pentest results takes place in the further course of the process, with the insights gained being used to optimize the achieved maturity level through the implementation of targeted measures. We refer to these as post-ex activities [1].

Below, we present our three solution approaches, each with its associated **OODA-Loop** framework, in a concise manner.

8.1   Observe-Orient-Decide-Act Loop (OODA-Loop)

To ensure adequate planning, implementation, and monitoring of defense activities, we use the modified OODA-Loop as part of our overall strategy. Before introducing the framework, however, we would like to familiarize you with the origin and rationale of the OODA-Loop.

8.1.1 Origin of the OODA Loop

During aerial combat in the Korean War, U.S. Air Force Colonel John Boyd developed the so-called OODA Loop [2]. The original idea was to create an unpretentious and simple cycle for decision support. Boyd initially presented the OODA Loop as a straightforward, linear four-step process (Fig. 8.1).

From a scientific perspective, the **OODA Loop** is regarded as a methodological framework designed to enable efficient and adaptive decision-making despite information deficits and unpredictable changes in the environment. In the first **phase (Observe)**, the environment is observed, taking into account both internal and external influences and factors. The observations are then analyzed and interpreted in the next **phase (Orient)**, where mental models—conceptual, strategic, and experience-based models—are used to interpret the factors.

In the third **phase (Decide)**, the most effective alternative is selected from the options developed based on observations and orientation, and is prepared for operationalization. The final **phase (Act)** implements the chosen decision. Subsequently, the outcomes of the actions taken are observed, and the cycle begins anew. **In the OODA Loop, success depends on efficient execution, which is reflected in the speed, quality, and timing of the decision.** The OODA Loop is thus deliberately employed to enable rapid, time-critical, and rational decisions even in the face of information deficits.

Let us now transfer this perspective to IT environments. IT environments are characterized by volatility, uncertainty, complexity, and ambiguity **(VUCA)**. These characteristics manifest in a range of challenges that influence decision-making.

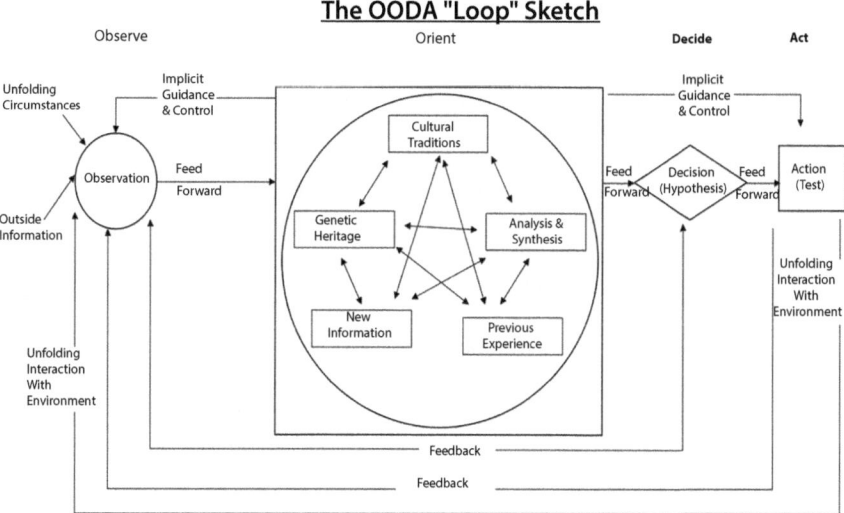

Fig. 8.1 John Boyd's OODA Loop. (Adapted from [2])

In particular, ambiguity—together with information overload and information deficits, sensory overload, speed, and ambiguity in such contexts—disrupts the rational assessment of situations.

These disruptive factors may lead to decisions being made increasingly on a subjective basis, thereby neglecting the factual situation and, in effect, the actual risk landscape. The increased tendency to make decisions subjectively can result in the real threat situation not being adequately considered. This means that objective information, evidence-based data, or precise analyses may not have the appropriate influence on the decision-making process.

Decision-makers may be inclined to rely more on personal beliefs or fixed assumptions, such as the belief that regular phishing campaigns are sufficient, without adequately considering or training for the actual threat of vishing attacks by phone. Even more problematic is the case when campaigns are conducted without prior clarification and definition of concrete objectives. In such cases, there is a risk that the effectiveness of the campaigns is not properly evaluated and the expected practical goals are not clearly defined. This can lead to inefficient use of resources and significantly impair the ability to improve the security posture in a targeted manner.

The human hacker benefits from such defense strategies, as they do not produce clearly recognizable security-compliant responses, which can result in suboptimal and ineffective defense.

The prevailing volatility in IT environments underscores that decisions are short-lived and require continuous review and adjustment. In such dynamic settings, the sustainability and objectivity of decisions are challenging. This also means that ongoing evaluation and identification of decisions are essential to ensure the effectiveness and relevance of the decisions made.

In IT environments where decisions are made selectively and sometimes subjectively due to information overload or information deficits, the need for frameworks that enable efficient, appropriate, and dynamic observation, selection, interpretation, and inference of factors becomes evident. This ensures well-founded and relevant decision-making despite prevailing uncertainties and fluctuations.

In this respect, the OODA Loop represents a suitable strategic and tactical framework. Through continuous observation and rapid orientation, the OODA Loop enables dynamic adaptation to changing circumstances.

The selective interpretation of relevant information and the rapid decision-making based on it make it possible to address the short-lived nature of decisions in IT environments and ensure sustainable effectiveness. In this sense, the OODA Loop functions as an instrumental mechanism that counters the challenges of the VUCA environment and provides the foundation for adequate decision-making processes.

Today, the OODA Loop is considered one of the most internationally recognized decision support models and is used by major companies such as Dell to gain competitive advantage.

The OODA Loop offers a wide range of applications and is regarded in various scientific contexts as a crucial tool for efficient and adaptive decision-making processes. In military science, the OODA Loop is used to accelerate tactical decision-making and outmaneuver the enemy through continuous adaptation and flexibility. This adaptability enables rapid adjustment to changing conditions and real-time optimization of strategies. In the field of corporate management and strategy, the OODA Loop is applied as a means of coping with uncertainty and adapting to changing market dynamics. Organizations use the OODA Loop to respond more quickly to market developments, develop innovative business models, and make effective strategic decisions. In the field of information security, the OODA Loop is used to respond to rapidly evolving threats in vulnerability management and incident response management. The rapid identification of attacks, interpretation of the threat landscape, swift decision-making, and prompt implementation of countermeasures are crucial to minimizing cyber risks.

Our defense concept is based on operationalizing our solution approaches using the OODA Loop as an overarching framework.

This strategic approach enables us to respond flexibly to changing threats and to continuously optimize the effectiveness of our social engineering defense measures.

8.1.2 Key Concepts of the OODA Loop

Before we introduce our modified OODA Loop, it is necessary to outline some fundamental concepts of the OODA Loop for better understanding.

Boyd combined military strategic principles with scientific fields and theorems such as neo-Darwinism, cybernetics, quantum mechanics, and chaos theory. To better understand the OODA Loop, it is necessary to become familiar with several scientific and philosophical principles that contributed to its development. In a broader sense, the OODA Loop is a learning system based on a method for overcoming ambiguity and a dedicated strategy for winning. In this sense, the OODA Loop aims to make the implicit explicit.

To this end, Boyd integrated mental models. These mental models are paradigms applied to consider and understand the correlated and coherent relationships between observed elements.

Mental models are multifaceted and are influenced by subjective cultural perceptions, empirical experiences, and genetics. According to Boyd, mental models refer to conceptual, strategic, and experience-based thought structures. These models serve to analyze and interpret the various factors in the environment.

They influence how observations are interpreted and help generate a variety of possible courses of action.

Mental models are thus paradigms or approaches to thinking that are applied to understand the interrelated and coherent relationships between observed elements. Boyd emphasized that these models are diverse and influenced by subjective cultural perceptions, empirical experiences, and genetic factors. Depending on their level of granularity, mental models can be specific or general and may relate to rules, behaviors, or even overarching principles.

In [3], Boyd referred to three additional philosophical and scientific principles to highlight the inconsistency, incompleteness, and volatility that play a relevant role in decision-making processes. Boyd points out that this deficit must be regarded as an integral part of the universe. These three principles refer to Gödel's incompleteness theorem, Heisenberg's uncertainty principle, and the second law of thermodynamics.

Insight 1 Based on Gödel's incompleteness theorems, Boyd defined a self-contained cycle that specifies the mutual interaction between concepts and observations. Through observations, concepts can be conceived. However, observations themselves are dynamic, volatile, and incomplete.

As a result, it becomes evident that the concepts derived from these observations exhibit the same degree of incompleteness as the underlying observations themselves. Therefore, every logical concept is imperfect and requires continuous refinement and adaptation to meet the demands of volatile and dynamic observations.

Insight 2 In further explanation, Boyd refers to the uncertainty principle. Heisenberg's uncertainty principle states that the position and velocity of particles cannot be measured and determined simultaneously. The more precisely one attempts to determine one value (e.g., velocity), the less precise the measurement or determination of the other value (e.g., position) becomes. The insights from these two principles led Boyd to conclude that more precise observations can only be made in an object-dependent and limited manner. This instinctively creates the risk of focusing on a central object of observation and consequently relying on a single mental model. In other words, the ability to perceive reality is limited.

Insight 3 At this point, the second law of thermodynamics comes into play. This law states that the entropy of an isolated system increases over time—entropy measures the disorder or irregularity of a system. The law implies that in a closed system, where no energy is added from outside, natural processes lead to an increase in disorder. It is often associated with the increasing "irreversibility" of natural processes, meaning that energy in a system tends to disperse in a way that cannot be spontaneously reversed.

Let us transfer this property to our problem: Isolated security strategies that do not observe their environment do not receive current and relevant information.

Here is an example for you: Conducting annual, ongoing phishing campaigns may serve to fulfill the requirement of "employee training," but the actual benefit in terms of risk reduction appears to be limited. Such campaigns may merely sharpen employees' awareness of phishing without effecting a profound behavioral change in the detection and avoidance of real threats.

It is evident that pure phishing training campaigns, without a holistic integration of security objectives, may not be sufficient to effectively reduce the actual risk level. Phishing campaigns should be considered as part of a comprehensive security approach that, in addition to raising employee awareness, also includes security-compliant behavior and the responsiveness of employees.

In such cases, decision-makers behave like a closed system. Closed systems, due to their isolated observations and orientations, are exposed to increasing entropy and imprecise information content. Therefore, the analogy of decision-makers with isolated mental models is also subject to mental entropy.

Let us examine this interpretation in more detail using another concrete example:

Boyd explains this universal and interdisciplinary perspective as follows: When a particular doctrine is repeated continuously, there is a tendency for it to become dogma over time. Doctrines tend to turn into dogmas, and dogmas, in turn, tend to trigger the "man with a hammer syndrome" among decision-makers. This creates the risk that mental security models become entrenched and rigid.

A cybersecurity engineer who maintains a consistent, isolated internal perspective or fails to adequately assess incoming external information behaves like a closed system. The isolated cybersecurity engineer possesses a security model for assessing cyber risks, vulnerabilities, and exposures, but the situation has changed since the last assessment.

Repeating the risk analysis does not seem meaningful here either, as the cybersecurity engineer continues to assess risks and threats using isolated mental models and security strategies, without incorporating new modifications and insights into the decision-making processes. As the cybersecurity engineer continues to operate against an evolving threat landscape with an outdated mental model, uncertainty, inconsistency, and system entropy are the natural result.

In this particular example, we are therefore talking about the "man with a hammer syndrome," which is a metaphor indicating that people tend to rely on what is most familiar to them or what they are most comfortable with when solving problems or interpreting information, even if it may not be the optimal solution. The term derives from the notion that someone who only has a hammer tends to see every problem as a nail.

Insight 4 In a NATO publication on operational planning, tempo is defined as "the speed or rhythm of activities compared to those of the adversary." [4] describes that the time span between perception and a decision **depends on two factors: the rate of activity (speed) and the rhythm of activity (timing).** To be well prepared for a social engineering attack, speed plays a crucial role, as decision-makers must possess the speed of perception or "coup d'oeil" to recognize and process a potential threat, an emerging danger, and the available options at an early stage. In practice, it is not sufficient to make decisions as quickly as possible, because beyond a certain point, this approach is no longer efficient.

How can this perspective be better explained? The following thought experiment supports this view, in which the speed of detection and the timing of a cyberattack can, for example, be derived using the OODA loop, enabling organizations to better prepare for a potential cyberattack. Let us consider the situation of an international service provider about to go public:

The cybersecurity engineers and decision-makers responsible for the availability of the provider's IT systems might, for example, assess the likelihood and timing of an attack in the period before and immediately after the IPO as very high. This could be due to the possibility that hostile competitors may commission such attacks. Based on our ongoing observations, we can formulate hypotheses, develop postulates, and generate suggestions. Using the OODA loop, these are systematically organized, placed in context, and presented as so-called evidence. This evidence, with an indicative effect, provides possible clues to existing threats.

Now that you are familiar with the basics and rationale of the OODA loop, we would like to introduce our modified version of the OODA loop, in which we relate the original phases to threat intelligence and resilience processes in social engineering.

8.1.3   Application Scenarios of the OODA Loop in Social Engineering

We divide the OODA loop into two areas (Fig. 8.2). The first, overarching area represents the tactical level, where the individual process steps must be carried out in a predetermined order. The process steps can be embedded within each other so that a complete process cycle is executed more quickly and intuitively. This is especially the case when observation, orientation, and decision-making are almost seamlessly interconnected. Based on previous observations and defined orientations, a decision can sometimes be fully made and derived.

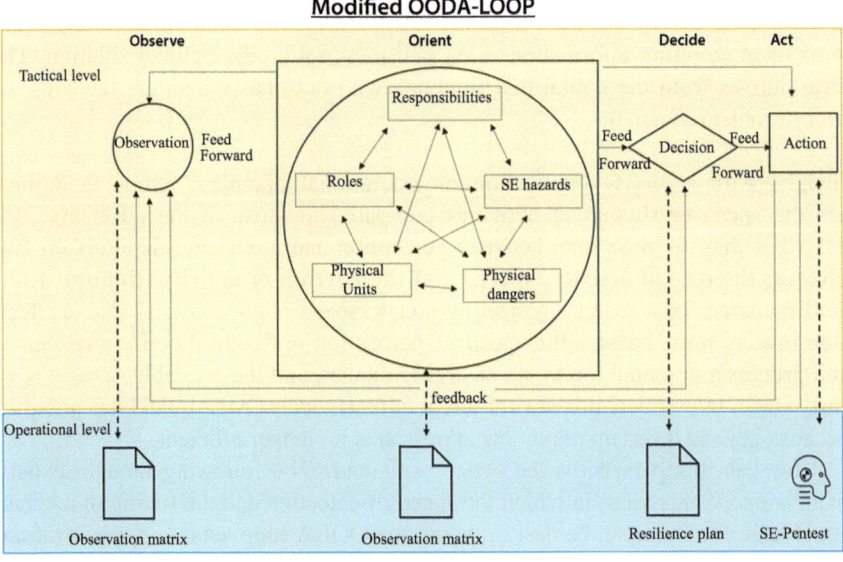

Fig. 8.2 Modified OODA loop. (Adapted from [2])

The second area concerns the operational level and encompasses the procedures and artifacts aimed at enabling efficient execution of the loop. These include the observation matrix, the resilience plan, and the social engineering penetration test [5].

By linking the tactical and operational levels, it becomes possible to use the OODA loop for the operational and targeted defense against social engineering attacks. In the following sections, we will discuss the individual process steps and explain how you can operationalize the OODA loop by applying the defined solution approaches.

Here, we focus on efficient action. In the field of information security, the key to efficient action lies not only in making quick decisions, but more importantly in making high-quality decisions at the right time. This enables preventive measures to significantly reduce both the likelihood and the impact of an event. In this sense, we strive to develop the ability to act appropriately both proactively and reactively.

The primary premise is to learn not only from one's own mistakes but—more importantly—from the mistakes of others.

8.1.4   Observe and Orient with the Observation Matrix

The "Observe" phase is not an isolated action, but rather a developing awareness based on constantly changing circumstances and incomplete information. This gives this phase an essential role in our defense processes. Through the "Observe" phase, we attempt to counteract—and possibly overcome—the challenges posed by the second law of thermodynamics.

This is achieved by continuously considering new information about our evolving IT environment and the social engineering threat landscape. We aim to capture the full spectrum of information gathering in an open system.

From a tactical perspective, specifying the sources of information is crucial to ensure effective observation. For this reason, we define a set of observation objectives and tools that have already proven to be effective in practice for "Observe" and "Orient," and incorporate them into the observation matrix (Fig. 8.3).

Process Step 1: Targeting
In the first step, targeting involves defining all roles and physical entities and assigning them to realistic attack and threat types. When identifying individual roles within an organization, it is necessary to recognize and embed not only internal roles but also those belonging to external organizations or temporarily working for the organization, such as suppliers, service providers, interns, etc., into the observation matrix. In a second step, using the same approach, physical entities are identified and incorporated into the observation matrix. After identifying the roles and physical entities, social engineering attacks and physical attack types can then be mapped and assigned to the already defined roles and physical entities.

Roles	human-based Threats (HT)						Clustering
	HT 1	HT 2	HT 3	HT 4	HT 5	HT 6	
R 1	x	x			x	x	Security Staff
R 2	x	x			x	x	
R 3			x				Engineering Maintenance
R 4		x			x	x	OT-Staff
R n+1		x			x	x	

Cluster	Department	security requirement
CR 1	Security Staff	Critical (3)
CR 2	Engineering Maintenance	High (2)
CR 3	OT-Staff	Critical (3)

phyiscal Units	phyiscals Threats (PT)						Clustering
	PT 1	PT 2	PT 3	PT 4	PT 5	PT 6	
P 1	x	x			x	x	Network interconnection point
P 2	x	x			x	x	
P 3	x	x	x		x	x	Network operation center

Cluster	Department	security requirement
CP 1	Network interconnection point	Critical (3)
CP 2	Network operation center	Critical (3)

Assessment	CP 1	Value	Matrix final value
CR 1	x	3 x 3	9
CR 2	x	2 x 3	6
CR 3	No allocation	No allocation	No allocation
	CP 2	Value	Matrix final value
CR 1	x	3 x 3	9
CR 2	No allocation	No allocation	No allocation
CR 3	x	3 x 3	9

Fig. 8.3 Meta-example of the observation matrix [1]

This makes the current potential threats, relevant roles, and physical entities visible for the first time.

Through continuous observation, the observation objectives can be supplemented and updated. The visibility of the current threat landscape, the affected roles and physical entities, and their mapping to each other ensures a coherent and transparent view, ultimately reducing the level of abstraction (e.g., Which actual threats affect me, and which specific roles and systems are targeted by these threats?).

By reducing the level of abstraction, it becomes possible to address the real threat landscape in a targeted manner.

Process Step 2: Clustering
In the second step, roles with similar task profiles and protection requirements (e.g., all roles assigned to a common set of attack types) are grouped together in a cluster. The same approach can be applied analogously to physical entities.

In this way, a large number of roles and physical entities exposed to similar attack vectors and types can be grouped into homogeneous groups [1].

Process Step 3: Assessment
Clustering homogeneous assets simplifies the processes for criticality assessment. After clustering, the next process step is to assess the individual role clusters and physical clusters, where the various role and building clusters can be evaluated using three scale values (moderate (1), high (2), critical (3)). However, the individual levels of the assessment system to be used must be defined specifically for the organization and interpreted qualitatively or quantitatively. The aim of determining criticality is to interpret the fragility, vulnerability, and impact of attacks on target individuals, target buildings, and the organization as a whole. This includes considering the potential effects on the security and functionality of the system, supply, and secure operations [1].

Process Step 4: Mapping
In the fourth step, the assessments of the role clusters and physical clusters are combined, resulting in an overall evaluation of the individual areas. This allows the overall criticality to be determined. The advantage is the visualization of the overall criticality of the roles and physical entities [1].

Application Scenario: CEO Fraud in the Home Office
In the observation phase, the matrix enables decision-makers to precisely focus on the specific social engineering threats that impact the reality of their organization. A practical example illustrates the relevance of this approach: With the global outbreak of the COVID-19 pandemic, numerous organizations were forced to establish home office workstations via VPN access and virtual collaborative software in order to maintain business operations. These measures led to a multitude of new technical and physical interfaces which, if inadequately protected, were potentially vulnerable to attacks and compromise. By applying the observation matrix, decision-makers can systematically capture and transparently visualize their threat landscape. This makes it possible to identify specific risk areas. For example, matrix analysis reveals that certain roles within the company became increasingly targeted by CEO fraud attacks, or that vulnerabilities in VPN access and remote connections were exploited more frequently. The matrix thus serves as an effective tool to first visualize and accurately assess the threat situation in a complex environment such as the home office, and, based on this, to implement proactive security measures.

In this context, the question arises: How can decision-makers take effective action to protect themselves against threats they may not even be aware of? The key component in addressing this problem lies in recognizing the value of an observation matrix.

Through the systematic collection and analysis of information, the matrix offers the opportunity to detect and understand potential threats in the context of targeting at an early stage, even if they do not initially manifest themselves directly.

The decisive advantage is that, by applying the observation matrix, decision-makers can adopt a proactive stance. They gain insights not only into already known threats, but can also be alerted to previously unknown or underestimated risks. This enables them to implement preventive protective measures before potential threats develop into actual risks.

In short, the observation matrix creates awareness of the threat landscape even before it becomes fully visible. It is therefore an indispensable tool for strengthening a company's protection mechanisms and ensuring that decision-makers are better prepared to respond even to threats that may not yet be fully recognized.

Application Scenario: Colonial Pipeline
Had the decision-makers at Colonial Pipeline [6] been aware of the mapping of their existing roles and IT systems to the threat landscape (e.g., misuse of VPN access in operational technology) as well as the mapping of vulnerabilities and threats to roles (e.g., operational technology admins with insecure handling of confidential authentication information), the cyberattack might have been prevented. It is postulated that by visualizing the threat situation, it can be assumed that the threat landscape can be made transparent in a role-, system-, and threat-specific manner. Decision-makers would thus be able to initiate targeted investigations and measures, such as:

a) deactivating unused VPN access,
b) allowing external remote access only with two-factor authentication, and
c) providing targeted training for maintenance personnel (e.g., a targeted information security awareness program on handling confidential authentication information).

Without adequate judgment, data and information have little significance, even if they are complete and consistent. This postulation is based on the premise that more information, data, and controls do not necessarily lead to better decisions. Well-developed judgment, which recognizes patterns and generates sustainable knowledge, is capable of extracting knowledge from available information and, on this basis, making sustainable and efficient decisions.

In this context, human perception plays a relevant role in the "Observe" and "Orient" phases. Perception describes the active acquisition, processing, and assignment of meaning through the senses. This cognitive, mental process enables understanding and interpretation of stimuli captured by the senses. This fundamental cognitive ability is of great importance in everyday life and especially in information security.

By specifically stimulating cognitive functions, it is indeed possible to train and enhance perception. Since this process is active, it is the responsibility of individuals to select, organize, and understand the relevant information.

Selection People are exposed to countless stimuli every day, which they can only process to a limited extent. This means that information must be selectively filtered so that it can be decided what exactly should be perceived. This is achieved through the use of matrices.

Organization Once it is clear what should be perceived (transparency through matrices), stimuli must be categorized so that meaning can be assigned to them. Synergy plays a special role here, as the amount of information received cannot be reduced to the properties of individual stimuli.

Interpretation Once the selected stimuli are categorized, they are processed so that meaning can be assigned to them. The perception process is then completed. Experience and expectations influence how this interpretation process unfolds.

The ability to create transparency in the selection of information and observation targets through the observation matrix makes it possible to deliberately decide which stimuli should be brought into focus. The organization of these selected stimuli is then carried out according to clear criteria in order to create a meaningful structure and better understand the overall information. Through this active and conscious perception, decision-makers can recognize relevant patterns and relationships, which in turn leads to an improved understanding of the threat situation.

It is emphasized that an overload of information and data alone does not necessarily lead to better decision-making. Rather, it is trained and experienced judgment that generates knowledge from the available information and, on this basis, makes sustainable and efficient decisions. Therefore, targeted training and development of perceptual abilities and judgment are crucial aspects for enabling well-founded and effective decision-making in the "Observe" and "Orient" phases.

8.1.5 Decide with Resilience Plan

Based on the results obtained, a resilience plan (Fig. 8.4) can now be used to implement proactive, reactive, and adaptive measures, each targeting the identified roles, buildings, and associated hazards. In this context, two fundamental areas of resilience can be defined [1].

Process Step 1: Cluster-Based Decision-Making

All identified and assigned social engineering attack types can now be addressed on a cluster-specific basis. For each embedded social engineering attack type, decisions can be made regarding the definition of information security training programs. It is possible to determine which social engineering threats need to be addressed preventively, and to what degree of granularity and intensity. In this way, organizational efforts to raise awareness and empower employees can be tailored to the complexity and intensity of the identified social engineering threats [1].

Resilience plan for CR 1

Threats	IS-Awareness	IS-Training	IS-Education
HT 1	x		
HT 2		x	x
HT 5	x		x
HT 6	x		x

Resilience plan for CP 1

Threats	camera surveillance	physical intrusion detection system	Physical Pentest
PT 1	x	x	
PT 2	x	x	x
PT 4	x	x	x
PT 5	x	x	

Meta informations — involved staff

	affiliation
R 1	Security Staff
R 2	Security Staff

Meta informations — involved physicals Units

	affiliation
P 1	Network interconnection point
P 2	Network interconnection point

operative treatment plan

Measure	due date	Responsible	Accountable
IS-Awareness	Prio B: 31.12.2023	CISO	CEO
IS-Training	Prio B: 31.12.2023	CISO	CEO
IS-Education	Prio B: 31.12.2023	CISO	CEO
camera surveillance	Prio A: 31.10.2023	CISO	CEO
physical intrusion detection system	Prio A: 31.10.2023	Chief Security Officer	CEO
Physical Pentest	Prio C: 31.03.2024	Chief Security Officer	CEO

human-based Threats (HT)

Roles	HT 1	HT 2	HT 3	HT 4	HT 5	HT 6	Clustering
R 1	x	x			x	x	
R 2	x	x			x	x	Security Staff
R 3			x				Engineering Maintenance
R 4		x			x	x	OT-Staff
R n+1		x			x	x	

Cluster	Department	security requirement	Clustering
CR 1	Security Staff	Critical (3)	
CR 2	Engineering Maintenance	High (2)	
CR 3	OT-Staff	Critical (3)	

physicals Threats (PT)

physical Units	PT 1	PT 2	PT 3	PT 4	PT 5	PT 6	Clustering
P 1	x	x			x	x	Network interconnection point
P 2	x	x			x	x	Network operation center
P 3	x	x	x		x	x	

Cluster	Department	security requirement	Clustering
CP 1	Network interconnection point	Critical (3)	
CP 2	Network operation center	Critical (3)	

Threats Matrix

Assessment	CP 1	Value	Matrix final value
CR 1	x	3 x 3	9
CR 2	x	2 x 3	6
CR 3	No allocation	No allocation	No allocation

Assessment	CP 2	Value	Matrix final value
CR 1	x	3 x 3	9
CR 2	No allocation	No allocation	No allocation
CR 3	x	3 x 3	9

Fig. 8.4 Integration of the observation matrix with the resilience plan [1]

Process Step 2: Selection of the Training Concept

To define concrete measures for raising awareness, training, and empowering employees against social engineering attacks, we refer to NIST Special Publication 800-50, titled "Building an information technology security awareness and training program" [7]. This guideline provides comprehensive instructions for developing security awareness and training programs in the IT domain.

NIST SP 800-50 distinguishes three essential levels of granularity: awareness, training, and education. These should be considered in implementation to ensure effective protection against various social engineering attacks [1].

Awareness

Awareness focuses on employees' understanding of fundamental security aspects and the associated risks. The goal is for employees to develop a general understanding of security concepts, policies, and threats. Corresponding measures include the implementation of regular communication campaigns, training materials, and sessions that convey basic security principles.

Training

Training is defined as the imparting of specific skills and knowledge required for the secure use of IT and the defense against relevant threats. The objective is for employees to be able to perform security-related tasks and respond appropriately to threats. Measures include the implementation of practical training, exercises, and simulations to prepare employees for concrete scenarios.

Education

Education goes beyond training and imparts a deeper understanding of the underlying principles of information security. The aim is for employees to understand information security defense concepts and to be able to make security-critical decisions. Measures include the implementation of formal training, certifications, and advanced courses that provide a comprehensive understanding of information security.

Distinguishing between these levels of granularity is crucial, as employees require different knowledge and skills to defend themselves effectively against various social engineering attacks. Awareness creates foundational understanding, training imparts specific skills, and education fosters in-depth knowledge and expertise.

Process Step 3: Definition of Defense Measures

All identified and assigned physical attack types can now be addressed on a cluster-specific basis. For each embedded physical attack type, decisions can be made regarding the definition of defense measures. It is possible to determine which physical threats need to be addressed preventively, reactively, correctively, or detectively, and to what degree of granularity and intensity. This process step can be carried out analogously to process step 1.

Process Step 4: Integration and Scheduling
All measures defined in process steps 2 and 3 can be integrated into the treatment plan for practical application and operationalization, and scheduled according to specific criticalities and resource capacities to enable their operational execution and monitoring. The resilience plan offers a variety of advantages. Its existence allows concrete, real threats identified in the "Observe" phase to be precisely reduced by specifically addressing causes and effects.

The flexible structure of the plan enables different implementation strategies that meet individual requirements and risks.

The planning of measures becomes more targeted through the resilience plan, enabling precise selection to maximize effectiveness against specific threats. Resources can be optimally allocated, resulting in efficient resource allocation. Transparent objectives improve understanding of the impact of each measure and facilitate communication.

Implementing the plan allows for more effective use of existing resources and enables precise monitoring and evaluation of the effectiveness of each implemented measure. A holistic approach provides protection against various attack vectors and scenarios. The resilience plan supports the early identification of objectives and can be continuously adapted to respond to changing threats and requirements.

8.1.6   Act and Information Security Awareness and Training

There are several fundamental aspects that, from a professional perspective, form the foundation of any conceivable awareness and training program. Hänsch et al. described three modular concepts (Fig. 8.5) of the term "security awareness" [8]. The primary concept describes the conscious action of users, i.e., they are aware of the threats to information security (perception). The secondary concept describes knowledge, i.e., users understand and know how to protect themselves against these threats (protection). The third concept states that users not only know and recognize threats and know what to do about them, but also integrate this knowledge into their behavior **(behavior).** Only the last concept promises a real increase in information security within an organization.

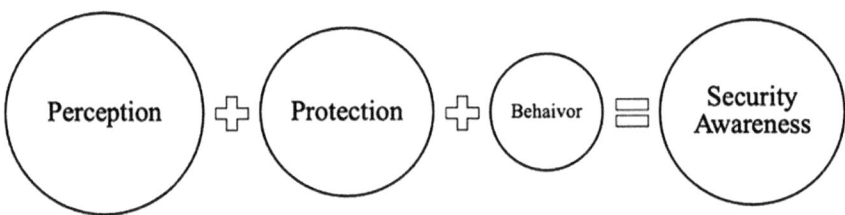

Fig. 8.5 Three concepts of security awareness

Accordingly, security awareness means that users know how to behave in a manner consistent with information security (**e.g., not clicking on links in phishing emails, not opening suspicious attachments, and not enabling macros**), and what consequences may result from non-compliance (e.g., reputational and financial damage in the event of data loss involving customers or employees).

In this context, strategic decision-makers must be trained and sensitized differently than operational staff.

Information security awareness refers to the conscious handling of information, regardless of the medium. A conscious approach to information security can be described as a construct of cognitive and affective processes (e.g., How can I behave in a security-compliant manner?; [7]). Therefore, psychological aspects, particularly social psychology, play a significant role. The field of social psychology can help to understand human behavior in the context of information security, as it considers various aspects such as attitudes, beliefs, and social norms, which can be leveraged for information security within organizations [9, 10].

The professional preparation and organization of an awareness program form the fundamental basis for its effectiveness. A key principle is to avoid provoking negative feelings and fears among employees. The targeted development of focused and actionable training content is crucial, ensuring that it is not only topic-specific but also tailored to the individual needs of specific groups. In this context, quality takes precedence over quantity, enabling a sustainable learning effect. The integration of new behaviors and policies takes place through a multi-stage process, supported by the use of case studies. To ensure the quality of the program, continuous interactivity and feedback are essential. These quality assurance features should be recursively embedded in the process to enable ongoing optimization. When considering cultural and individual characteristics, the focus is on fostering awareness of diversity and adapting standardized training content to the needs of different groups.

A well-considered procedural model is indispensable for the definition and implementation of awareness programs. The following process steps provide a structured guide for successful implementation:

Process Step 1: Defining a Goal (What do we want to achieve?)
Defining a clear goal forms the starting point of the procedural model. This includes both qualitative and quantitative objectives aimed at a comprehensive improvement of the information security level. This holistic approach begins with the clear definition of both qualitative and quantitative goals.

The focus here is on raising the fundamental level of information security within the company and defining measurable indicators such as training coverage, reduction of incidents, and successful defense against simulated attacks.

Process Step 2: Environmental Analysis (Organizational Capability)
After defining the goals, an in-depth environmental analysis is conducted to assess
the organizational conditions for their suitability for training measures.

This involves establishing the necessary organizational prerequisites and implementing technical as well as organizational measures that serve as the foundation
for training. Analyzing the organizational conditions is crucial to ensure the feasibility of training measures. This includes creating the necessary organizational
prerequisites and integrating technical and organizational measures.

Process Step 3: Reducing Complexity (Topic Segmentation)
Reducing complexity is carried out in a multi-stage process, with topics such as
password security serving as exemplary focal points. Various aspects are considered, including employees' level of knowledge and behavioral intentions.
Additionally, training groups are divided into general and group-specific units to
ensure targeted training.

Process Step 4: Reducing Complexity (Segmentation of Training Groups)
Developing the training concept at the effectiveness level sets the strategic framework
for training and awareness measures. It adapts the target state, defines responsibilities, schedules, topic- and group-specific training, as well as evaluation mechanisms.
The segmentation of training groups is carried out into general and group-specific
units. In this process, different employee groups, such as regular users, IT administrators, or staff in high-security areas, are specifically addressed and trained.

Process Step 5: Development of the Training Concept
Operational implementation takes place at the efficiency level, where comprehensive campaign planning is crucial. Strategic decision-makers are involved at
an early stage, sufficient time is allocated for employee participation, and a mix
of in-person and online training as well as various social marketing components
are considered. The training concept at the effectiveness level defines the strategic
direction of training and awareness measures, specifying objectives, responsibilities, implementation cycles, topic-specific training, and training formats.

Process Step 6: Operational Implementation
The evaluation process completes the holistic approach by considering both
employee feedback and the achievement of objectives at the organizational level.
Practical experience is used to drive continuous improvements and adapt the training process to changing requirements. Operational implementation at the efficiency
level requires careful planning and execution. This includes involving strategic
decision-makers, selecting appropriate training formats (in-person and online training), utilizing gamification elements, and regularly evaluating the measures.

Process Step 7: Evaluation of the Entire Process
The evaluation process completes the holistic approach by considering both employee feedback and the achievement of objectives at the organizational level. Practical experience is used to drive continuous improvements and adapt the training process to changing requirements. The final evaluation considers the overall process and the goals achieved. Employee feedback is incorporated into the ongoing improvement of training measures. An objective and unbiased evaluation ensures the continuous adaptation and optimization of awareness programs. This systematic approach combines qualitative and quantitative aspects to design and continuously improve a comprehensive information security awareness program. The focus is not only on knowledge transfer but also on specifically influencing behavioral intentions to establish sustainable security habits within the organization.

Integrating these process steps into an inclusive procedural model provides a solid foundation for defining and implementing information security awareness programs. This model ensures not only the delivery of theoretical knowledge but also its practical application in the workplace. By incorporating fundamental rules, a positive learning environment is created that fosters understanding and internalization of security principles. The iterative nature of the model enables continuous adaptation to evolving requirements and threats in the field of information security.

8.1.7   Act with the Social Engineering Penetration Test

The **social engineering penetration test** [11] is a comprehensive analysis of security measures in a socio-technical environment, particularly in the area of human-machine interaction. Its purpose is to identify vulnerabilities in an organization's information and IT security concept as well as in its resilience measures, and to assess their effectiveness and efficiency. This test serves as a measurable indicator of the organization's resilience level in the area of social engineering.

The social engineering penetration test includes a targeted vulnerability analysis of the human and physical factors in information security. It serves as a tool for auditing and simulating realistic social engineering attacks or acts of sabotage. Logical attack methods such as SOCMINT, OSINT, and physical attack vectors such as tailgating are used in this context.

The test follows a structured approach, carried out in four modular process steps:

Pre-preparation Phase: Detailed Planning
In this phase, the framework conditions for the social engineering penetration test are established. Clear objectives are defined, such as persuading employees to click on a link in a phishing email, enter credentials on spoofed login pages (pharming), disclose information, absorb and internally disseminate misinformation, release

or ship goods without authorization, transfer money, alter master data, gain access to the client's premises, and, beyond that, infiltrate special protection zones and (high-)security areas undetected in order to simulate a physical or logical attack. In addition to the objectives, procedural workflows must also be clearly discussed in advance, such as how the pentesters should behave if discovered by employees or security staff. For purely digital social engineering penetration tests, the entities responsible for information security should always be informed in advance of the exact timing of the attack, so that in the event of an incident, they can always distinguish between the simulated social engineering test and a potential real attack. Further detailed planning should also include the integration of additional actors and stakeholders from cross-sectional areas such as data protection, compliance, and the works council, in order to align any questions and expectations [1].

Preparation Phase: Reconnaissance
During the preparation phase of a physical social engineering penetration test, an on-site analysis is conducted to gain a direct impression of the target organization. Physical and environmental security perimeters, processes, routines, responsibilities, and similar factors play a major role in the development of the actual **attack scenarios**.

For all digital social engineering penetration tests, specific initial analyses are operationalized using OSINT and SOCMINT methods to enable targeted and precise information gathering as a basis for developing attack scenarios. As a result of the preparation phase, the **Course of Action (COA)** is defined, specifying and refining the nature of the attack scenarios [1].

Attack Phase: Execution
In the attack phase, the actual attack is carried out based on the groundwork and COA developed in the previous phases. For a physical social engineering penetration test, cover stories—i.e., identities—are created to enable the social engineering pentester to infiltrate the target site undetected and gain unrestricted freedom of movement.

The social engineering pentester then attempts, for example, to gain access to the IT system via a physical attack vector. Depending on the agreement with the target organization, prepared removable media such as USB sticks, physical keyloggers, Wi-Fi sniffers, eavesdropping devices (in a broad sense), and similar tools may be used.

Analog information is also reviewed, recorded, and, if necessary, stolen (photographed) on site by the social engineering pentester. **The physical social engineering penetration test (Variant I) is completed once the target site has been successfully and covertly exfiltrated.** In a digital social engineering penetration test, the respective COA is considered complete whenever one of the defined objectives is achieved, another COA is initiated or supported, or the attack is thwarted. **In Variant II, physical social engineering penetration tests conclude after the actual attack simulation with the initiation of measures to raise information security awareness** [1]. For example, at the end of a social engineering penetration test, one can move increasingly subtly within the target organization until finally being approached by an employee (deliberate tactical exposure). At this point, the social engineering pentester can persist with their cover story, requiring the employee to file a report and escalate the incident. Here, the focus is not only on the employees' response but also on the functionality and efficiency of reporting channels, escalation chains, alerting plans, and contactability. Alternatively, the social engineering pentester can resolve the situation, explain to the employee what is happening, and transition into an active real-time awareness training session. This approach can also be applied analogously to logical social engineering penetration tests, where, for example, a vishing attack is used to illicitly obtain critical information or to induce improper behavior. In Variant II of a logical social engineering penetration test, the social engineering pentester may pose as an employee of a well-known company and typically request assistance with an urgent business problem. Shortly thereafter, the social engineering pentester resolves the situation, briefly introduces themselves, explains the purpose of the attack simulation, and thereby becomes a social engineering awareness trainer [1].

Post Phase: Follow-up and Results Discussion
This phase marks the conclusion of a social engineering pentest and includes a detailed description of the execution and results of the scenarios carried out, as well as the approach taken by the social engineering pentesters. Each attack is documented in writing with a situational description, and all identified vulnerabilities are assessed in a thorough analysis. To protect employees from discreditation, the report is anonymized and delivered to the target organizations as a secure digital PDF. After the in-depth analysis, the results are discussed in so-called post-workshops, based on the written report, with information security decision-makers and affected employees as part of the debriefing, in order to analyze the observed human behavior, identify possible individual causes, and derive appropriate mitigation actions. Through dialogue with employees, the true underlying issues often come to light [1].

In the post-pentest phase, various causes for identified vulnerabilities can be derived. These causes serve as the basis for operationalizing remediation measures. Below are some exemplary causes that may arise after a physical pentest (Table 8.1).

Table 8.1 Findings from the Post-Pentest Phase

Empirical Observation	Findings from the Attack Phase
The pentester is noticed by employees as an unknown and apparently external person, but is not approached, even though their behavior is at times very conspicuous	→ {**Deficient or absent error culture:** Uncertainty and fear of making mistakes} → {**Deficient security culture or lack of collective information security awareness:** That's not my responsibility, we have a reception desk and security for that} → {**Lack of knowledge and skills – perceived behavioral control:** I wouldn't even know what to say} → {**Human factors – self-efficacy expectation:** What if I approach them and it turns out to be an auditor or another external consultant, or even worse, a supervisor?}
The pentester is simply let in through a side entrance by an employee, even though they do not know each other (tailgating)	→{**Human factors – injunctive perceived norm:** I didn't want to be rude} → {**Lack of communication and insufficient training and awareness among employees:** I wasn't aware that it was my responsibility to pay attention to who is allowed in and who isn't} → {**Lack of knowledge – behavioral intention and salience:** Why would anyone want to get in here, what do we have to hide, we're just a municipal administration?}
The pentester is able to bypass a turnstile because an employee hands over their ID badge	→{**Human factors – injunctive perceived norm:** I didn't want to be rude} → {**Human factors – behavioral intention and habit:** That's what we always do at lunchtime, we only bring one card when we go to eat together}

References

1. Erfan Koza, Asiye Öztürk, Michael Willer, Physische Penetrationstests im Kontext des bevorstehenden KRITIS-Dachgesetzes: Ein praxiserprobter Ansatz zur Resilienzerhöhung. In: Die Themen des 20. Deutschen IT-Sicherheitskongresses, pp. 318–332.
2. John Boyd, zitiert nach Grant, T. Hammond, A Discourse on Winning and Losing, Maxwell, AFB, Alabama, 2018.
3. John Boyd, The Essence of Winning and Losing, 1996, edited by C. Richards and C. Spinney, Bluffton, South Carolina, USA, 2012.
4. Ministry of Defence, Allied Joint Doctrine for the Planning of Operations, NATO Standard AJP-5, Edition A Version 2 + UK national elements (Change 1), 2019, unter: https://assets.publishing.service.gov.uk/government/uploads/system/uploads/attachment_data/file/971390/20210310-AJP_5_with_UK_elem_final_web.pdf (Zugriff 07.07.2023).
5. Erfan Koza, An Assessment Model for Prioritizing CVEs in Critical Infrastructures in the Context of Time and Fault Criticality. In: Hämmerli, B., Helmbrecht, U., Hommel, W., Kunczik, L., Pickl, S. (eds) Critical Information Infrastructures Security. CRITIS 2022. Lecture Notes in Computer Science, vol 13723. Springer, Cham. In Proceedings of the 17th International Conference on Critical Infrastructures Security (CRITIS 2022), Springer Lecture Notes in Computer Science, Deutschland, München.
6. Cybersecurity & Infrastructure Security Agency, The Attack on Colonial Pipeline: What We've Learned & What We've Done Over the Past Two Years, unter: https://www.cisa.gov/news-events/news/attack-colonial-pipeline-what-weve-learned-what-weve-done-over-past-two-years (Zugriff: 07.08.2023).

7. National Institute of Standards and Technology, Building an Information Technology Security Awareness and Training Program U.S. Department of Commerce, Washington, D.C., Federal Information Security Management Act (FISMA), Special Publication 800-50, October 2003, unter: https://nvlpubs.nist.gov/nistpubs/legacy/sp/nistspecialpublication800-50.pdf.
8. Norman Hänsch, Zinaida Benenson, Specifying IT Security Awareness, in IEEE 2014: Proceedings of the 25th International Workshop on Database and Expert System Applications, 2014, pp. 326–330.
9. M. E. Kabay, Using Social Psychology to Implement Security Policies, in S. Boworth & M. E. Kabay: Computer Security Handbook, Wiley, 2002, pp. 1–22.
10. Kristin Weber, Andreas E. Schütz, Tobias Fertig, Insider Threats – Der Feind in den eigenen Reihen, in: Weber, K., Reinheimer, S. (eds) Faktor Mensch. Edition HMD. Springer Vieweg, Wiesbaden, 2022.
11. Erfan Koza, Asiye Öztürk, Michael Willer, Social Engineering Penetration Testing Within the OODCA Cycle–Approaches to Detect and Remediate Human Vulnerabilities and Risks in Proceedings of the 14th International Conference on Applied Human Factors and Ergonomics (AHFE 2023), Vol. 91, 2023, France, pp. 72–82.

Part II

Black Chapter: Attack Techniques

Business Email Compromise (BEC)

9

Business Email Compromise (BEC) refers to an email-based fraud in which attackers impersonate supervisors, employees, service providers, partners, or customers with the aim of redirecting business financial transactions to their own accounts. The disclosure of confidential or sensitive data can also be the target of a BEC attack. To achieve this, the attacker typically uses a forged email address or resorts to email spoofing.

Email spoofing represents a sophisticated method of identity deception, in which an attacker manipulates the sender information of an email to create the impression that the message originates from a legitimate source. This technique is frequently used in various social engineering-based attacks, including phishing and BEC.

Advanced spoofing methods can also alter the entire header, the mail domain, and other attributes of the email to create the appearance of a trustworthy source. This enables an attacker to pose as a legitimate sender and thus gain the recipient's trust.

In addition to email spoofing, a human hacker may have already gained unauthorized access to a business email account through a prior hacking attack or may have acquired login credentials via the darknet. In such cases, this is referred to as Email Account Compromise (EAC).

The attacker uses the illegally obtained credentials of a legitimate email account to impersonate its owner in a BEC attack, thereby bypassing email spoofing and the use of forged email addresses.

In 2022, the American Federal Bureau of Investigation (FBI) identified BEC as one of the fastest-growing and most financially damaging internet-based crimes. This is partly attributable to changes resulting from the COVID-19 pandemic, such as the increased virtualization of routine business processes and virtual communication.

E. Koza et al., *Social Engineering and Human Hacking*,
https://doi.org/10.1007/978-3-662-72084-4_9

From October 2013 to the end of 2022, the FBI recorded over 277,000 cases of BEC/EAC worldwide, including both successful attacks and attempted fraud [1]. The attackers attempted to steal more than 50 billion USD.

However, the actual number of cases is likely to be significantly higher, as many incidents go unreported due to concerns over reputational damage, or smaller cases of fraud may remain entirely undetected.

Statistics from the FBI's Internet Crime Complaint Center (IC3) also clearly show that BEC is not a regionally limited type of attack.

Cases of BEC have been reported in over 177 countries worldwide. In more than 140 countries, unauthorized payments resulting from BEC attacks have already been recorded [1].

The top transaction destinations include banks in Thailand, Hong Kong, China, the United Kingdom, Mexico, and Singapore, where attackers set up target accounts. Attackers employ various attack scenarios to persuade their victims to transfer funds [1]. Most BEC attacks can be assigned to one of the following five main groups, although dynamic variations are possible:

CEO Fraud
Attackers impersonate executives and instruct employees in accounting or finance departments to make unauthorized payments, or attempt to obtain confidential information.

Account Compromise
Attackers hack employee accounts, such as email accounts (EAC), to request unauthorized financial transactions—e.g., from vendors and external providers—using the compromised accounts.

Fake Invoices
Attackers pose, for example, as suppliers and use forged invoices to request payments to fraudulent accounts. With professional attackers, these fake invoices are often indistinguishable from genuine ones.

Data Theft
Attackers attempt to obtain confidential data, which they may subsequently resell or use directly for further attacks. A possible scenario would be an attack on the HR department to obtain personal, sensitive employee data, or on the finance department to acquire important information about customers and suppliers. Gathering information about executives can also be a preparatory step for a subsequent CEO fraud attack.

Attorney Impersonation
Attackers pose as legal counsel or the company's legal representative to request information or instruct transfers. The primary targets of this attack are often lower-level employees, who are less likely to have the necessary knowledge to verify the

request or the sender's identity. In all five main groups, attackers rely on social engineering.

In the following, we will take a closer look at CEO fraud as an example and analyze it to develop a better understanding of the social engineering techniques used in such attacks.

References

1. Federal Bureau of Investigation (FBI), Public Service Announcement. Business Email Compromise: The $50 Billion Scam, unter: https://www.ic3.gov/Media/Y2023/PSA230609 (Zugriff: 04.01.2024).

CEO Fraud

10

CEO fraud, a globally widespread form of BEC, is characterized by attackers, as previously described, assuming the identity of a CEO or other high-ranking executives. Their goal is to manipulate susceptible employees in accounting into authorizing transfers of sometimes substantial sums of money.

Without the use of social engineering techniques, this attack method is rarely successful. For the human hacker to achieve their objective, extensive preparation and information gathering are required, which will be explained in more detail below.

CEO fraud typically begins with an apparent email from the executive to the victim (**target individual**) in the finance department. Alternatively, a voice message via messenger or a message left on an answering machine may be used. This presupposes that the human hacker is technically capable of simulating the executive's voice—a capability that can already be achieved using specialized software and AI. In this context, the human hacker employs the deepfake attack method. A deepfake refers to machine learning technology, particularly the use of AI to create deceptively realistic synthetic content, including fake audio recordings of human voices.

In this message, the target individual is presented with a scenario (**illusion**), which, for example, might involve a planned corporate acquisition abroad. (**Pressure and urgency**) are emphasized, making it clear that an immediate payment is required to ensure the completion of the acquisition before legal deadlines expire (**stress**). To prevent possible follow-up questions from the target, strict confidentiality is explicitly requested, even within the company itself. Especially in publicly traded companies, it is often pointed out that disclosing the information to third parties could have undesirable effects on the share price (risk mitigation tactic).

To understand why this form of fraud remains successful despite being widely known, it is necessary to become familiar with the details and the social

© The Author(s), under exclusive license to Springer-Verlag GmbH, DE, part of
Springer Nature 2025
E. Koza et al., *Social Engineering and Human Hacking*,
https://doi.org/10.1007/978-3-662-72084-4_10

engineering methods employed. For an email purporting to be from the CEO to be perceived as authentic and not recognized as fraud, the human hacker must possess at least the following information:

- *Which executive is to be impersonated?*
- *What is the executive's email address and what does the original signature look like?*
- *Who is an appropriate target individual and what is their email address?*
- *How do the executive and the target individual usually communicate via email? This includes the form of address, language/writing style, and closing.*
- *Ideally, is there a current business case involving the target company abroad that the attacker can reference? Perhaps a press article about a potential business development, opening of a branch office abroad, partnership talks or acquisition negotiations abroad, planned investments, etc.?*
- *What is the maximum amount of money that the target individual is authorized to transfer abroad independently without additional approvals?*
- *Are technical measures required to spoof the executive's email address, or does a domain need to be registered that closely resembles the original domain?*

Note:
In the latter case, this is tactically smarter, as a fake email address allows for ongoing communication with the target individual. With a spoofed email, there is also a significant risk that the target might reply—something the attacker may not have intended—potentially alerting the real executive to the attack.

- *Will the executive be out of the office and ideally also unreachable by phone at the time of the attack?*

To obtain this necessary information during the preparation phase of the attack, attackers often use publicly available sources with the help of OSINT, but vishing calls are also an effective means of gathering key information. For the CEO fake email to have the desired effect on the target, social engineering techniques are used to trigger an emotional rollercoaster in the victim. Below is a sample attack email, with the corresponding emotions that are intended to be triggered and exploited by the content (Fig. 10.1).

The target individual will likely experience a series of emotional reactions:

Brief moment of shock
The message signals an unexpected problem abroad, which may trigger a brief moment of shock.

Praise and recognition from management
Mentioning a corporate matter abroad may elicit praise and recognition from the target, as they appear to be involved in strategic company decisions.

Good morning Ms. Müller,

As you probably know, we are planning to acquire a company in Asia. Unfortunately, we have made an embarrassing mistake and have failed to transfer the purchase price to the trustee who is overseeing this purchase on time, which directly jeopardizes the purchase. (Fear)

Due to your discretion and impeccable work in our company to date (praise and recognition), I would like to give you responsibility for this extremely important project. (Helpfulness)

As the transaction must be treated with absolute confidentiality, I would ask you to discuss the status of the transaction only with me and without exception by e-mail. No one in our company may find out about this. Should this become public knowledge, the company acquisition will fail. (Pressure and urgency)

I count on your discretion and thank you in advance for your cooperation. (Discretion)

Please find attached all relevant information for the transfer.

With best regards

Your name
Signature &Logo

Fig. 10.1 CEO fraud—example

Exploitation of gullibility
The target may be inclined to trust the message due to its apparent authenticity and the authority of the executive.

Triggering helpfulness
Emphasizing urgency and the need for immediate payment may trigger the target's willingness to help.

Pressure from the demand for confidentiality
The demand for absolute confidentiality may create pressure, especially if it is implied that sharing the information could have negative consequences for the company.

No room for questions or seeking advice, increasing the pressure
Restricting the scope for action and emphasizing urgency may intensify the pressure, as the target has no opportunity to seek advice or obtain further information.

Fear of personal and organizational consequences
The target may fear personal consequences due to lack of support or organizational consequences in the event of possible failure.

Fear or respect for authority (executive/lawyer)
Mentioning the executive and a lawyer may trigger fear or respect for authority in the target individual.

Overall, targeted emotional manipulation is used to persuade the target not to question anything and to act immediately.

In some cases, CEO fraud is not limited to text-based attacks but is combined with other social engineering methods. Human hackers continue their deception by having the target receive a phone call shortly after opening the email from someone posing as the company's lawyer. In this call, explicit reference is made to the recently received, time-critical email, which further increases the pressure on the target to act.

In the following section, we take a detailed look at the mechanisms of these emotional reactions using a concrete precedent case.

10.1   Case Description: CEO Fraud at Sparkasse Pforzheim Calw

"CEO fraud involving a transfer of 1.7 million euros at a corporate client of Sparkasse Pforzheim Calw—Sparkasse held liable"
(Handelsblatt, 2018 [1]).

The accountant of a company receives a forged email from her supposed CEO, who claims to be in China for the acquisition of a company. Citing alleged time pressure and the need for strict confidentiality, he instructs the accountant to check the available account balance at the bank.

Two hours later, she receives instructions to prepare a transfer to China, along with a request to send a sample signature of the actual CEO to BaFin (Federal Financial Supervisory Authority) via email. The attacker uses a BaFin email address under his control for this purpose.

The accountant, acting on telephone instructions, prepares a transfer form bearing the company stamp of Sparkasse and forwards it to the attacker. The attacker adds the signature obtained via the BaFin email address to the transfer form and sends it back. Within three days, the bank transfers approximately 1.7 million euros.

The deception is only discovered later, when the employee notices the forged email address uses **.st** instead of **.de**.

The company successfully sues the bank, as the accountant was not contractually authorized to initiate the transfer. The financial institution is held liable for the resulting loss of 1.7 million euros.

10.2   Analysis

In the following case analysis, only a single attacker is referenced, as the reporting does not provide information regarding the possible number of perpetrators. However, based on the efforts described in the case analysis, it cannot be ruled out that a criminal group planned and executed this attack.

The affected family business was successfully attacked via the email attack vector using the methods of spear phishing and CEO fraud. In this context, spear phishing refers to a targeted attack through email communication, in which the content and process are carefully tailored to a specific individual. **The spear phishing method is combined here with the CEO fraud attack pattern.**

To ensure a successful three-day attack, careful preparation is required to control and manage potential success factors.

Identification of the Appropriate Target
To identify the appropriate target within the company, the attacker must carefully select individuals, taking into account their contact details, positions, and authorizations. The chosen target should be capable of obtaining the signature of the correct managing director.

Analysis of the Relationship Level
After identifying the target, the attacker analyzes the relationship between the managing director and the target individual. This analysis enables a targeted adaptation of the attacker's communication strategy, taking into account examples of the typical wording and communication style of the real managing director.

Acquisition of Authentic Emails
For convincing communication, authentic emails from the managing director are required, which the attacker can obtain through dumpster diving or by accessing digital email histories. Imitating the appearance of the emails requires relatively little effort, especially after obtaining original emails.

Determining the Optimal Timing
Determining the optimal timing for the attack requires thorough research and reconnaissance of company processes. Communication should take place exclusively via email to maintain consistent deception. The target must not use any other communication channels to prevent identity theft from being uncovered.

Blocking the Managing Director's Availability
Completely blocking the managing director's availability during the attack is crucial to maintaining credibility. The attacker uses an email address that closely resembles the original address of the managing director, but with the ending **.st** instead of .de.

To implement all the factors mentioned for a successful attack, extensive preparatory steps are required on the part of the attackers. This includes gathering relevant background and key information, which serves as the basis for developing attack strategies and tactics. This information acts as an amplifier to intensify the persuasive effect of the correspondence. To focus on the various amplifiers used in this attack, we will examine further elements of this manipulative approach below.

The human hacker instructs the employee to send a sample signature of the managing director to the Federal Financial Supervisory Authority (BaFin). For this purpose, he provides her with a fake email address, which presumably resembled BaFin's actual email address.

In doing so, he exploits the powerful position and authority of the federal agency, as well as the general reporting obligation for such large transactions, using this as an amplifier. **The human hacker thus leverages the authority of an institution as an amplifier.** Here, an **amplifier** refers to a manipulative tool used to reinforce the impression created in a social engineering attack.

The goal is for the target to have as little doubt as possible about the legitimacy of the situation. To achieve this, the information must be as realistic as possible and reinforced with key details. This, in turn, requires careful reconnaissance during the preparation phase, including spying on the target organization and possibly other social engineering or hacking attacks.

By choosing this amplifier, the employee can continue to be deceived and controlled, as reflected in her subsequent actions—namely, sending the original signature to the specified email address and initiating preparations with the savings bank for the transfer.

In addition to these aspects, **human characteristics and, presumably, the insufficient awareness of employees** are also identified as exploitable and vulnerable points. In our analysis, these are incorporated into the chain of causality according to the cause-and-effect principle, which can be specified as follows:

The first email emphasizes urgency and the need for discretion. By directly addressing the employee as the "fake managing director," natural human traits are deliberately exploited.

Mentioning discretion likely conveys a sense of pride and recognition to the employee, as the managing director personally places trust in her ability to discreetly handle such an important task.

Recognition is one of the most fundamental needs of humans as social beings. It creates a sense of belonging and can sometimes influence one's position within a social hierarchy. The target feels praised and encouraged by the attention and recognition she receives. Human hackers attempt to exploit this natural emotional response to suppress rational questioning of the circumstances. The curiosity aroused by the sensitive subject further reinforces this suppression.

Another typical human behavior in this context is the **creation of pressure.** The fraudster emphasizes in the email that this unique opportunity will not last much longer. This creates time pressure on the target and, at the same time, hierarchical pressure due to the disparity between the accountant and the managing director. Most people find it difficult to make decisions under pressure, as it limits their ability to thoroughly analyze the situation and compare and weigh possible courses of action.

Time pressure and hierarchical pressure thus serve the attacker's intent to suppress rational questioning by the target and to prevent her from considering alternative courses of action, such as making an independent decision contrary to the supposed boss's instructions. Instead of acting rationally, the attacker leads the target to accept the seemingly harmless situation and act obediently.

Such behaviors frequently occur in cases where targets have received little or no awareness training in the area of social engineering. Social engineering awareness measures include, among other things, education about typical attack patterns, such as CEO fraud and spear phishing attacks. Social engineering training provides explanations of how human hackers exploit human traits and how to protect oneself. Training in safe and stress-free environments can help develop useful behaviors, which could have led to this attack being quickly detected.

In our case analysis, the primary focus is to analyze the behavior of the employee of the corporate client of the savings bank, as the attack took place within her area of responsibility.

Nevertheless, the savings bank was held legally responsible because its employees accepted the transfer order from the accountant. The court's decision was based on the contractual agreements between the savings bank and the corporate client regarding authorization to initiate transfers.

These agreements specified which individuals were authorized, and the accountant was not among them. As a result, there was a breach of contract by the savings bank's employees, which established the corporate client's claim for liability. Thus, the attack on the corporate client had significant consequences for the savings bank, even though the attacker had not selected it as the primary target. Nevertheless, banks are not immune to such attacks. While current reporting may not document any known incidents within a bank, in our assessment, similar attack patterns using the CEO fraud method with a bank as the direct target appear highly realistic.

10.3 Summary

As a subtype of BEC attacks, CEO fraud thus makes a significant contribution to the global annual losses amounting to billions. The most well-known German victim of CEO fraud to date is the automotive supplier Leoni AG, which suffered a loss of 40 million EUR in 2016 [2]. However, attackers also use this method to fraudulently obtain smaller amounts.

In conclusion, it should be emphasized that CEO fraud is a form of attack that requires extensive preparation. This fraud mechanism involves not only the execution of financial transactions, but also a sophisticated strategy that specifically exploits human characteristics of the targeted individuals.

The deception begins with detailed reconnaissance during the preparation phase, in which the attacker carefully analyzes potential victims and their positions within the organization.

By deliberately selecting targets and identifying hierarchy and communication structures, a foundation of trust is established. The emphasis on urgency, the skillful approach to targets by supposed authorities, and the use of psychological reinforcement such as recognition or pressure are steps aimed at the targeted manipulation of human behavior.

The methodology of CEO fraud thus highlights not only the financial risks, but also the subtle and precise targeting of human vulnerabilities.

The high number of successful attacks underscores the need for a holistic security strategy that, in addition to technical safeguards, also focuses on comprehensive employee awareness. Only through this integrated approach can the complexity and sophistication of CEO fraud be effectively countered.

References

1. Handelsblatt, Falscher Chef kassiert knapp 1,7 Millionen Euro—Sparkasse haftet für die Überweisung, unter: https://www.handelsblatt.com/finanzen/banken-versicherungen/banken/betrugsmasche-falscher-chef-kassiert-knapp-1-7-millionen-euro-sparkasse-haftet-fuer-die-ueberweisung/22835478.html (Zugriff: 11.11.2023).
2. Golem, CEO-FRAUD: Autozulieferer Leoni um 40 Millionen Euro betrogen, unter: https://www.golem.de/news/ceo-fraud-autozulieferer-leoni-um-40-millionen-euro-betrogen-1608-122741.html (Zugriff: 11.11.2023).

Shoulder Surfing

The social engineering attack method known as **shoulder surfing** can be classified as an attack or surveillance vector and, in this context, refers to the deliberate observation of a victim in order to obtain information.

Shoulder surfing is particularly mentioned in connection with debit or credit card fraud, as perpetrators attempt to obtain PINs and access credentials to illegally withdraw or transfer money, or—prior to the introduction of multi-factor authentication—to take over bank or other online accounts.

However, the relevance of shoulder surfing is not limited to attackers targeting private bank accounts of individuals. In addition to the possibility of obtaining critical information such as PINs or login credentials, this method also enables perpetrators to access other sensitive information belonging to their victims.

With the proliferation of smartphones, which are often equipped with high-resolution cameras, a single photo or short video is sufficient to capture relevant information. The attacker can then calmly analyze and, if necessary, edit the collected material. Advancing technology, especially high-resolution smartphone cameras, extends the reach of shoulder surfing and underscores the importance of security measures to protect personal information from this subtle yet effective attack method. Consequently, the human hacker can subsequently review and process the gathered material at their leisure.

However, even a brief glance at a laptop, for example on public transport, can reveal information about the operating system in use. An experienced human hacker immediately recognizes the open programs, while the desktop icons disclose information about the installed software. In this context, two fundamental shoulder surfing attack techniques can be distinguished:

The **active variant** involves direct observation, where the attacker discreetly and unnoticed collects personal information, and the **passive variant,** in which the human hacker uses technical aids to spy on information.

E. Koza et al., *Social Engineering and Human Hacking*,
https://doi.org/10.1007/978-3-662-72084-4_11

11.1   Active Versus Passive Variant

A detailed analysis of this attack method also highlights its diverse areas of application. **The active variant requires the human hacker to be in close physical proximity to the victim.**

Everyday situations offer numerous opportunities for this—whether at ATMs, on public transport, at bus stops, airports, supermarkets, cafés, libraries, or during events.

Even in virtual meetings, carelessly shared screen content often reveals information about the software in use or possibly even the emails of the virtual conversation partner.

When technical aids are used as part of the **passive variant, human hackers generally require a certain amount of preparation time, making this a more static attack.** Technologies such as cameras, binoculars, or spotting scopes are employed. This technique can also be used on the move and can be operated manually or installed in a fixed position. In practice, this means that a person does not even need to be visibly half a meter behind or beside the target to obtain information through shoulder surfing.

In most cases, victims of shoulder surfing practically offer a buffet of information to potential attackers—often without the need to overcome any access controls, and all at no cost. Basic shoulder surfing requires little to no skill set on the part of the human hacker and is difficult, if not impossible, to detect. For this reason, shoulder surfing is an extremely attractive technique for information gathering, especially in the context of social engineering.

11.2   Analysis

But why do so many people fail to perceive this threat? There is likely more than one possible answer. One reason may be the apparent triviality of the situations in which shoulder surfing can occur. People tend to perceive their surroundings as safe and harmless in familiar, everyday situations, which often leads them to overlook the potential danger of shoulder surfing.

In addition, the often underestimated technique of the attack, which in its active form requires little to no technical skill, contributes to the widespread underestimation of this threat. Below, we examine some of the reasons that help answer our initial question.

Ignorance
Many people are simply unaware of the dangers of shoulder surfing and lack the necessary knowledge about this technique. They may also be unwilling to accept that there are indeed individuals who are ready to make them victims whenever the opportunity arises. In most cases, perpetrators do not care whom they target. As the saying goes: **opportunity makes the thief.** In this context, we offer

criminals daily opportunities to attack us, for example while working on the go, without being aware of the associated risks or taking appropriate countermeasures.

Indifference

Some people are indeed aware of the dangers associated with shoulder surfing, but simply do not care. In their daily routines and within their own bubble, they ignore the lurking threats that are present every day. Through their carelessness, they not only endanger their own data security but also put their company's security at risk.

Stress

Stress acts as a perception killer. In stressful situations, we unconsciously prioritize what we perceive. Perceptual filters, which now only allow what seems important to pass through, unconsciously eliminate everything else to conserve cognitive resources. As a result, a stressed person often does not consciously perceive a low-level threat, especially if they have never heard of it before **(ignorance).** In such moments, they focus on the immediate task or challenge and block out everything else that seems unimportant. The glance of the person sitting next to them at their open laptop goes unnoticed, and working on the go—for example, on a train—unconsciously becomes a potential threat to information security.

Everyday examples of such behavior are easy to find. People linger in cafés, on trains, in hotel lounges, or at conferences in seemingly quiet corners and feel safe. Stress forces them to focus exclusively on what is essential. **But what is essential in such situations, especially when working on a train? Completing the task at hand or safeguarding the security of one's company? The more stress or time pressure a person feels in this situation, the less likely they are to keep an eye on their surroundings to check whether someone nearby might be able to see their screen.** If someone simply refuses to accept that something like this could happen to them, they will not take the necessary precautions.

Another common phenomenon is the delegation of responsibility to other people or technical measures in order to avoid having to deal with it themselves.

An illustrative experience at the airport highlights this: While business travelers are particularly vigilant about their laptop bags at the terminal, their alertness often wanes after checking into the business lounge. The seemingly elite environment creates a sense of security. **How fortunate that criminals and industrial spies never frequent airport or train lounges, golf clubs, or yacht clubs …**

The phenomenon of **unwelcome delegation of responsibility** is something we have also encountered outside the context of shoulder surfing in various companies.

After one of our social engineering penetration tests, employees of a large midsized company commented as follows:

"We really don't understand why there's so much fuss about this. We have a security service that checks everyone who comes in. I don't have to do that as well, do I?"

If only it were that simple. One must remain vigilant within the company and at one's own workplace, because neither a security department—no matter how extensive—nor technical security solutions alone can guarantee security.

11.3   Summary

Shoulder surfing is a subtle attack method in which attackers attempt to carry out illegal transactions by deliberately observing sensitive information such as PINs and access credentials. Advancing technology expands the reach of shoulder surfing and highlights the need for security measures. The attack technique can be divided into active and passive variants, and it is particularly prevalent in everyday situations where the attacker is in close physical proximity to the victim.

Victims provide attackers with a wealth of information without the need to bypass access controls. Shoulder surfing requires minimal skills and is difficult to detect, making it an attractive attack technique in the field of social engineering.

The low awareness of the risk among individuals may be due to the seemingly trivial nature of the situations in which shoulder surfing can occur. Lack of knowledge about the technique and ignorance also play a role. Stress as a perception inhibitor and the tendency to delegate responsibility further increase the risk.

The following discussion of "dumpster diving" further explores the topic of social engineering attack techniques at the physical level.

Dumpster Diving

In the realm of information theft, a frequently underestimated yet highly effective practice comes to light: **dumpster diving.** This method refers to the systematic search of waste containers with the aim of obtaining confidential information. Criminal actors, potential competitors, or simply curious individuals sift through trash bins for any material that could potentially yield valuable insights. This includes confidential documents, unshredded papers, outdated hard drives, technical devices, and more. The information obtained is then used for various purposes such as identity theft, fraud, or gaining competitive advantages. In the following, we will take an in-depth look at this subtle yet highly effective technique of dumpster diving.

In contrast to digital threats, which focus on virtual domains, the dumpster diver operates by directly targeting physical data carriers.

Dumpster diving is a technique closely intertwined with the field of social engineering. **During the preparation phase** (Preparation Phase), attackers draw on both digital and analog information sources (referred to as information gathering in English) and use the information obtained to orchestrate targeted attacks. These attacks can be multi-layered and may include, for example, the creation of fake identities based on the collected information. These identities are used to gain access to secured areas, deceive employees, or to generate and execute spear-phishing emails or vishing attacks. The insights gained allow attackers to deepen their understanding of the target individuals or organizations and to tailor their attacks with greater precision.

An example of this might be the compilation of an invoice listing specific contacts, services rendered, customer numbers, and other relevant information. This seemingly trivial invoice could serve as the starting point for developing a customized attack scenario. In the following sections, we will comprehensively analyze these complex interactions and their implications for information security.

© The Author(s), under exclusive license to Springer-Verlag GmbH, DE, part of Springer Nature 2025
E. Koza et al., *Social Engineering and Human Hacking*,
https://doi.org/10.1007/978-3-662-72084-4_12

12.1 Dumpster Diving Techniques and Their Applications

The method of selective document extraction represents a sophisticated approach within dumpster diving, in which attackers specifically search for certain documents to obtain valuable information. This information gathering can be based on both digital and analog data carriers. Unlike digital media, analog data carriers allow for the almost immediate breakdown and extraction of information in near real-time.

In such scenarios, attackers may search for information either randomly or in a targeted manner after illegally entering a company.

They can extract a wide range of information, from general to highly specific content such as research results, strategic documents, formulas, and more. This information can be obtained in various ways, either by physically taking it or by using modern digital recording technologies such as integrated micro-cameras. The use of integrated micro-cameras offers two key advantages. First, modern recording technologies enable the covert collection of large amounts of data while minimizing any obvious attention. In this context, the attack technique involves integrating micro-cameras into discreet devices, such as a writing instrument, which primarily serves to document information unnoticed, without attracting significant attention or suspicion.

Furthermore, if discovered, the attacker can simply point to an inconspicuous pen that is, in reality, equipped with a camera.

Carrying such a pen is not illegal in itself, and this subtle approach allows the attacker, if confronted, to claim to have entered the company by mistake.

The integration of modern digital technologies thus significantly facilitates an attacker's approach and at the same time increases the likelihood of remaining undetected.

Dumpster divers are adept at adapting to their environment and use carefully crafted cover stories to avoid drawing attention. In a bank, for example, a well-groomed suit and inconspicuous, confident demeanor may be enough to seemingly unnoticed search through inadequately secured areas. The effectiveness of such cover stories is illustrated by the following example:

Two men, dressed in blue overalls and apparently posing as technicians, enter a busy area of a hospital. Equipped with the appropriate tools and devices, they openly dismantle a large flat-screen television and take it with them. The staff did notice the action, but because of the men's appearance, which was typical for technicians, they harbored no suspicions. The employees' lack of concern, as they automatically assumed the actions of the supposed technicians were legitimate, highlights the power of outward appearance and underscores the importance of critical security assessment even in seemingly familiar situations.

This example (based on a true incident) vividly illustrates the effectiveness of cover stories. Visual perception, as described by Daniel Kahneman's "System 1," quickly processes visual stimuli and makes rapid decisions. The automatic identification of the two men in blue overalls as technicians demonstrates that our perception and decision-making are often based on prompt, intuitive assumptions.

This underscores the relevance of the fact that our perception is influenced by pre-established concepts and preconceived images, and highlights the need for conscious security assessment to critically challenge such implicit assumptions.

The theft of physical artifacts from the trash is not limited to information alone. Employee badges, batches, access cards, or transponders can also be stolen. This enables attackers to construct identities and gain unauthorized access to secured areas.

In addition to extracting information from analog data carriers, attackers may also deliberately or opportunistically search for digital media, such as USB sticks, while passing through office spaces. These small, inconspicuous sources of information often contain unencrypted and diverse data. In the absence of a clear screen and desk policy in a bank, these inconspicuous items can easily be left on desks or even thrown away, where they can ultimately be stolen by a skilled dump-ster diver.

In contrast to analog data sets, which are immediately visible and readable, digital data carriers first require a reading procedure and, in some cases, even reconstruction in order to access the information they contain. The reconstruction of digital media from the trash provides attackers with a rich source of sensitive information.

This example provides an apt opportunity to further explain the statement from Chap. 8 of the White Chapter. It states that an adequate defense can only be defined if holistic information security is taken into account. In this context, defense concepts must interlock and address all three levels of the informa-tion security triad—human, organization, and technology. To defend against the scenario presented, mechanisms for physical access control and visitor manage-ment must be integrated, trained, and practiced. Measures must be implemented in the areas of clear screen 1, 2 and desk policies, hard drive encryption, and the proper disposal of data carriers in accordance with standards such as DIN 66399 3. Effective defense thus requires a skillful combination of technical, organizational, and individual practices, which only achieve their full effectiveness when they are interlinked and implemented as a holistic concept.

12.2 Analysis

Dumpster diving represents a subversive method of information theft that demon-strates remarkable effectiveness in many respects. From an analytical perspective, several factors play a decisive role, including human, organizational, and techno-logical aspects. These factors help explain why dumpster diving is such a notably successful method of information theft.

Vulnerabilities in Attention and Perception
Humans tend to focus on certain activities while neglecting others.

This primarily results from the fact that our cognitive orientation and process-ing of stimuli are determined by the given task. This means that concentrating on a specific task is always accompanied by certain opportunity costs. While attention is directed toward a particular core area, perceptual processes are sensitized and executed according to the task at hand. This also implies that other stimuli, which may not be related to the actual task, are ignored. Dumpster divers exploit this weakness by searching for information in areas that are often overlooked.

Trust and Authority
Deliberately imitating roles and personas, for example by adopting the appearance of inspectors, technicians, or cleaning staff, enables attackers to gain the trust of their environment and operate inconspicuously.

By outwardly adapting to common and familiar figures within a particular environment, attackers are able to create an aura of authenticity. This appearance of familiarity not only grants them access to sensitive areas but also allows them to carry out their activities without arousing much suspicion or distrust. The deliberate imitation of roles and the creation of personas are strategies based on psychological mechanisms of trust and authority. By assuming an apparently legitimate position within the target environment, attackers can disguise their actions and achieve their objectives more effectively. This illustrates that people's trust in the apparent authority of a role often serves as a gateway for inconspicuous but potentially harmful activities.

Lack of Security Zones
The absence of clearly defined security zones in companies and organizations means that there are no distinctly demarcated areas where sensitive and classified information can be securely stored. This creates the risk that confidential data is improperly stored or easily accessible, especially in areas open to unauthorized individuals.

Lack of Clear Desk and Screen Policies
The absence of clear guidelines for maintaining tidy workspaces means there are no explicit instructions on how employees should organize their work areas to ensure the protection of sensitive information. This can lead to an unstructured environment in which confidential documents are easily accessible or inadvertently discarded. Furthermore, the lack of clear regulations for handling classified information and data can also result in companies lacking uniform standards to ensure that sensitive data is adequately protected and classified. This can create uncertainty about what constitutes confidential information and how such information should be handled.

Lack of Visitor Management
The absence of an effective visitor management system in companies can have serious consequences for the security of sensitive areas. An effective visitor management system should enable the identification, monitoring, and control of external individuals entering company premises.

Difficulties in monitoring and controlling access by external individuals can take various forms.

Without clear guidelines and procedures for registering and identifying visitors, as well as partner companies, unauthorized individuals can easily enter the company undetected and unsupervised. This could lead to unauthorized access to sensitive areas where confidential information is stored. A deficient visitor management system can also make it difficult to adequately monitor visitor activities. This includes aspects such as escorting visitors by authorized staff or working in high-security areas to ensure that only authorized areas are accessed, as well as limiting the duration of visitors' stays.

Moreover, the lack of clear documentation and logging of visitor activities can result in an inability to trace who was present in the company at any given time and which areas were visited. This significantly complicates forensic analysis in the event of a security incident. Overall, an inadequate visitor management system provides an entry point for unauthorized individuals who may intentionally or accidentally access sensitive areas. From a scientific perspective, this underscores the necessity of establishing clear and effective visitor management policies that improve the identification and monitoring of visitors and strictly control access to sensitive areas.

Unregulated Handling of IT Assets
The lack of appropriate procedures for handling IT assets, including the disposal of analog and digital storage media, means that companies have no clear guidelines or practical processes for securely disposing of old hardware and storage devices. This can result in sensitive information being disclosed inappropriately, especially if these storage devices end up in the trash.

Lack of Encryption and Secure Disposal
The absence of encryption and inadequate security measures during disposal represent a vulnerability that can be specifically exploited by dumpster divers. These attackers make use of both analog and digital sources of information. While analog information is immediately readable, analyzing digital storage media may require additional effort. Neglecting encryption practices significantly increases the risk of data leaks and unauthorized access to information.

Improper disposal of storage media further exacerbates this problem. Dumpster divers can specifically search for unprotected storage media, whether in physical form such as paper documents or digital formats like unencrypted USB sticks. The lack of attention to secure disposal procedures facilitates the unauthorized acquisition of information, as such data is easily accessible and unprotected.

The success formula of dumpster diving thus lies in the skillful combinatorial exploitation of human, organizational, and technological factors. A thorough analytical examination of this method reveals how seemingly trivial vulnerabilities can lead to significant security risks. Therefore, the analysis of dumpster diving highlights not only the necessity of comprehensive security concepts but also the importance of continuous awareness, training, and exercises for all relevant stakeholders.

12.3 Summary

The dumpster diver poses a significant threat to the security of companies and individuals by extracting sensitive information from analog and digital storage media. It is crucial to recognize that dumpster diving not only serves as a direct attack but often also as preparation for more extensive chain attacks.

Effective protection against such attacks requires a differentiated approach at all three levels of the information security triad. It is not sufficient to merely formulate policies—these must be implemented through concrete mechanisms and actively practiced. A security culture that goes beyond theoretical concepts is of critical importance.

The practical implementation of training, awareness, and exercises is essential to create a deep-rooted security consciousness and integrate it into daily routines. It is not enough to simply know security policies; they must also be actively put into practice. Security should not exist only on paper but must be embedded in daily operations and decision-making. This means that security principles must be practically applied in every action and decision. Only by integrating security into everyday business processes can organizations ensure effective defense against social engineering attacks such as dumpster diving.

Effective defense against social engineering attacks, including dumpster diving, also requires not only individual secure behavior but a collective security culture. Establishing such a security culture is an ongoing process characterized by continuous learning, adaptation, and refinement.

The next chapter is dedicated to analyzing attack vectors related to unauthorized physical access to secure areas, with a focus on the specific social engineering attack method known as tailgating.

References

1. Deutsches Institut für Normung (DIN), Informationssicherheit, Cybersicherheit und Datenschutz—Informationssicherheitsmanagementsysteme—Anforderungen (ISO/IEC 27001:2022).
2. Deutsches Institut für Normung (DIN), Informationssicherheit, Cybersicherheit und Schutz der Privatsphäre—Informationssicherheitsmaßnahmen (ISO/IEC 27002:2022).
3. Deutsches Institut für Normung (DIN), DIN 66399-1:2012-10 Büro- und Datentechnik—Vernichten von Datenträgern—Teil 1: Grundlagen und Begriffe, pp. 1–8.

Tailgating

<big>**13**</big>

The social engineering attack method **tailgating,** also known as **piggybacking,** is based on the strategy of choosing the path of least resistance, whereby an attacker gains unnoticed access to a secured area.

Much like a burglar looks for the easiest way in by exploiting a house's vulnerabilities, the attacker seeks loopholes and weaknesses in access to protected rooms and areas.

Consider, for example, a house with comprehensive protection at all entry points, including windows and doors secured with special security doors and windows. But what if the homeowner or one of the children comes home and the attacker simply walks in with them? Although this may seem odd at first glance, this is precisely how tailgating works.

In our example, an attacker naturally needs a convincing cover story to be let in. Suppose there is a garden party taking place and the attacker pretends to be a friend of a guest who invited him. The size of the garden party plays a crucial role here. The smaller the event, the harder it is for the attacker to enter unnoticed. But what about a wedding with 200 guests? Who would turn him away at the door in a festive suit or evening gown, especially if he is carrying a gift?

In the corporate context, tailgating is particularly effective as a social engineering technique. The larger the company and the more impersonal the internal interactions, the more favorable the conditions for an attacker. Office buildings, laboratories, or warehouses can all be potential targets for this tactic. The goal is to gain unauthorized access to a secured area with minimal effort by blending in behind an authorized person.

13.1   Tailgating Techniques and Their Applications

Human hackers skillfully exploit the **(innate) trust** that employees place in others to gain unnoticed entry and access to sensitive information, systems, or physical resources. *The trust that generally prevails in social and interpersonal interactions is deliberately and insidiously exploited here. For most people, a basic trust in others and a certain degree of politeness are essentially the default mode.*

This implies that people generally do not initially assume malicious or illegitimate intent on the part of others. Even in situations where someone politely holds a door open for another person, this seemingly positive act can be tactically exploited by attackers to gain unnoticed access to secured areas.

The methods used by attackers can be extremely diverse.

Cover Story Tactic

For example, an attacker might pose as a delivery person, technician, courier, or new employee and politely ask to be let through the security checkpoint by an authorized staff member. If the attacker is carrying heavy-looking boxes, employees' willingness to help is often increased, as we tend to hold the door for people whose hands are full.

Hustle Tactic

In situations where there is hustle and bustle at the entrance, attackers can simply push past employees to gain access. If the attacker is on the phone during the unauthorized entry and appears highly focused and busy, the likelihood of being challenged decreases further. People are often socialized to consider it impolite to interrupt someone who appears to be on an important call.

Rapport Tactic

Another tactic involves building rapport with the target person before entry. This can be done, for example, by sharing a cigarette and engaging in small talk in the unsecured area outside the security door. An example would be wearing a white coat and specific medical attire, along with carrying stethoscopes and other medical instruments. By posing as a peer member of the medical staff, the attacker can easily gain the trust of employees. Smoking together outside the hospital could serve as an opportunity to informally connect with supposed colleagues and even gain joint access to sensitive areas of nuclear medicine.

Mass Tactic

Sometimes, it is enough for an attacker to blend into the crowd, for example during a factory tour.

Authority Tactic

A particularly sophisticated method involves posting a notice on the target door in the corporate identity of the target company, requesting that the door be left open today so that cleaning staff or technicians can carry out their work. This tactic cleverly exploits people's tendency to follow authoritative instructions. If an authorized employee finds the door closed contrary to the notice, they will likely assume it was a mistake and leave the door open after entering. This method requires no direct interpersonal interaction but still leverages the principles of social engineering.

This could be described as passive tailgating, which ultimately poses the same risk: an unauthorized person can move freely within the company or secured areas. Once the door is open, it also becomes easy for multiple attackers to enter. The effectiveness of this approach can be tested in practice to assess the security of a company or organization.

13.2 Analysis

The success factors of tailgating are diverse, ranging from psychological aspects to organizational vulnerabilities. A detailed analysis of these factors is crucial to increase the effectiveness of measures aimed at preventing tailgating. The following section examines some of the key reasons for the effectiveness of tailgating, with a particular focus on psychological aspects.

Lack of Collective Security Awareness

A central challenge is that many employees may not be sufficiently informed about the subtle psychological tactics used in tailgating. Psychological manipulation by attackers plays a decisive role in this context. A lack of awareness regarding the psychology of social engineering may result in employees not being fully conscious of the associated risks.

Social Conventions

Social norms and the drive for conformity are also significant psychological factors. People tend to align with social norms and do not want to appear rude or suspicious. This can lead to obvious anomalies and "red flags" in an attacker's behavior being ignored, even when a more security-conscious response would be appropriate. The tendency toward conformity is heightened in hectic situations, where tailgating is particularly easy to carry out. In such moments, employees may be less inclined to act against the perceived social norm.

Lack of Responsibility for Identity Verification

Additionally, employees generally do not feel directly responsible for verifying the identities of people moving within the building. This task is often considered a low priority, especially when there is high staff turnover or when external parties such as service providers and temporary workers regularly access the company. The complexity increases further when employees, out of politeness or reluctance to confront an unfamiliar person, avoid pointing out suspicious behavior.

Breach of Perimeter Security

Furthermore, doors may be left open for convenience. In some cases, it is also a combination of technical misconfigurations and lack of awareness. In particular, if the closing time of security devices is set too generously, it creates a potential entry opportunity for an attacker. For example, if the opening time of a security gate is set to 15 seconds after successful verification and authorization, a skilled attacker can use this window to follow a legitimate person through the gate unnoticed and exploit this relatively long period to enter the building undetected. This allows the attacker to benefit from the authorization of a legitimate person and gain access to the secured area without being detected by security systems. Therefore, correctly configuring the closing time is crucial to minimize such potential vulnerabilities and improve protection against tailgating.

Physical access to protected areas poses a significant threat, as attackers may gain access to confidential information and cause substantial damage. This affects various premises such as offices, server rooms, warehouses, and other secured areas. Sensitive data thus becomes vulnerable to unauthorized viewing, theft, or manipulation. Attackers often use specialized hacker hardware tools such as acoustic eavesdropping devices or keyloggers, or install malware to achieve their objectives.

By carrying out tailgating, attackers gain the opportunity to steal valuables—both personal and corporate—damage equipment, and disrupt or manipulate business processes. Tailgating is considered one of the simplest and most cost-effective methods to gain physical access to a building or secure area undetected.

Overall, tailgating poses the risk of significant financial losses for companies, as well as reputational damage, loss of trust, successful cyberattacks, data leaks, and other disruptions to business operations. It is therefore essential to implement adequate security measures to minimize the risk of tailgating attacks and ensure the protection of sensitive information and resources.

13.3 Summary

Tailgating represents an often underestimated threat in the context of social engineering that companies and individuals should take seriously. Strengthening the security culture, vigilant observation of suspicious behavior, and targeted control of access to sensitive information and resources are essential. Through awareness-raising, training, and the implementation of appropriate technical and organizational security measures, we can best protect ourselves against the threat of tailgating.

Vishing

14

Within the realm of social engineering, human hackers have developed a wide range of methods to gain access to and obtain sensitive information. One particularly sophisticated tactic among these strategies is **vishing (voice phishing).** In vishing, human hackers use targeted phone calls to elicit valuable key information or to manipulate the called individual into actions that may be harmful to themselves or their organization.

This chapter is dedicated to analyzing the art of deceptive phone calls in the context of social engineering. It examines why vishing is highly successful for attackers and the risks it poses to organizations and personal security.

14.1   Vishing versus Spear-Vishing

Analogous to phishing attack tactics, vishing attacks in practice manifest both as broadly distributed **shotgun attacks** and as highly specialized, targeted spear attacks. The accuracy of a shotgun depends on various factors, including the shot pattern, distance to the target, type of ammunition, and the construction of the weapon. In general, shotguns are designed to fire shot shells containing numerous small pellets. However, at longer distances, accuracy decreases as the shot pattern spreads. The specific ballistic properties vary depending on the type of ammunition and the shotgun's caliber. The purpose of a shotgun is often to cover a larger area.

Thus, shotgun attacks or shotgun tactics focus more on the quantity of attack activities rather than detailed preparation for a specific target individual. In shotgun vishing attacks, the emphasis is on the volume of attacks carried out rather than extensive preparation for a particular target.

This means that attackers conduct broad-based actions and targeting without gathering specific information about the intended individuals in advance. The approach is to increase the likelihood of successful manipulation through the sheer number of attacks, rather than focusing intensively on individual targets.

© The Author(s), under exclusive license to Springer-Verlag GmbH, DE, part of
Springer Nature 2025
E. Koza et al., *Social Engineering and Human Hacking*,
https://doi.org/10.1007/978-3-662-72084-4_14

Notable examples of shotgun tactics include the fraudulent calls made in the name of Europol during the summer months of 2022, which, despite an assumed number of unreported cases, led to numerous reports and complaints to the Federal Network Agency [1]. In these scam calls, a computer-generated voice initiates contact by instructing the called person to press 1. This serves to connect the victim to an apparent caseworker from Europol (occasionally also Interpol, the Federal Criminal Police Office, or the Office for the Protection of the Constitution).

As the conversation progresses, human hackers ask targeted questions to obtain personal information or persuade victims to hand over money. In such attacks, the quantity of calls is paramount, aiming to reach individuals who will follow the attackers' instructions. In contrast, spear-vishing attacks are more subtle and harder to detect, targeting a specific organization or individual.

Spear-vishing refers to a highly specialized form of vishing attack in which the call is directed at a specific individual or organization. This type of attack is typically executed based on precise information gathering through OSINT and SOCMINT. Through this prior analysis, individual characteristics, professional roles, or other relevant details about the target person or organization are identified to make the vishing call even more targeted and convincing.

Let us take a closer look at a spear-vishing scenario. Suppose a human hacker needs specific key information about a target company for their main attack, such as details about the firewall in use. To obtain this information, the attacker might pose as a sales representative from a firewall manufacturer. In a phone call with the target company, they explain and promote the manufacturer's products. The response of the person on the phone will be crucial for the further course of the attack.

Disguised as a simple sales call, it becomes challenging for the recipient not to mention the firewall in use. The effectiveness depends on the human hacker's conversational skills and whether the recipient is even willing to engage in the conversation.

The creativity of the human hacker knows no bounds. They may pose as a colleague, customer, applicant, outsourced support, regulatory authority, and much more. In addition to the psychological manipulation techniques employed by human hackers, technical manipulation techniques are also used. This again underscores our definition in Sect. 2.5 of the White Chapter, which defines social engineering as involving both human and technical manipulation methods playing a decisive role.

In the context of vishing, the risk is significantly heightened by the targeted technical use of manipulation techniques. This practice makes vishing particularly dangerous, as it relies on advanced technical mechanisms designed to reinforce the illusion created by the human hacker for the target and to draw them deeper into the manipulation.

The targeted use of technical manipulation techniques in vishing attacks enables the human hacker to make anonymous calls from anywhere in the world. By spoofing phone numbers, they can also impersonate any desired person or organization. This form of deception is known as call ID spoofing [2].

Additionally, applications can be used to play background noises that technically distort or even manipulate the attacker's voice so that it resembles the original voice of the person the human hacker is impersonating.

For the human brain, it is nearly impossible to ignore the perceived auditory stimuli and not draw its own conclusions about the supposed reality.

If, during a phone call, a seemingly stressed person urgently requests certain information while appropriate background noises such as traffic sounds, announcements at an airport or train station, or lively office noise can be heard, these acoustic elements exert a significant influence on our emotional responses and our assessment of the situation. This, in turn, decisively shapes the course of the conversation and affects the perception of urgency and authenticity of the presented situation.

14.2   Analysis

Why does vishing, despite its potential danger, not receive the same level of attention as other attack vectors?

The limited awareness of vishing as an attack vector, despite its considerable danger, could be explained by various factors. Two possible theories are as follows:

First, the relative obscurity of vishing may be due to the subtle nature of this attack vector. Compared to well-known attack methods such as phishing or ransomware attacks, vishing often operates covertly by relying on deception via phone calls without leaving immediate visible effects. This inconspicuousness may result in vishing receiving less attention.

Second, it is possible that the general public, organizations, and even security experts are not sufficiently informed about the technical sophistication and effectiveness of vishing. This could lead to an underestimated perception, as vishing is considered less "spectacular" or threatening.

In this chapter, we will examine the various aspects of vishing in detail to provide a comprehensive understanding of this underestimated but extremely dangerous form of social engineering.

14.2.1 Invisible Threat

Typically, after a cyberattack or another security incident, a team of digital forensic experts is deployed to analyze the affected systems and reconstruct the attack path in detail. The objective is to trace the exact sequence of the attack, identify the type of attack, locate the exploited vulnerability, and determine the extent of the damage.

These experts secure critical evidence to define appropriate recovery measures and restore the systems to their original qualitative and quantitative state through targeted recovery processes. However, their responsibilities do not end there. Additional activities in this field include so-called lessons learned or post-incident activities. These are intended to derive preventive measures from the analysis conducted, aiming to prevent the recurrence of similar attacks. Thus, forensic investigations contribute not only to damage mitigation but also to the continuous improvement of a company's security infrastructure. This process is similar to police procedures following a burglary, where the investigation seeks to determine how the intruder gained access to the house.

In the case of a vishing attack, however, **post-mortem traceability proves to be extremely challenging,** especially if the attack was not recognized as such. In information technology, post mortem refers to a retrospective analysis conducted after an event has concluded. In the context of security incidents, this means a detailed investigation to identify causes, draw lessons, and develop preventive measures for the future. In the context of vishing attacks, the difficulty of post-mortem traceability underscores the need for a thorough debriefing to determine whether a vishing attack occurred, particularly if it was not recognized as such.

A comprehensive debriefing, however, could provide insight into whether a vishing attack may have taken place. Debriefing is a process in which a systematic assessment and analysis is conducted after an event. It often involves gathering information, sharing insights, and discussing experiences. In the context of vishing attacks, debriefing serves to review responses, decisions, and procedures. It enables those involved to share their perspectives.

Let us now consider a concrete scenario together to deepen our understanding:

A medium-sized company was confronted with the consequences of a ransomware attack in which all data was encrypted. Although forensic experts were able to identify the compromised system user and the system node, the entry point of a malicious email remained undiscovered. Further in-depth analysis and so-called dead forensics revealed that the affected system user had received a call from an alleged external IT support representative. This individual persuaded the user to manually enter a domain in the browser and, by clicking a specific link on the compromised website, to initiate the attack.

In such scenarios, the challenge lies in the fact that a "call" is generally not immediately identified or localized as an "attack" and is therefore considered irrelevant to the course of the attack.

As explained in Sect. 4.7 of the White Chapter, the assumption is that anything that can be perceived can also be addressed. This perspective can also be applied to vishing attacks. The central problem is that vishing calls are often neither recognized nor reported by the targeted system users as potential attack attempts. One reason for this may be that employees are not sufficiently informed about the various types of attacks and the associated risk situations, making it difficult to identify such attack vectors **(lack of awareness).** Another possible reason may be employees' reluctance to report anomalies in such calls out of fear of possible repercussions (**lack of security culture**). This contributes to the fact that the threat of vishing largely goes undetected and remains under the radar.

The assessment and analysis of vishing attacks within a company is particularly challenging due to the covert nature of these attacks. This challenge arises not only from technical aspects, but also from the fact that many companies have not yet fully internalized the potential dangers of vishing. As a result, this specific form of attack often remains overlooked on the security awareness agenda.

14.2.2 Hidden Threat

If no one talks about a threat, does that threat even exist? If dangers and threats are not discussed, one could argue that they remain, in a sense, hidden in the shadows. **Vishing as a hidden threat suggests that the danger is intentionally or unintentionally concealed or obscured.**

Let us take a closer look at the mechanisms and actors in the security market. The security market in Germany is saturated with service providers and technology vendors aiming to sell their security products and services—a perfectly understandable objective.

When actively searching for such solutions, one encounters a wide range of approaches that address various security issues, but not necessarily vishing. A simple interpretation might suggest that the broad spectrum of offerings leads to discussions only about problems and threats for which the market provides concrete solutions. In the case of vishing, however, there is only a comparatively small niche of highly specialized companies. This may result in this specific problem being less widely known than its more prominent relative, email phishing.

It is important to emphasize that human hackers do not necessarily aim to obtain passwords or highly sensitive internal information through phone calls. Rather, they often focus on seemingly trivial details that allow a human hacker to form a clearer overall picture with each piece of information obtained, much like assembling a puzzle.

In the domain of social engineering, this principle is often referred to as the jigsaw puzzle or treasure hunt. Even the most seemingly insignificant information that the called party may inadvertently or carelessly reveal during a phone conversation can serve as the basis for a potentially successful follow-up attack with far-reaching consequences.

14.2.3 Successful Threat

Why do attackers use vishing? Attackers choose vishing as an effective attack vector to obtain targeted key information, thereby facilitating access to corporate targets.

Key information comprises fundamental details about the target system or organization. For human hackers, these serve as crucial resources for optimizing their attack strategies. The range of information may include technical aspects such as the operating system in use, firewall, antivirus software, browser, or specialized software solutions like SAP, ERP, or DMS. In addition, sensitive banking and financial data, highly sensitive customer data, information about suppliers, insights into internal business processes, assignment of responsibilities, knowledge of executives' vacation periods, and insights into corporate culture can also be targeted. Obtaining such key information enables human hackers to tailor their attacks with high precision and exploit existing vulnerabilities in the target organization's security system more effectively. This targeted approach significantly increases the efficiency and likelihood of successful attacks.

Compared to elaborate exploit techniques, human hackers invest less time and resources by persuading employees to engage in phone conversations under plausible pretexts. During these calls, attackers skillfully elicit information or induce the called individuals to voluntarily disclose sensitive data.

Additionally, human hackers use vishing to prompt the called person to perform certain actions, either during or after the conversation. They often combine various attack vectors, such as vishing calls with spear-phishing emails or smishing. Smishing is a form of phishing that involves sending fraudulent messages via SMS (short message service). This type of attack cleverly combines the widespread use of mobile phones with phishing tactics to deceive victims and steal sensitive information. Smishing messages often contain links or phone numbers that victims are prompted to respond to. When victims click on these links, they are redirected to fake websites that closely resemble legitimate ones, where they are asked to enter confidential information such as passwords, credit card details, or personal identification data.

The intended actions may include opening malicious links, entering harmful URLs, or downloading infected software.

Instructing victims to carry out unauthorized financial transactions is also among the objectives of vishing attacks, as seen in BEC or grandparent scams.

By specifically using the telephone, attackers can impersonate trusted individuals, enabling a more personal contact compared to phishing emails. Direct contact provides attackers with additional manipulation opportunities and makes defense significantly more difficult by applying social engineering techniques in real time. This typically makes vishing attacks more successful than phishing attacks. In many cases, subtle vishing calls may not even be recognized as attacks and thus remain undetected.

14.3   Summary

The landscape of vishing attacks is shaped by broad shotgun-style attacks and highly specialized spear attacks. The shotgun tactic is characterized by wide distribution and a high volume of attack activities, focusing on quantity to increase the chances of successful manipulation. In contrast, spear vishing is a highly specialized variant that targets specific individuals or organizations.

The shotgun tactic is marked by its broad distribution and little to no preparation compared to targeted attacks. An example is scam calls made in the name of Europol, which are conducted on a large scale. In contrast, spear vishing is based on precise information gathering through OSINT and SOCMINT to make the attack more targeted and convincing.

The creativity of the human hacker is evident in various disguises, ranging from colleagues and customers to authorities, using both psychological and technical manipulation techniques. The targeted use of technical manipulation methods, such as caller ID spoofing and background noise, enhances the illusion created by the human hacker and makes vishing particularly dangerous.

Overall, vishing attacks employ a variety of tactics, with the shotgun approach focusing on quantity and spear vishing proceeding in a targeted and precise manner. The diversity of disguises and technical means make vishing a serious threat that must be addressed through awareness and improved security measures.

References

1. Spiegel, Betrug am Telefon, Behörden verzeichnen große Welle von falschen Europol-Anrufen, unter: https://www.spiegel.de/netzwelt/web/europol-masche-behoerden-verzeichnen-welle-von-betrugs-anrufen-a-392d3286-c372-41d9-ad41-fff5995ae34f. (Accessed: 21.12.2023).
2. Bundesnetzagentur, Manipulation von Rufnummern, unter: https://www.bundesnetzagentur.de/DE/Vportal/TK/Aerger/Faelle/Manipulation/start.html. (Accessed: 14.12.2023).

Grandchild Scam

15

The term **grandchild scam** refers to a form of fraud in which, in its classic form, elderly people—especially grandparents—are contacted by criminals posing as their grandchildren. These fraudsters employ manipulation techniques from social engineering to gain the trust of older individuals and persuade them to hand over money or disclose personal information.

15.1   Forms of the Grandchild Scam

Typically, the grandchild scam takes the form of a phone call in which the fraudster claims to be in an emergency situation, such as an accident, an arrest, or a time-critical financial problem. The perpetrator pretends to be the victim's grandchild and asks for financial assistance, without arousing the grandparents' suspicion.

The tactic of the grandchild scam is based on emotional manipulation and the trust that older people place in their grandchildren. In many cases, age-related circumstances such as memory loss or hearing difficulties, and the associated uncertainty or even shame, are deliberately exploited. The fraudsters may also use personal information from social media or other sources to make their story more convincing.

In addition to direct phone calls, there has been an increase in fraudulent attacks via SMS. In these scenarios, the fraudster claims to be the child of the potential victim and states that they have lost or damaged their mobile phone.

The execution of the fraudulent scheme via SMS involves sending a supposedly new phone number, followed by communication exclusively in writing through a messenger app. In numerous cases, this approach is characterized by a shotgun tactic, in which automated SMS delivery waves are used to reach, for example, up to 1,000 recipients simultaneously. The criminals rely on arithmetic and stochastic *principles. Assuming a 1-percent success rate, represented by the response rate to the delivered SMS, this results in exactly (1000 * 0.01 = 10) a victim count of ten people who fall into the fraudster's trap.*

In the course of our research activities, we deliberately engaged with such an attack and actively managed the communication with the fraudster (Fig. 15.1).

We established contact with the supposed attacker and engaged with their approach. We implied that the sudden change of phone number was accepted without question, and then followed the attacker's initial instructions by moving the conversation to WhatsApp. We allowed the attacker to take the initiative in the conversation and initially remained passive (Fig. 15.2).

Our approach was to wait until the attacker felt sufficiently secure and only then made their actual demand, namely the transfer of money. After the explicit statement of their demand, which was: "to pay for the phone and laptop," we carefully initiated a reversal of the dynamic. We signaled general agreement but

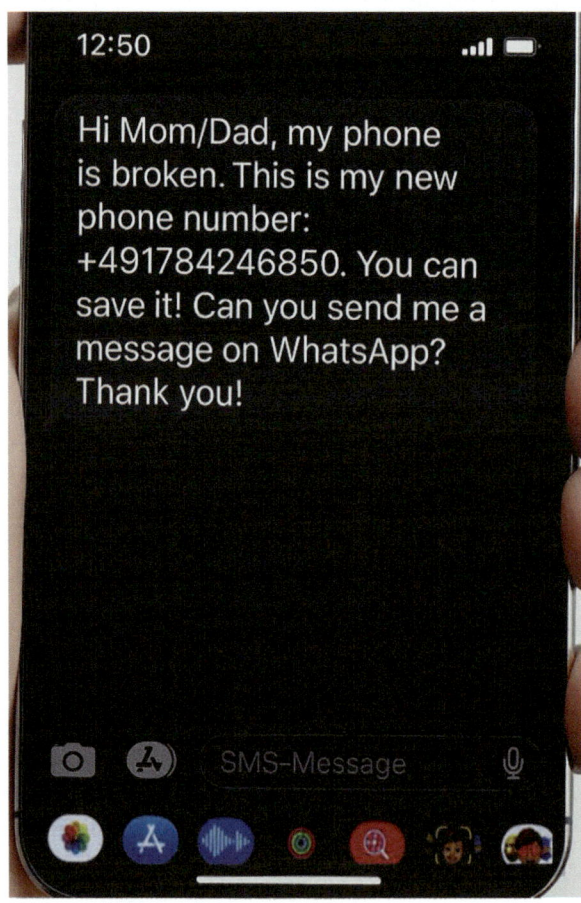

Fig. 15.1 Spam via SMS—Part 1

Fig. 15.2 Spam via SMS—Part 2

emphasized that we were currently on the move and could not fulfill the request immediately (Fig. 15.3).

As the conversation progressed, we suggested that we had complied with the request. Subsequently, the supposed attacker demanded proof in the form of a screenshot of the completed payment. At this point, we had the opportunity to manipulate the course of the attack. We claimed that we had successfully uploaded the requested proof photo to a shared Dropbox folder. We then sent the Dropbox link (Fig. 15.4).

As you may have noticed—but the attacker did not—the link we sent looked almost like a real Dropbox link, but only almost. In fact, it was a tracking link we had prepared. The attacker seemed not to notice this manipulation, clicked on the link, and thus revealed their location to us: Amsterdam.

The attack variants described above were (seemingly) anonymous attacks. This approach appears particularly sensible from the fraudster's perspective, as it

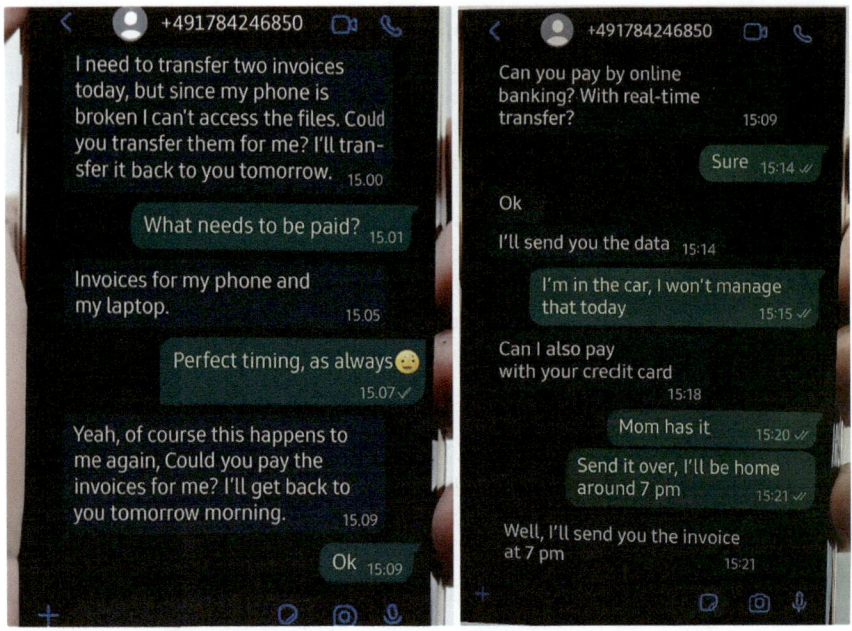

Fig. 15.3 Spam via SMS—Part 3

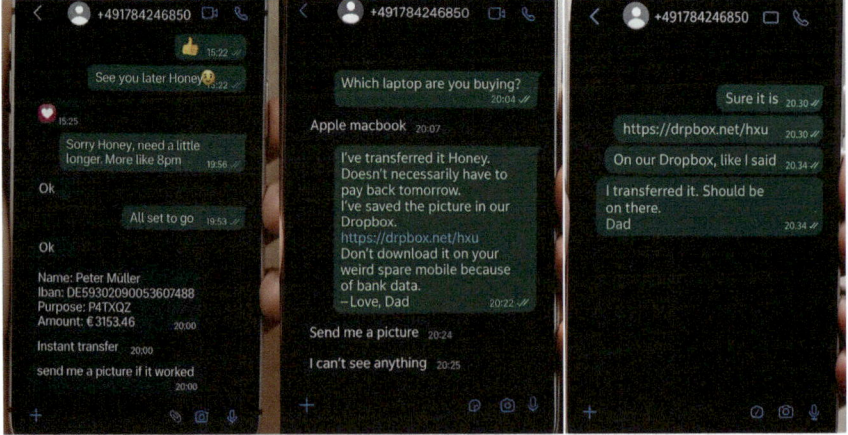

Fig. 15.4 Spam via SMS—Part 4

allows them to conceal their own identity and carry out attacks from virtually anywhere in the world.

However, there are also fraud attempts in which direct communication with the victim takes place. In these cases, the attacker often substitutes the supposed grandchild with an authority figure, such as a police officer. Especially with older people, manipulation by supposed authorities often proves more effective than with younger individuals.

An exemplary scenario for this is the **fake police officer:**

The day began seemingly as usual for a retired couple from northern Germany, until they suddenly received a call from a supposed BKA officer. He claimed that, as part of an alleged phone surveillance operation targeting dangerous serial burglars, he had learned that their home was to be targeted for a burglary that very day. The news sent the couple into a state of panic.

The fraudulent BKA officer pressured the retirees to immediately secure all their cash and valuable jewelry in order to supposedly protect them from the imminent burglary. They were assured that a police officer from the local criminal police would arrive shortly to collect the valuables and issue a receipt. This measure was said to ensure that the valuables would be returned after the alleged burglar was apprehended.

During the phone call, the doorbell suddenly rang and the supposed police officer from the local criminal police was at the door. In their fear-driven state, the retirees were convinced that this was the expected officer. They handed over cash and valuables worth a total of about 60,000 EUR without resistance.

The fake police officer further emphasized the supposed danger posed by the burglar and urged the couple to leave their apartment immediately for safety reasons. It was allegedly claimed that their house was already under BKA surveillance and that the couple's safety must not be jeopardized under any circumstances.

In their haste, the retirees left their beloved home. However, after a few minutes, doubts about the situation began to arise, and they decided to visit the local police station to clarify the matter. There, they quickly realized they had fallen victim to a devious scam.

Despite a vague description of the perpetrator, they were unable to provide any concrete information regarding the identity of the fraudster.

The issue of grandchild fraud is highly multifaceted and cannot be reduced to simple types of attacks. Rather, it is important to understand that there are currently two particularly vulnerable groups who, due to their naivety, gullibility, and potentially heightened cognitive and emotional susceptibility, are especially prone to criminal schemes. This concerns both elderly individuals of retirement age and children in primary and secondary school, that is, the younger population group.

It should be emphasized that the challenges and risks for these two vulnerable groups manifest in different ways. Among older people of retirement age, vulnerabilities often stem from a general lack of knowledge about modern fraud methods, pronounced gullibility, and a possible cognitive and emotional disposition that increases their susceptibility to fraudulent activities.

In contrast, children and adolescents in primary and secondary school are particularly at risk due to their not yet fully developed cognitive abilities and limited life experience. Their gullibility and lack of awareness regarding the various types of fraud make them targets for criminal actors who deliberately exploit the emotional and social development of these young people.

Given these differing risk profiles, a differentiated approach and preventive measures are required to effectively protect both vulnerable groups.

15.2 Analysis

In our analysis, we arrive at the following clarifications:

Clarification of the term "grandchild fraud" reveals that this term is used more broadly in the context of fraudulent acts that exploit emotional relationships within family systems. The target group of such scams extends to various family members, including grandparents, grandchildren, parents, and children. The fraudsters adopt different roles within the family structure to gain trust and conceal their fraudulent intentions.

It is essential to recognize that fraudulent attacks can take various forms and may focus on a wide range of familial relationships. The basic concept is to manipulate trust and emotional bonds within the family structure with the aim of achieving financial gain.

In our analytical review, we identify the challenge faced by grandparents, who, despite using modern technologies, may have difficulty distinguishing between fraudulent and non-fraudulent actions. This complexity largely results from the fact that grandparents represent a demographic group that may lack the knowledge and skills to keep pace with the rapid evolution of attack vectors. As a result, they may not knowingly be able to identify such requests as attacks.

The dimensions of knowledge and ability are central in this context. Knowledge refers to theoretical understanding of modern technologies, security aspects, and fraud patterns. Grandparents may have difficulty grasping the subtle nuances of fraudulent methods due to their potentially limited knowledge in this area. Ability, on the other hand, refers to the practical application of this knowledge, particularly regarding the implementation of security practices and the capacity to recognize fraudulent requests and respond appropriately.

In addition to these factors, cultural influences and the behavioral intentions cultivated by grandparents over the years also play a significant role. Behavioral intention, as an evolutionarily developed intuitive behavior, is activated when one's own child or grandchild appears to be in danger or trouble. The cultural dimension of behavioral intention is rooted in the "help each other" mentality, which holds particular social value for our older population. This attitude became an integral part of the value system, especially after the war years.

The fraudulent approach in which perpetrators pose as authority figures also deliberately targets older people, who are particularly vulnerable due to their credulity (naivety) and trust in state institutions.

The perpetrators' approach is characterized by a high degree of professionalism, with initial contact usually made by telephone. In these conversations, the fraudsters act extremely convincingly and eloquently, place their frightened victims under considerable pressure, and in many cases even arrange for a contact between an accomplice and the victim during the first call in order to collect valuables in person. The victims often find themselves in a helpless situation without sufficient time for critical reflection, leaving them defenseless against the supposed representatives of the authorities. In numerous tragic cases, the victims' entire savings are stolen.

Successful manipulation is based on two key factors: First, the criminals assume the role of an authority figure, thereby creating a high level of trust that is rarely questioned. Second, they create artificial time pressure situations to exert pressure on the victims and leave no opportunity for a considered response. This means that a carefully prepared story or role meets a very short reaction window, which often leads to the fraudsters' success.

The perpetrators can receive the valuables directly and at the same time gain access to the empty apartment or house. This enables them to search the premises for valuables undisturbed within a limited time frame.

15.3   Summary

Grandchild fraud, in which criminals pretend to be relatives of elderly people, typically occurs through phone calls in which financial assistance is requested under the pretense of emergency situations. This tactic exploits emotional manipulation and the trust of older individuals, often exacerbated by age-related vulnerabilities. In addition to phone contact, fraudulent SMS attacks have also become increasingly common. A manipulative response to such a scam attempt was carried out by simulating a "catch-and-release" scenario, during which the attacker unknowingly revealed their location. Grandchild fraud is multifaceted, employs various roles within family relationships, and requires differentiated preventive measures for vulnerable groups such as the elderly.

Phishing

16

In the current era of digital connectivity, email has become an indispensable means of communication. Unfortunately, the growing importance of email has also facilitated the spread of cybercrime, particularly email phishing.

This chapter therefore highlights a crucial insight: Despite advanced security technologies, the human factor remains central in the context of email phishing. Even sophisticated security measures such as email filters, Sender Policy Framework (SPF), Domain-based Message Authentication, Reporting, and Conformance (DMARC), and DomainKeys Identified Mail (DKIM) cannot guarantee that a user will not receive a fraudulent email, open it, click on a malicious link, or disclose confidential information—unless they act vigilantly and with security awareness.

16.1 Forms of Phishing

The term **phishing** *is derived from the English word* **fishing**, *with the* **phishers—** *the attackers—attempting to catch their victims using carefully crafted digital bait.* Typically, fake communication channels such as emails, websites, or text messages are used, which pretend to originate from trusted sources. We will maintain this analogy with fishing for a moment, as there are fundamentally different types or approaches among anglers as well.

Approach 1: One-against-many Tactic
The angler displays an indifferent preference regarding the type of fish and is simply aiming for a successful catch. The choice of bait is made strategically to maximize the probability of success.

Approach 2: One-on-one Tactic
With this tactic, the angler specifically targets a particular species of fish, deliberately selects the appropriate bait, and pursues clearly defined objectives regarding the intended catch.

Approach 3: Catch-and-release Tactic
The angler's primary motivation is not to keep the catch; rather, other motives drive them to release the fish after a successful catch (catch and release). The main interest lies in the enjoyment of fishing itself, perhaps in recounting the experience to fellow anglers or sharing photos of the catch.

These three types are also present in the context of cybercrime.

Approach 1: One-against-many Tactic
In contrast to the individual one-on-one tactic, the broad-based strategy can be described as "one against many," often referred to as "mass phishing" or "shotgun phishing." In this method, fake communications are sent out on a large scale to reach as many potential victims as possible. The focus is on developing up-to-date narratives by the criminals, often leveraging emotional topics such as COVID-19 bonuses or inflation compensation payments. The goal is to maximize the probability of success by appealing to a broad audience with emotionally charged topics, some of which have also been presented in the media by government actors.

Approach 2: One-on-one Tactic
The one-on-one tactic, in turn, refers to the so-called spear phishing method. Spear phishing is a specific form of phishing attack in which the attacker targets a particular individual, organization, or group. The term "spear" underscores the targeted nature of this attack, comparable to the precise throw of a spear at a single target. As you may have noticed, there are parallels here as well. In this analogy, a specific target is identified and then manipulated and compromised using tailored narratives and illusions (a specific type of fish and bait that are matched to each other).

Approach 3: Catch-and-release Tactic
In the context of phishing, the term "catch and release" refers to an approach in which attackers aim to showcase their skills rather than achieve direct financial gain or personal benefit. This tactic is similar to the principle of catch and release in fishing, where the focus is not on keeping the "fish" permanently. In phishing scenarios, attackers select specific targets, not necessarily to obtain money or personal information, but to demonstrate their technical abilities. After the "catch"— the successful execution of the phishing attack—they may choose not to use the acquired data for malicious purposes.

Instead, they might use this information as proof of their skills within the hacker community or even report security vulnerabilities to the affected parties so they can be addressed. This catch-and-release tactic stands apart from purely financially motivated phishing attacks and is more about self-promotion and show-casing the attackers' technical prowess.

In the following, we will examine each of these approaches in detail.

16.1.1 One-against-many Tactic

Email is undoubtedly the most dangerous external attack vector in this context. This assertion is based on the observation that emails are used more frequently and in a greater variety of ways than other electronic communication channels. The widespread use of email in various online interactions—whether in business relationships, information exchange, or transactions—makes it a prominent attack vector for criminals. Furthermore, email is used in both private and professional contexts for platform registrations, magazine or newsletter subscriptions, online purchases, registrations and memberships, platform notifications, job applications and professional communication, event announcements, and communication between companies and individuals. This versatility offers attackers a wide range of opportunities to employ different deceptions and pretexts. The extensive use of email in diverse contexts increases the likelihood that people will fall for fraudulent attempts. The fact that emails are ubiquitous and used in numerous situations creates significant potential for attacks. The diversity and high frequency of email usage thus create considerable potential for phishing attacks. Despite investments in technical IT security measures, there remains a residual risk, as the user ultimately makes the final decision on how to interact with the technology. A typical scenario might involve an email in which the attacker poses as a parcel delivery service. In this regard, the chosen methods and lures are crucial in reaching the largest possible number of potential victims.

Figure (16.1) shows that organizations in the service sector such as DHL, PayPal, Amazon, and banking institutions—which have acquired and retained a substantial customer base—are widely abused as purported senders in large-scale one-against-many phishing campaigns. Emails that appear to originate from Microsoft or reference its products are also highly popular due to their widespread use. In 2022 alone, we recorded a concerning number of over 30 million malicious messages that unlawfully used the Microsoft logo or referenced its products. These insidious messages concealed potentially dangerous elements, including Excel spreadsheets with hidden malicious code, devious links to shared OneDrive folders, or deceptive Microsoft update links that could be activated with a seemingly harmless click [1].

The theoretical probability of recognizing a phishing email with a one-against-many character in time is high compared to the one-on-one tactic, since it is not specifically tailored to the recipient and the context or sender may not align with the individual's situation. Nevertheless, our behavior regarding phishing emails is strongly influenced by the circumstances under which we encounter them, and not solely by the content of the email itself.

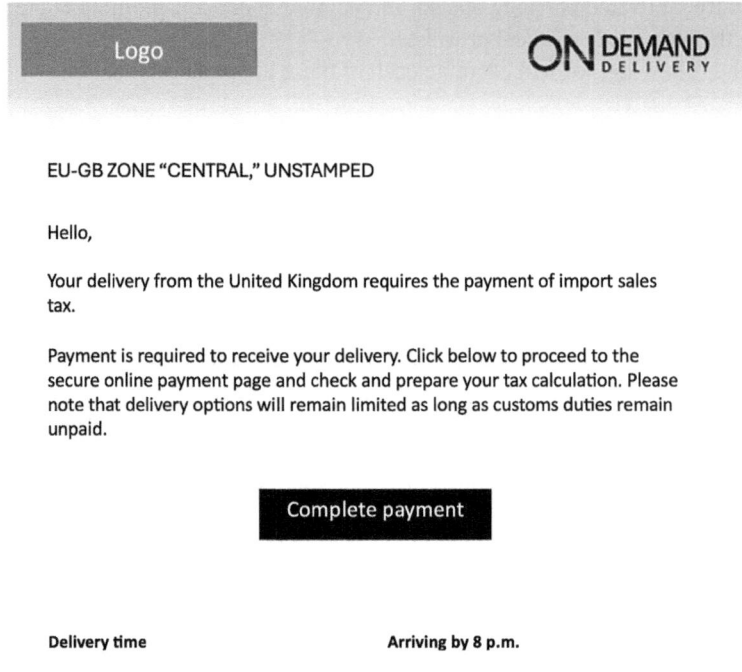

Fig. 16.1 One-against-many tactic

For example, if we are expecting a long-awaited package, we may feel pleased about the apparent opportunity to track the shipment via a link in the email, even if the specified delivery service is incorrect. In a situation where we have recently experienced technical issues with our online banking account, a purported message from our bank announcing an important update may seem like a welcome and urgently needed notice.

Criminals tend to skillfully incorporate current topics into their phishing emails. During the COVID pandemic, for instance, it was observed that they quickly crafted phishing emails referencing the coronavirus or alleged COVID support payments in order to exploit the period of uncertainty and fear in society.

Moreover, it is evident that many people are unfamiliar with technical methods such as spoofing and continue to place considerable trust in the visual design of emails. *This can be attributed to the fact that our perception, especially in simple and seemingly trivial contexts, is based on direct connections to System 1 as described by Kahneman. System 1 enables us to make quick decisions. In this case, System 1—similar to the perception of the mail carrier (**see Sect. 4.6 of the White Chapter**), may conclude that an email is legitimate solely based on familiar branding and external appearance.*

In addition, experienced readers no longer process a text or a passage step by step, letter by letter, as beginners do. Instead, they recognize a word and its meaning instantly at first glance.

Even when words are jumbled, they can still recognize them, as the brain remembers words by their specific sequence.

In simple situations, it is sufficient to capture the correct order of the first and last letter for the brain to recognize the correct word, even if the letters in between are scrambled.

Instead of reading letter by letter, the brain groups already learned words into meaningful units—it anticipates the correct word.

This tendency of the human brain to identify familiar patterns (in this case: familiar words) even in random arrangements (also known as pareidolia) is evident even when these patterns do not actually exist. The expectation of a familiar word enables identification in a similar arrangement.

Nevertheless, this alone is not sufficient to understand the text at hand; the context of the entire text is crucial. If these words are viewed in isolation and not read in the context of a complete sentence, it becomes significantly more difficult to infer their meaning.

Phishing emails often exploit mechanisms of urgency, pressure, and fear to trigger stress responses in recipients. This impairs perception in stressful situations and causes the brain to favor and accept familiar patterns. Under such stress, the introduction of a manipulated link, such as "www.BeipsielBank.de," may be mistakenly perceived as "www.Beispielbank.de" and the link clicked without a second thought. The concept of rapid word recognition and anticipation discussed above reinforces this tendency, as the brain is inclined to highlight and respond to familiar elements in stressful situations. This illustrates how the deliberate manipulation of emotions and stress in phishing attacks can specifically influence the victim's perception to provoke misleading actions.

16.1.2 One-on-one Tactic (Spear Phishing)

In the **one-on-one tactic**, criminals employ the spear phishing approach, using specifically crafted emails that target a particular individual or entity. In this tactic, the attacker has a specific target in mind and, metaphorically speaking, fishes with a spear for a particular organization or person.

Much like an angler who sets out to catch a specific species of fish, the attacker must conduct intensive research on the target to be successful. This involves gathering information about the target's whereabouts and environment, living conditions, behavior and habits, appearance, and preferred food in order to bait it effectively. Analogously, criminals collect information about their targets.

To acquire this knowledge, they use a variety of sources. One of the most effective methods for obtaining background information about a target individual or organization is OSINT (see Sect. 2.4 of the White Chapter) and SOCMINT.

Social media provide criminals with a rich environment. The more information a target discloses about themselves online, the more opportunities arise for the criminal to exploit.

This facilitates the development of successful attack scenarios and enables a more precise prediction of the target's behavior.

In social engineering, the aim is to analyze and deliberately influence the target's perception, interpretation of situations, and thus their behavior in advance. There are various methods for integrating the collected information into a spear-phishing attack. From the attacker's perspective, differentiating and categorizing the gathered background information into specific context categories is a veritable goldmine.

Business Context
- Information or clues about daily work routines
- Working conditions
- Tasks
- Routines
- Level of training
- Career stages
- Internal work contacts
- Connections to other companies
- Communication channels used, preferred communication styles, and much more

Private Context
- Information or clues about place of residence
- Living conditions
- Family
- Social environment
- Friends and acquaintances
- Hobbies and interests
- Purchasing or consumption behavior, and much more

Personal Context
- Information or clues about personality traits
- Life motives
- Attitudes
- Norms and values
- Social behavior
- Personal strengths and weaknesses
- Communication styles, and much more

The effectiveness of a spear-phishing attack depends on various factors, and not all key information required is easily researched by the attacker in advance.

Sometimes, seemingly minor details can have a decisive impact on the success of an attack. A concrete example with an illustrative interpretation demonstrates this (Fig. 16.2):

The presented email appears to be ordinary business correspondence between two business partners. At first glance, nothing unusual or suspicious can be inferred from the email context. If the victim focuses solely on the factual content of the email, there is a likelihood they will fall for the attack. However, if aspects such as the salutation, writing style, and level of formality do not match the sender—for example, if the sender and recipient usually communicate informally—this may arouse the recipient's suspicion and even prompt the target to address the supposed sender personally about the received email.

For a criminal, seemingly minor details often represent crucial key information that can significantly increase the likelihood of a successful attack.

Questions about the nature of the relationship between sender and recipient (victim), as well as about the written salutation and closing, can provide relevant clues in this context.

A recipient who focuses exclusively on the factual email context and neglects other aspects due to time constraints *(stress, routine)* can quickly become a victim of a spear-phishing attack. The true art of social engineering using the external

From: Lisa Mustermann <lm@beispiel-gmbh.com>
Date: Friday, October 6 at 09:45
To: Max Müller <m.mueller@dienstleister-ag.com>
Subject: Invoice for last delivery

Dear Mr. Müller,

Thank you for your renewed delivery yesterday morning.

Unfortunately, we must have somehow lost your invoice in the current hectic rush... I am very sorry about that! Could I ask you to please send it to me again? Preferably directly by e-mail so that there are no long delays in payment.

Thank you very much in advance and have a nice weekend!

Yours sincerely

Lisa Mustermann
Accounting

Signature & Logo

Fig. 16.2 Spear Phishing—Example 1

From: IT
Date: Friday, October 6 at 09:45
To: Anne Sorglos <annesorglos@beispiel-ag.de>
Subject: Problems with ZE software

Good morning Ms. Sorglos,

Recently our time recording software has been causing problems again and
again. We would need to know which employees have already been affected
so that we can check the account settings again for those affected.

It would be a great help to us if you could forward this form to your department
and ask them to complete the survey so that we can resolve the problem as
quickly as possible:

 Important_SurveyZE-Software.xlsm

Many thanks and best regards

Jan-Ole Meier
IT Manager

Signature & Logo

Fig. 16.3 Spear Phishing—Example: Helpfulness

attack vector of email communication lies in deliberately influencing a victim's
behavior. Not only can a realistic-looking business correspondence be exploited,
but also the personal characteristics of the victim. If the attacker has information
about the victim's personality type, motives, and traits, they can use this information to their advantage.

Below, we provide further examples to give you a deeper insight into the topic.
This serves to underscore the practical relevance of the concepts presented and to
offer you a more comprehensive overview of the variety of spear-phishing scenarios and the exploitation of human emotions (Fig. 16.3, 16.4, 16.5 and 16.6).

16.2   Analysis

In all the examples cited, the individual degree of critical thinking, caution, or gullibility undoubtedly plays a significant role. *The topic of perception is discussed in
detail in the White Chapter of this work, which we would like to reference at this
point.*

Phishing and spear-phishing attacks can target us not only in professional settings but also in our private lives. For the purpose of analysis and as an explanatory basis, we would like to present an example from one of our social engineering

From: Lisa Müller <lmueller@beispiel-ag.de>
Date: Friday, October 6 at 09:50
To: Peter Schlau <pschlau@beispiel-ag.de>
Subject: Promotion planning

Hello Mr. Schlau,

please ignore the last email, I accidentally sent it to you instead of
Ms. Petra Schau, the Managing Director. I am sorry about that!
Please treat the information confidentially!

Thank you very much and sorry again!
LG Lisa Müller

Signature & Logo

From: Lisa Müller <lmueller@beispiel-ag.de>
Date: Friday, October 6 at 09:45
To: Peter Schlau <pschlau@beispiel-ag.de>
Subject: Promotion planning

 Dear Mr. Schlau,

As discussed in our last round of voting, here is an overview
the expected promotion planning for the next 24 months
promotion planning for the next 24 months.

Promotion planning_v.3.xlsm

Yours sincerely

Lisa Müller
Head of Human Resources Department

Signature & Logo

Fig. 16.4 Spear Phishing—Example: Curiosity

penetration tests, which illustrates the critical importance of not using a business email address for private matters:

Case Description
An employee subscribed to a hiking club newsletter and used their business email address instead of a personal one. Over time, the club was compromised by cybercriminal activity, and the email addresses from the newsletter list were published on the dark web. While preparing our digital penetration test, we

From: Lisa Lieb <lisa.lieb@beispiel-ag.de>
Date: Friday, August 31 at 15:15
To: Ingo Igel <ingo.igel@beispiel-ag.de>
Subject: Coupon

Hello Ingo,

good news today! :-)

At the beginning of the year we were lucky enough to win Amazon as a
cooperation partner and since the last few months have been so great
(thanks again at this point, you did a really great job!), we have decided
to provide a € 250 voucher for the next Amazon shopping tour for
September as a small token of appreciation!

Here you will receive your personalized voucher code, which you can
easily redeem with your next order:

  www.beispiel-ag.deingutscheincode.de/amazon

If you have any problems accessing the code, please contact me.

We hope you enjoy redeeming your code - and thank you once
again for your hard work! :-)

Sunny greetings

Lisa Lieb
Personnel Department

Signature & Logo

Fig. 16.5 Spear Phishing—Example: Praise and Recognition

discovered this data breach. Although we did not have access to complete login
credentials, the clear connection between the business email address and the hiking club's newsletter list enabled us to craft a targeted spear-phishing email. The
affected employee received a convincing email from the hiking club referencing
their hobby and offering a guided hiking tour as a prize—the recipient simply
had to register via a provided link to book the free tour. Trusting the message, the
employee clicked the link without hesitation, thereby unknowingly putting their
company's security at significant risk—had this not been a penetration test conducted in the spirit of "white hat hacking."
   *In this example, a personal interest and a lack of caution during newsletter reg-
istration were deliberately exploited to carry out a successful attack on a business*

From: Hartmut Hart <h.hart@beispiel-ag.de>
Date: Friday, March 15 at 17:45
To: Lisa Müller <l.mueller@beispiel-ag.de>
Subject: URGENT!

Good evening Ms. Müller,

please make sure you transfer the money to Beispiel GmbH before the end of
the day! Otherwise we will lose our cooperation here! We can't afford that right
now. I have assured Mr. Schmidt that the money will be transferred by this evening!

I'm on a plane for the next 7 hours, so I've attached the information. Everything
is detailed there.

Please do it as soon as possible! Thank you very much.

Hard
Managing Director
Signature & Logo

Fig. 16.6 Spear Phishing—Example: Hierarchical Pressure

*email account. This authentic scenario highlights the urgency and importance of
establishing clear guidelines for the use of business email addresses, communicating these policies effectively, and adhering to them in accordance with security
awareness protocols.*

In general, anyone can become the target of a phishing attack. However, certain personal characteristics and circumstances influence how susceptible we are
to phishing emails, especially spear-phishing emails. Various studies have shown
that, in addition to gender and age, specific personality traits such as impulsivity, conscientiousness, and neuroticism affect our vulnerability to spear-phishing
attacks [2–6].

Furthermore, the level of training regarding social engineering attacks has a
significant impact on our ability to recognize and defend against attacks and red
flags.

In the White Chapter, we discuss in greater detail the role of personality traits
in resilience to social engineering attacks.

The challenge of providing a definitive analytical explanation for the success of
phishing arises from the complexity of causes and effects, which are determined
by the principle of the causality chain. The mechanism that makes people susceptible to phishing is embedded in diverse contexts and depends on numerous factors.

The interplay of psychological, social, and cognitive aspects creates a multitude
of influences that can reinforce each other. Curiosity, trust in authority, emotional
triggers such as urgency and fear, as well as general inattentiveness in digital communication, are just some elements of this complex structure.

In addition, individual differences in personality and cybersecurity knowledge play a decisive role. People respond differently to phishing tactics based on their temperament, impulsivity, and critical thinking skills.

The complexity of these mechanisms makes it difficult to identify a clear cause-and-effect relationship. Rather, various elements interact within a network, and their significance can vary depending on the context. Therefore, comprehensive awareness and training are necessary to address the multifaceted challenges of phishing and to develop a holistic security strategy.

16.3 Summary

Despite advanced security technologies, emails remain vulnerable to phishing attacks, with the human factor continuing to play a decisive role. Phishing manifests in various approaches, comparable to fishing techniques. The "one-against-many tactic" targets broad-based attacks, the "one-on-one tactic" focuses on specific targets, and the "catch-and-release tactic" demonstrates technical skills without immediate financial gain. In the email context, these approaches are known as mass phishing, spear phishing, and catch-and-release phishing. Emails remain a dangerous attack vector due to their diverse uses, despite implemented security measures. The interaction of psychological, social, and cognitive aspects creates a multitude of influences that can reinforce each other.

References

1. Proofpoint, State of the Phish-Bericht 2023, unter: https://www.proofpoint.com/sites/default/files/infographics/pfpt-de-ig-state-of-the-phish-2023.pdf (Accessed: 10.10.2023).
2. Mohamad Alhaddad, Masnizah Mohd, Faizan Qamar, Mohsin Imam, Study of Student Personality Trait on Spear-Phishing Susceptibility Behavior, in: International Journal of Advanced Computer Science and Application, Bd. 14, No. 5, 2023, pp. 667–678.
3. Steve Sheng, Mandy Holbrook, Ponnurangam Kumaraguru, Lorrie Faith Cranor, Julie Downs, Who falls for phish?: a demographic analysis of phishing susceptibility and effectiveness of interventions, in: CHI '10: Proceedings of the SIGCHI Conference on Human Factors in Computing Systems, 2010, pp. 373–382.
4. Tian Lin, Danel E Capecci, Donovan M Ellis, Harold A Rocha, Sandeep Dommaraju, Daniela S Oliviera, Natalie C Ebner, Susceptibility to Spear-Phishing Emails: Effects of Internet User Demographics and Email Content, in: ACM Transactions on Computer-Human Interaction (TOCHI), Vol. 26, 2018, S. 1–28.
5. Tzipora Halevi, Nasir D. Memon, Oded Nov, Spear-Phishing in the Wild: A Real-World Study of Personality, Phishing Self-Efficacy and Vulnerability to Spear-Phishing Attacks, in: SSRN Electronic Journal, 2015.
6. Marcus Butavicius, Kathryn Parsons, Malcolm Pattinson, Agata McCormac, Breaching the Human Firewall: Social engineering in Phishing and Spear-Phishing Emails, in: Australasian Conference on Information Systems, 2015.

Smishing

17

In the context of mobile communications, a new threat has emerged alongside traditional phishing methods: **smishing, a portmanteau of SMS-phishing.** *This specific type of phishing attack targets mobile users via SMS and other instant messaging services. Similar to traditional phishing and spear phishing, the goal of smishing is to steal sensitive information, manipulate recipients into taking certain actions, and infect mobile devices with malware.*

17.1 Forms of Smishing

Smishing attacks can take the form of mass attacks using the **one-against-many tactic**, comparable to phishing, or through targeted manipulation, similar to spear phishing. Commonly impersonated senders in mass smishing attacks include:

- banks and financial institutions,
- governments,
- authorities, national or international, usually from the security sector such as Federal Office for Information Security or Federal Criminal Police Office,
- customer support,
- shipping service providers,
- mobile network operators, and also
- the user's own voicemail with a new message.

Spear smishing attacks, on the other hand, involve researching target individuals to craft personalized and convincing messages. An example of this is CEO fraud, which we examined in detail in the Black Chapter.

In high-profile cases such as the SMS-based malware attack FluBot, which occurred in 2020/2021, numerous mobile devices worldwide were compromised.

E. Koza et al., *Social Engineering and Human Hacking*, https://doi.org/10.1007/978-3-662-72084-4_17

These attacks were carried out by sending malware via fake links or malicious attachments in smishing messages. By opening these links or attachments, victims enabled attackers to perform harmful actions such as stealing login credentials or spying on personal data from infected mobile phones. The FluBot attack lured recipients into opening a link and installing an app. During installation, access permissions were requested, which most users did not scrutinize. As a result, attackers gained access to highly sensitive information such as online banking credentials. With the granted permissions to the address book, the malware also sent smishing messages to stored contacts, spreading virally. International investigations in eleven countries eventually led to law enforcement control of FluBot [1].

The deceptive power of smishing lies in the skillful exploitation of mobile phones as everyday companions. Smartphones have evolved into versatile devices used not only for personal activities such as communication, social media, banking, and professional tasks, but also for business purposes. This duality can potentially lead to fluctuations in users' security awareness. The frequent and rapid switching between private and professional contexts on the same device makes the psychological methods of phishing particularly effective on mobile phones.

Analysis also shows that even individuals who use their phones exclusively for private purposes can fall victim to smishing.

This can be explained by various factors, including widespread digital complacency. Many users who use their mobile phones only for personal purposes tend to adopt a relaxed attitude toward digital security. **This mentality is often reflected in thoughts such as: "my data isn't really important" or "nothing has happened so far."**

The underlying assumption that personal data is of little value or interest to attackers leads to negligent behavior. Users may be inclined to neglect security precautions and be less critical of suspicious messages or links. This approach can result in private users being less vigilant and more likely to fall for convincing smishing messages.

The classic: "nothing has happened so far," reflects a certain indifference to potential dangers. Such users may believe themselves to be in a supposed safety bubble and assume they are immune to cyberattacks. This mindset increases the effectiveness of smishing attacks, as victims are less likely to take proactive steps to strengthen their digital security.

A key explanatory factor for susceptibility to smishing attacks also lies in insufficient knowledge about different types of attacks and attack vectors.

Many users are not sufficiently informed about the various types of cyberattacks and the methods employed by attackers. The knowledge factor plays a crucial role, as an informed user base is better able to recognize threats and respond appropriately.

In addition to this knowledge gap, there is the skills factor, which concerns uncertainty about how to effectively defend against such attacks, even when one is aware of potential dangers. It is not only important to know that threats exist, but also to understand how to protect oneself both proactively and reactively. This requires specific skills, including the ability to detect anomalies and identify red flags that may indicate potential smishing attacks. This also involves developing a personal sensitivity to suspicious elements in messages and recognizing deviations from the norm.

The ability to respond appropriately and defend oneself is equally important and requires a personal touch, as not all smishing attacks follow the same pattern. Users must learn how to react appropriately in different situations, whether by ignoring suspicious messages, verifying senders, or reporting suspicious behavior.

In addition to personal skills, technical competence also plays a role. Users should be able to utilize existing security features and harden their own systems to minimize the attack surface. This requires an understanding of available security mechanisms as well as the ability to implement and maintain them effectively.

Given the increasing use of smartphones for sensitive activities such as online banking, this underscores the need for heightened security awareness and technical safeguards against smishing attacks.

17.2 Analysis

Susceptibility to smishing, especially in the modern era of mobile communications, is influenced by various factors. The use of smartphones for a wide range of activities, combined with psychological and contextual elements, plays a decisive role. Recipients of smishing messages are often torn between private and business use of their smartphones. The rapid switching between personal and professional use affects perception and may reduce security awareness. Smartphones may also be perceived less as a target for attacks.

The deceptive power of smishing exploits not only technical vulnerabilities, but also psychological and social factors. The daily use of smartphones in various scenarios leads to different mental states, which influence the perception of security threats. The risks of smishing go beyond simply clicking on links and can result in access to sensitive data and extortion attempts.

The effectiveness of smishing is based on the skillful exploitation of psychological vulnerabilities and contextual dependencies. Cybersecurity awareness on smartphones should be strengthened by promoting both technical security measures and personal resilience. A comprehensive understanding of these dynamics is essential for establishing effective security protocols.

17.3 Summary

With the unauthorized infiltration of a hacker into a smartphone, extensive insights into the private life of the affected individual become possible. This includes viewing photos, accessing stored contacts, and reading written correspondence. At the same time, the attacker gains the ability to manipulate two-factor authentication, eavesdrop on phone calls, and covertly use the video camera and microphone for secret recordings. Subsequent confrontation and extortion using compromising material represent only one of many options from the criminals' perspective.

References

1. Europol, Takedown of SMS-based FluBot spyware infecting Android phones, unter: https://www.europol.europa.eu/media-press/newsroom/news/takedown-of-sms-based-flubot-spyware-infecting-android-phones (Accessed: 02.12.2023).

Part III

Yellow Chapter: Anomaly Detection and Defense Strategies

Technical Basic Defense Concept

18

The scope of influence of human hacking and social engineering demonstrates that criminal activities are not limited to unauthorized information gathering or credential theft. Rather, they are also used to initiate advanced attack types and operations aimed at disrupting processes, up to and including the complete paralysis of networks. As outlined in the White Chapter, it becomes clear that a well-thought-out and comprehensive security concept is required—one that integrates the three core elements of information security in a coherent combination and operationalizes them in a practice-oriented manner. *This holistic security concept serves not only as prevention and response to specific attacks, but also as a proactive line of defense against potential threats in accordance with the all-hazard approach*[1]. *This perspective is reflected in the realization that, in addition to specific and attack-oriented precautions and defense strategies, a global baseline defense concept is indispensable. This forms the fundamental framework that enables the integration and implementation of specific defense concepts in the first place. In the present context, we first outline what such a global technical baseline security concept might look like:*

Technical Baseline Defense Concept

Designation:
Access control through Identity Access Management (IAM)
Measure:
Implementation of IAM platforms
Application:
Use of tools such as Microsoft Azure Active Directory or Okta for centralized management of user identities and access rights
Norm references:
C. 5.15, C. 5.16 ISO/EC 27001:2022 and 27002:2022 [2, 3]
ORP 4 IT-Grundschutz Compendium [4]

Designation:
Role and permission concept
Measure:
Implementation of Role-based Access Control (RBAC)
Application:
Implementation of RBAC to precisely control permissions in various IT systems, for example in corporate networks, to ensure granular access control
Norm references:
C. 5.18 ISO/EC 27001:2022 and 27002:2022 [2, 3]
ORP 4 IT-Grundschutz Compendium [4]

Designation:
Network separation and segmentation
Measure:
Use of a two-tier firewall concept: firewall – DMZ – firewall; use of Virtual Local Area Networks (VLANs) and additional firewalls to separate network zones and segments
Application:
Segmentation of the network into different VLANs, protected by firewalls, to prevent unauthorized access
Norm references:
C. 8.22 ISO/EC 27001:2022 and 27002:2022 [2, 3]
NET.1 IT-Grundschutz Compendium [4]

Designation:
Data backup and backup systems
Measure:
Automated backup solutions for redundant data protection
Application:
Use of backup tools such as Veeam or Acronis for regular backup of critical data. Various paradigms are available for implementing data backups, including full backup, incremental backup, differential backup, and offline backup (tape backup)
Norm references:
C. 8.13 ISO/EC 27001:2022 and 27002:2022 [2, 3]
CON.8 IT-Grundschutz Compendium [4]

Designation:
Patch management
Measure:
Technical process for identifying, implementing, monitoring, and managing software and system updates, also known as patches. Patches are updates provided by software vendors to close security gaps, fix bugs, and improve the performance of applications or operating systems
Application:
The implementation of systems such as Microsoft SCCM (System Center Configuration Manager) for the automatic distribution of security patches is essential for maintaining a robust security posture. Alternatively, a manual patching process can be established, especially in the context of so-called Operational Technology (OT), where automated patching is often critical WSUS (Windows Server Update Services) is a service provided by Microsoft that enables IT administrators to manage the distribution of updates, patches, and service packs for Microsoft products within a Windows environment. WSUS acts as a central update server, locally managing the traffic from Microsoft update services within the organization
Norm references:
C. 8.19, C. 8.31 ISO/EC 27001:2022 and 27002:2022 [2, 3]
OPS. 1.1.3 IT-Grundschutz Compendium [4]

Designation:
Capacity management
Measure:
Technical process for comprehensive planning, monitoring, and optimization of resource utilization in an IT infrastructure, such as storage capacities or monitoring CPU usage
Application:
Use of monitoring systems such as Nagios or Prometheus for continuous resource monitoring
Note: Capacity management enables comprehensive monitoring of CPU utilization and storage consumption. This ongoing monitoring can serve as an evidence-based method for detecting anomalies. Malicious software such as viruses, trojans, ransomware, or worms often access a computer's logical capacities without authorization. Unexplained CPU usage or storage overload can be interpreted as evidence of unauthorized use. Furthermore, systems can operate with so-called "baselining." By defining standard values that trigger an alert when reached or exceeded, effective early detection of unusual activities can be achieved
Norm references:
C. 8.6 ISO/EC 27001:2022 and 27002:2022 [2, 3]
OPS.1.2.2., DER.1., SYS1.1., SYS.1.5., SYS2.1., NET.1.1., NET.1.2., NET.3.2. IT-Grundschutz Compendium [4]

Designation:
Secure installation and operation of software and hardware systems
Measure:
Strict separation of roles and privileges between regular users and superusers to prevent unauthorized software installations
Application:
Technical separation of front-end and back-end components to ensure secure and controlled software deployment
Standards references:
C. 8.19 ISO/EC 27001:2022 and 27002:2022 [2, 3]
APP.6 IT-Grundschutz Compendium [4]

Designation:
Software whitelisting or blacklisting
Measure:
Implementation of a software blacklist to prohibit insecure applications
Application:
Implementation of technical restrictions to ensure that only validated and approved software (or source code) can be executed within the network, as well as the use of application control tools
Standards references:
C. 8.7 ISO/EC 27001:2022 and 27002:2022 [2, 3]
SYS.1.1 IT-Grundschutz Compendium [4]

After outlining the technical basic defense concept, we now turn to specific defense strategies tailored to particular types of attacks.

References

1. Bundesamt des Innern, Nationale Strategie zum Schutz Kritischer Infrastrukturen (KRITIS-Strategie), Bonifatius GmbH, Paderborn, 2009.
2. Deutsches Institut für Normung (DIN), Informationssicherheit, Cybersicherheit und Datenschutz – Informationssicherheitsmanagementsysteme – Anforderungen (ISO/IEC 27001:2022).

3. Deutsches Institut für Normung (DIN), Informationssicherheit, Cybersicherheit und Schutz der Privatsphäre – Informationssicherheitsmaßnahmen (ISO/IEC 27002:2022).
4. Bundesamt für Sicherheit in der Informationstechnik (BSI), IT-Grundschutz-Kompendium, 2023.

Technical Defense Tactics

19

19.1 Technical Countermeasures Against BEC

Technical protection against BEC requires a variety of approaches and technologies. The following presents alternative and additional measures that provide a fundamental defense against BEC attacks.

19.1.1 Technical Behavioral Analysis

The introduction of mechanisms that analyze typical user behavior offers the opportunity to identify irregularities compared to normal activity patterns. In this way, anomalies can be detected that may indicate a possible BEC attack. In other words, by implementing such solutions, suspicious behaviors that deviate from standard procedures can be identified, thus pointing to a potential BEC threat.

In the context of analyzing normal user behavior to detect deviations that may indicate a potential BEC attack, various types of anomalies can be considered. Here are some examples (Tab. 19.1).

19.1.2 Email Encryption

The use of end-to-end encryption for confidential emails ensures that even in the event of a compromised email account, the contents remain protected from unauthorized access. This type of encryption means that the transmitted information remains encrypted throughout the entire transmission path, from the sender to the recipient. In other words, even if an attacker gains access to the transmission or the email account, the actual contents are protected by impenetrable encryption. This

Tab. 19.1 Anomalies and Indicators

Anomaly	Indicator
Unusual Access	Sudden or unusual access to protected resources or files, especially outside normal working hours or from atypical locations
Changed Communication Behavior	Noticeable changes in communication patterns, such as unusually frequent or infrequent emails to external parties, especially when they contain financial information
Deviations in File Access Patterns	Unusual patterns in accessing files or databases, particularly when confidential information is involved
Unusual Transactions	Sudden or unexpected financial transactions, especially those that do not follow usual patterns or approval processes
External Manipulation of Emails	Suspicious changes to emails, such as adding new recipients, modifying payment details, or the appearance of unusual attachments
Exceptional Access Attempts	Repeated unsuccessful attempts to access sensitive systems or applications may indicate unauthorized access attempts
Unusual Device Connections	Connections from unusual or non-standard devices to the corporate network may be a sign of compromise
Suspicious Communication Patterns	Noticeable communication patterns, such as a sudden increase in interest in confidential information or unusual requests for access rights

provides an additional layer of security, ensuring that even in the event of potential security breaches, the confidentiality of sensitive information is maintained.

19.1.3 Email Whitelisting

Creating a list of trusted email addresses from which legitimate communication is expected plays an important role in minimizing phishing attacks. With email whitelisting, specific sender addresses are marked as trusted. This signals that emails from these addresses should be considered legitimate. When a company or organization establishes such a whitelist, it means that only emails from the listed addresses can reach the regular inbox, while emails from unauthorized senders are blocked or moved to the spam folder.

This measure significantly reduces the attack surface for BEC attacks, as only pre-authorized senders are able to gain direct access to the inbox. In this way, the likelihood that employees will fall for fraudulent emails is greatly reduced, since communication is limited to trusted sources. Whitelisting is therefore an effective approach to strengthening security against phishing attacks and maintaining the integrity of email communication.

19.1.4 E-mail Security Technology

The implementation of solutions for e-mail authentication and security at the application level ensures secure and reliable communication. This measure is designed to guarantee the authenticity of e-mails by deploying specific mechanisms at the application layer. In this way, it is ensured that communication between sender and recipient is trustworthy and not compromised by forged identities.

E-mail authentication at the application level often involves technologies *such as SPF (Sender Policy Framework), DKIM (DomainKeys Identified Mail), and DMARC (Domain-based Message Authentication, Reporting, and Conformance). These standards verify the origin of e-mails and validate the sender's identity. In this way,* the integrity *of communication is ensured, and recipients can be confident that the e-mails they receive originate from authenticated sources. This approach helps to minimize phishing attacks and strengthen the security of e-mail communication.*

Tagging e-mails that originate from external sources but are delivered to the internal mailbox is a technical measure to identify potentially forged e-mails. This approach enables early warning of users about a potential social engineering attack, especially when the e-mail attempts to simulate internal communication.

By marking external e-mails in the internal mailbox, it becomes possible to distinguish between internal and external sources. This facilitates the detection of spoofing, where an attacker pretends to be a trusted internal source. This technical identification provides users with an additional indication that a received e-mail may not have the expected internal origin. As a result, attention is drawn to potentially fraudulent e-mails, enabling users to take appropriate precautions to prevent a possible attack.

The implementation of a phishing alert button in Outlook or other e-mail clients is a proactive measure that allows users to flag suspicious e-mails and easily move them to an IT security quarantine folder.

This plug-in enables users to quickly identify potential threats and place them in a dedicated area for further review by an IT security expert.

Within this quarantine folder, a thorough review of the e-mails marked as suspicious can be conducted. If their safety is confirmed, the e-mail can be returned to the user. In the event of an actual threat, the e-mail can be deleted or further security measures can be taken as appropriate.

This feature facilitates the active involvement of end users in identifying and reporting potentially harmful e-mails, thereby increasing collective vigilance against phishing attacks. It underscores the importance of a collaborative defense strategy, in which both technological solutions and the active participation of users play an integral role.

19.1.5 Identity Verification through Technical Verification Chain

The intensification of identity verification, particularly in the context of financial transactions, may require the introduction of multi-factor authentication methods or additional verification procedures. This approach aims to enhance security for sensitive transactions by going beyond conventional authentication methods.

Multi-factor authentication methods may, for example, involve the use of multiple identification factors such as passwords, biometric data, or tokens. These additional layers of identity verification increase the difficulty for potential attackers to gain unauthorized access, even if basic authentication information is compromised.

Additional verification procedures may include requiring authorized individuals to confirm or approve transactions before they are executed. This could involve, for example, the use of separate, secure communication channels or the implementation of automated alerts in the case of unusual transaction patterns.

Overall, enhanced identity verification is intended to ensure the integrity and authenticity of transactions, particularly in situations that carry an increased risk of fraudulent activity, as is the case with financial operations.

19.2 Technical Countermeasures Against Shoulder Surfing

Technical countermeasures against shoulder surfing, in which an attacker attempts to obtain confidential information by covertly observing keyboard input or screen content, can encompass several strategies.

19.2.1 Privacy Screen Technologies

Some contemporary laptops and monitors are equipped with built-in privacy screen technologies. These advanced technologies use polarized light to ensure that the screen content is clearly visible only from an optimal viewing angle. By employing polarized filters, the light is aligned in such a way that it is significantly diminished or distorted for individuals outside the defined viewing angle.

The primary purpose of these technologies is to protect the user's visual privacy, especially in environments where potential visibility by side observers could pose a security risk. By limiting the viewing angle of the screen content, these integrated privacy solutions allow users to view confidential information more discreetly, without having to worry about it being seen by curious eyes outside the intended viewing area.

19.2.2 Automatic Screen Dimming

Automatic screen dimming is a feature that allows smartphones and tablets to be configured so that the screen automatically dims as soon as the device is not viewed from the front. This configuration is intended to prevent people standing to the side from reading information from the screen.

This technical measure reduces the visibility of the screen content to a minimum when the device is not held at a specific viewing angle. The automatic dimming serves to protect the user's privacy and makes it more difficult for people nearby to read the screen.

This mechanism helps to maintain the confidentiality of information, especially in situations where unauthorized individuals might be able to view the screen from the side.

19.2.3 Motion Sensors and Facial Recognition

Motion sensors and facial recognition are used in some devices to ensure that screen content is displayed only when the authorized user is directly in front of the device.

This technology uses motion sensors to detect the physical presence of the user, combined with facial recognition to verify identity. Only when both factors match is the screen content released. This approach provides an additional layer of security to ensure that the screen is activated only when the legitimate user is physically present and has been identified. This helps prevent unauthorized access and the display of information to unauthorized individuals.

19.2.4 Distortion Technologies

Modern technologies have the capability to slightly distort screen content as soon as it is viewed from a side angle. This innovative approach is designed to make it significantly more difficult for unauthorized viewers to read the information.

When the screen is viewed from a side angle, the technology intervenes and applies a slight distortion to the displayed content. This effect impairs the clarity and comprehensibility of the information for individuals who are not looking directly at the screen. Through this targeted distortion, the perception of content from side angles is significantly hindered, thereby protecting sensitive information from unauthorized disclosure.

This advanced technology thus represents a proactive measure to ensure the security of screen content and to maintain the confidentiality of information even in environments with potential side observers.

19.2.5 Active Screen Masking

Systems based on eye-tracking technology have the capability to automatically mask or blur screen content as soon as they detect that the user's gaze is outside the authorized area. These advanced systems use cameras or sensors to track the user's gaze direction and determine whether visual attention is within the approved area.

When the eye-tracking system detects that the user has diverted their gaze from the authorized view, a reactive measure is triggered. This may include, for example, the automatic application of blur effects to the screen content or the complete masking of sensitive information. In this way, the confidentiality of the displayed data is maintained and unauthorized reading by side observers is prevented.

This technology represents an innovative security measure specifically designed to protect the integrity of screen content in environments with potentially curious onlookers, thereby providing effective protection against unwanted shoulder surfing. The combination of several of these technical countermeasures offers comprehensive defense against shoulder surfing by significantly restricting or preventing the visibility of screen content from side angles.

19.3   Technical Countermeasures Against Dumpster Diving

Techniques against dumpster diving (searching through waste containers for sensitive information) focus on ensuring the security of discarded or disposed documents and preventing unauthorized access. The following are some IT-based techniques.

19.3.1 Data and Disk Encryption

Data encryption is a critical protective mechanism designed to secure information stored on data carriers through robust encryption. Even if physical data carriers are accidentally discarded, the data stored on them remains unreadable to unauthorized individuals. This security measure ensures that access to sensitive information is significantly hindered, even in cases of physical loss or improper disposal. In particular, the implementation of disk encryption is crucial for data stored on hard drives. This specific form of data encryption ensures that all data stored on the hard drive is encrypted. Advanced encryption algorithms are used in disk encryption to guarantee that, even with physical access to the hard drive, the stored data cannot be interpreted without the correct decryption key. This additional security mechanism helps minimize potential risks from accidental data loss or unauthorized physical access.

19.3.2 Remote Data Wiping

Remote data wiping is a valuable preventive security measure that enables the remote deletion of data on stolen or lost devices. This feature allows sensitive information to be removed from remote locations if devices are improperly disposed of or fall into unauthorized hands.

Remote data wiping ensures the security of data even after physical loss or theft. This measure provides a proactive approach to ensure that, in the event of device loss or theft, no confidential information falls into the wrong hands. The ability to delete data remotely helps comply with data protection regulations and significantly reduces the risk of data breaches. Such a feature should be integrated into a comprehensive security strategy to ensure effective protection of sensitive information.

19.3.3 Secure File Deletion

Secure file deletion represents an essential security practice aimed at the permanent removal of files from digital storage media. Secure deletion algorithms are applied to ensure that files cannot be recovered even after disposal.

The use of secure deletion algorithms is crucial to ensure that sensitive information cannot be recovered or reconstructed after being removed from a digital storage medium. This measure helps fulfill data protection requirements and minimize the risk of data leaks, especially when digital storage media are decommissioned or recycled.

Consistent use of secure deletion algorithms should be considered an integral part of a comprehensive data security strategy to ensure that sensitive information can be effectively and permanently deleted.

19.3.4 Geofencing for Digital Devices

The implementation of geofencing technologies is an advanced security measure aimed at defining the geographic areas in which certain devices are permitted to operate. This technology can trigger automatic data deletion on devices that move outside these defined areas. Geofencing enables the control of digital devices based on their geographic location. If a device leaves a predefined area, a deletion function can be automatically activated. This approach provides an additional layer of security to ensure that sensitive information does not inadvertently remain in insecure environments. Geofencing is particularly suitable for mobile devices or those that frequently change their physical location, such as laptops or tablets. Integrating geofencing technologies into the security strategy enables precise control over data access, thereby strengthening data protection and security.

19.3.5 Data Loss Prevention (DLP) Software

The implementation of Data Loss Prevention (DLP) solutions is an essential preventive security measure aimed at monitoring data flows and ensuring that sensitive information is not copied or moved without authorization.

DLP software provides proactive control over the handling of sensitive data within a company or organization. By monitoring data streams, DLP software can detect potentially harmful activities and prevent sensitive information from being copied, moved, or transmitted without authorization. Implementing these solutions enables comprehensive data security by ensuring compliance with policies and data protection standards. DLP is particularly relevant for minimizing insider threats and ensuring that sensitive information is adequately protected both within and outside organizational boundaries.

19.3.6 Encrypted Communication During Disposal

With regard to the disposal process, it is essential to use encrypted channels or secure protocols when transmitting information. This security measure is intended to thwart eavesdropping attempts during the disposal process.

The use of encrypted channels ensures that sensitive information is protected during transport via secure protocols. This approach aims to counteract potential eavesdropping attempts by third parties by protecting the transmitted data from unauthorized access. Especially during the disposal process, when confidential information may be transported, encrypted communication helps maintain the integrity and confidentiality of the data. Integrating this security practice into the disposal process ensures that an appropriate level of security is maintained even during the transport of data.

19.3.7 Monitoring Device Activities

The implementation of systems for monitoring IT device activities is an essential security measure for detecting suspicious activities that may indicate improper disposal.

Continuous monitoring of IT device activity can detect potential anomalies and suspicious actions that may indicate insecure disposal practices or unauthorized access. These monitoring systems can log activities, trigger notifications in the event of unusual behavior, and thus enable an early response to potential security risks. Monitoring device activities is an integral part of a comprehensive security concept aimed at protecting the entire lifecycle of IT devices. This measure helps ensure that devices are appropriately monitored during their use and especially during the disposal process to guarantee the integrity and security of data.

These technical solutions focus on protecting digital data and systems to ensure that an adequate level of IT security is maintained even during physical disposal.

19.4   Technical Countermeasures Against Tailgating

Techniques against tailgating (unauthorized entry into secured areas by following an authorized user) focus on controlling physical access and detecting unauthorized individuals. The following are some IT-based techniques.

19.4.1   Multi-factor Authentication (MFA) for Access to Sensitive Areas

The implementation of MFA for access to sensitive IT rooms or critical areas is a key security mechanism that extends traditional single-factor authentication. In an MFA system, users must present a second authentication factor in addition to their regular login credentials to verify their identity. Below are some technical details and implementations (Table 19.2).

Implementing MFA not only provides robust protection against tailgating, but also against various other threats such as phishing or password theft. MFA makes it more difficult for attackers to use credentials stolen through phishing. Even if a

Tab. 19.2   Technologies and Implementations

Technology	Implementations
Authentication Factors	MFA uses at least two of the following authentication factors: • **Knowledge-based factors:** regular login credentials such as username and password • **Possession-based factors:** something the user possesses, e.g., a token, smart card, or mobile device • **Biometric factors:** physical characteristics such as fingerprints, facial or iris scans
Token-based MFA	A common second authentication factor is a token. This can be a physical device that generates a one-time password (OTP) or a virtual token displayed on a mobile device
Mobile App-based MFA	Many organizations implement MFA via mobile apps. Users receive a time-based code through the app, which is used to verify their identity
Time-based Codes	MFA systems, especially those based on mobile apps, often use time-based codes. These codes are valid only for a short period, which increases their effectiveness in preventing unauthorized access
Integrated Systems	Modern MFA solutions integrate seamlessly with existing authentication infrastructures. They often work in conjunction with single sign-on (SSO) systems to ensure a smooth and secure login experience
Biometric Integration	Advanced MFA systems integrate biometric technologies such as fingerprint scans or facial recognition. These provide an additional layer of security and eliminate the risk of loss or theft of physical tokens

user clicks on a phishing link and enters their credentials, the additional authentication step will prevent the attacker from taking over the account. In the case of password theft, whether through leaks or insecure practices, MFA provides an extra layer of protection. Even if the password is compromised, the attacker still needs the second authentication factor to access the account. It creates an effective barrier that ensures access to sensitive areas is granted only to authorized users, while also taking user convenience into account.

19.4.2 Access Logging and Monitoring

Monitoring systems can log and monitor access to specific areas.

Access logging and monitoring are therefore fundamental elements of the security infrastructure, serving to monitor and record access to specific areas for potential irregularities. These monitoring systems capture precise data on access activities, enable the identification of suspicious patterns, and contribute to the early detection of security risks. For example, repeated logins by the same user within a short period or multiple individuals accessing an area with a single valid badge may indicate a potential form of unauthorized entry, also known as tailgating.

Access logging provides comprehensive records of the temporal and spatial dimensions of access.

Careful analysis of these logs makes it possible to identify unusual activities that could indicate potential security breaches. In particular, it is important to monitor shared access credentials in order to respond appropriately to security threats such as tailgating.

19.4.3 Biometric Authentication for IT Rooms

The implementation of biometric access controls for specific IT rooms can ensure that only authorized users with the correct biometric characteristics are granted access. Biometric authentication for IT rooms as well as critical security zones and areas ensures, through the integration of biometric access controls, a precise verification of the identity of individuals seeking access to specific IT rooms or critical areas. This security measure ensures that only authorized users with the correct biometric features are granted access.

Biometric authentication technologies, such as fingerprint or facial recognition systems, serve as reliable methods to control access rights while ensuring that only individuals with predefined biometric characteristics can access sensitive IT rooms.

19.4.4 Video Analysis and AI Surveillance

The implementation of video surveillance in entry areas, particularly in sensitive zones, primarily aims to detect tailgating attempts and retrospectively identify unauthorized individuals. As a detection measure, video surveillance enables visual monitoring of activities and the identification of deviations from authorized access behavior. By definition, however, video surveillance cannot be considered a preventive measure, as it is based on detection and identification rather than prevention or reduction.

The preventive aspect refers to measures designed to prevent potential violations in advance or to reduce the associated risks. In contrast, video surveillance operates in a detective-reactive manner by uncovering incidents after they occur.

Under optimal conditions, such measures—especially when combined with real-time analysis and response—can be regarded as corrective to reactive approaches.

With regard to the potential preventive effect of video surveillance, it must be noted that this also depends on the assumption that the mere visibility of cameras acts as a deterrent. However, this assumption is not clearly confirmed, as criminals continue to infiltrate physical premises despite widespread camera surveillance.

It should also be noted that the effectiveness of video surveillance depends not only on its technical implementation, but also on other factors such as the perception of surveillance, the type of areas covered, and the existing security measures.

For effective implementation of video surveillance, organizations should pursue a comprehensive security strategy that goes beyond mere visual monitoring technologies. Video surveillance systems, especially when supported by AI, offer the capability for precise analysis of behavioral patterns and anomaly detection. Supported by AI, these systems can trigger early alarms in situations where multiple individuals follow an authorized user without the necessary permissions (tailgating). These advanced surveillance technologies enable proactive identification of unauthorized access and allow for timely responses to potential security risks. In this context, it is crucial that technological measures are part of a broader security strategy that includes organizational aspects and employee training.

19.4.5 Automated Access Control

The implementation of automated access control systems based on authentication factors is aimed at minimizing tailgating. These systems grant access to only one user per authentication process. These advanced door access control mechanisms utilize various authentication factors, such as biometric features or personalized access cards, to ensure that only authorized individuals are granted entry. This measure helps to secure the integrity of access and simultaneously minimize the risk of unauthorized entry, particularly through tailgating.

The implementation of effective physical access control, for example through security gates or turnstiles at all entry points, forms the foundation for protection against tailgating. Particular attention must be paid to defining appropriate parameters, such as short closing times or preventing attempts to bypass the access control system.

The latter could occur through additional uncontrolled entry points or by bypassing a security turnstile without authentication.

In combination with appropriate sensors, it can thus be largely ensured that an authorized person cannot grant access to another individual to the protected area without their individual authentication. Access authorization is therefore always granted to only one authorized person at a time.

19.4.6 RFID Access Cards with Time Zone Restrictions

Restrictions enable precise control of access at specific times. By programming RFID access cards, time-based restrictions can be set to allow access only during defined periods. This approach effectively prevents unauthorized individuals from entering outside regular working hours. The time-based programming of RFID access cards thus serves as an effective security measure to specifically and controllably regulate access to certain areas.

19.5   Technical Countermeasures against Vishing

To protect against vishing, technical countermeasures focus on securing IT and communication systems. Here are some IT-based techniques.

19.5.1 Call Authentication Systems

Call authentication systems represent advanced technological approaches for verifying the legitimacy of telephone calls and ensuring that they originate from authenticated sources. A concrete example of such systems is STIR/SHAKEN, which stands for "Secure Telephone Identity Revisited/Signature-based Handling of Asserted Information Using Tokens." These technologies rely on a combined application of established standards and protocols to verify the caller's identity.

STIR/SHAKEN uses digital signatures and certificates to secure the authenticity of telephone calls. Each call is assigned a unique digital signature generated by the call source. The recipient of the call verifies this signature to ensure that the call originates from a source classified as trustworthy and authentic.

The process is based on the use of certificates, similar to those used for identity verification on secure websites. STIR/SHAKEN implements a hierarchical model of certification authorities to ensure that the generated signatures can be considered credible and trustworthy.

19.5.2 Whitelisting for Legitimate Call Sources

Implementing whitelisting for legitimate call sources involves creating lists containing the phone numbers of trusted and recognized sources. The main objective is to ensure that calls from known and accepted sources are not mistakenly blocked or flagged as suspicious. This whitelist serves as a reference point for verifying incoming calls. Here, the security objective of "authenticity" is emphasized. The authenticity objective concerns ensuring the genuineness or credibility of information, identities, or entities in a communication or information system. It refers to ensuring that the claimed identity or origin of data, messages, individuals, or other elements is correct and trustworthy. Authenticity is a key aspect of information security and plays a central role in preventing forgery, fraud, or unauthorized access to sensitive information.

The goal is to ensure that information genuinely originates from the source it claims to come from and that it has not been manipulated during transmission or processing.

In practical implementation of authenticity verification, the phone numbers of trusted call sources are included in a predefined whitelist. For an incoming call, this list is used to check whether the caller's number is on the list of accepted sources. If there is a match, the call is considered legitimate and is allowed through accordingly.

This approach can be regarded as a form of access control for the communication channel, where only pre-authorized numbers are granted access while others are blocked.

19.5.3 Call Filtering Technologies

Call filtering technologies provide an innovative solution to specifically counter vishing attacks. These tools employ advanced algorithms and pattern recognition technologies to identify and block fraudulent calls. They analyze incoming calls based on predefined vishing patterns that include typical characteristics of fraudulent calls.

The implementation of such systems makes it possible to detect suspicious calls in real time and automatically block them. These technologies can access extensive databases of known vishing patterns and are continuously updated to keep pace with new fraud techniques.

In addition, call filtering tools can utilize advanced analytical methods to learn call patterns and identify anomalies that may indicate potential vishing attempts. The integration of machine learning enables an adaptive and effective response to constantly evolving vishing attacks.

Overall, call filtering technologies provide a proactive line of defense against vishing by protecting users from fraudulent calls and thereby enhancing the level of security in the communication environment.

19.6   Technical Countermeasures Against Phishing

In addressing the ever-increasing threat posed by phishing attacks, the implementation of targeted technical countermeasures is of critical importance. These measures are designed to minimize the attack surface and protect users from deceptive or fraudulent activities. In the context of IT security, the following technical defense strategies play a key role.

19.6.1 Email Authentication at the Application Level

The technique of email authentication at the application level is intended to ensure the integrity of communications. Various standards and protocols such as SPF (Sender Policy Framework), DKIM (DomainKeys Identified Mail), and DMARC (Domain-based Message Authentication, Reporting, and Conformance) are employed for this purpose.

SPF checks whether the server sending the email is authorized for the specified domain. This ensures that the email actually originates from a legitimate server of the stated domain. SPF thus helps to minimize spoofing attacks.

DKIM relies on digital signatures to guarantee the authenticity of the email. The sending server signs parts of the email and adds a signature. The receiving server can verify this signature using the domain's public key to ensure that the email has not been altered and genuinely comes from the sender.

DMARC is a policy that integrates SPF and DKIM. It defines how receiving servers should handle emails that do not have valid SPF or DKIM authentication. DMARC provides an additional layer of protection against emails that use forged sender addresses.

In combination, these technologies help ensure the authenticity of emails and thus protect the integrity of communication at the application level.

19.6.2 Identification of Spoofed Emails

The identification of spoofed emails is achieved by flagging emails that have been sent from outside the organization but still appear in the internal mailbox. This measure enables the detection of spoofed emails and thus serves as an early warning for potential social engineering attacks.

An example of this technique would be receiving an email from a trusted domain that does not meet external authentication requirements. This could indicate that the email is forged and does not actually originate from the claimed trusted source. By identifying such inconsistencies, users can be warned in time about potential spoofing attacks.

19.6.3   Enhanced Identity Verification

Enhanced identity verification aims to increase security, especially in financial transactions. This may require the implementation of multi-factor authentication methods or additional checks to ensure that the user's identity is reliably confirmed.

For example, in addition to conventional login credentials such as username and password, an additional authentication method may be required. This could include the use of a one-time password or biometric data such as fingerprints or facial recognition. These multi-layered authentication mechanisms strengthen identity verification and achieve a higher level of security for sensitive transactions.

19.6.4   Technical Solutions for Malware Scanning

Technical solutions for malware scanning at the email level are based on advanced antivirus and anti-phishing mechanisms. These systems aim to identify and isolate malicious software before it gains access to the user's mailbox. This process is carried out using sophisticated security algorithms and protocols. An exemplary implementation of this approach could be the deployment of robust security software that analyzes emails for suspicious content using real-time scanning. Various techniques such as signature detection, heuristic analysis, and machine learning are employed. Signature detection identifies known patterns of malicious software, while heuristic analysis is based on behavioral patterns to detect potentially harmful activities. In addition, machine learning can be used to identify new threats by recognizing patterns and anomalies in real time and responding accordingly.

19.6.5   Phishing Alert Button

The integration of a phishing alert button in email clients such as Outlook represents an additional security measure against phishing attacks. This feature enables users to identify suspicious emails and move them to a dedicated IT security quarantine folder by marking them. In this folder, emails marked as suspicious are thoroughly examined by security experts.

A concrete example would be a user receiving an email they consider suspicious and marking it using the phishing alert button. The IT department can then verify the authenticity of the email in question and take appropriate protective measures. This technology focuses on enhancing human interaction in the email context and empowering end users to recognize potentially fraudulent activities. This approach adopts a proactive strategy by involving users in the decision-making process while also providing a mechanism for subsequent review by security experts. In this way, the phishing alert button helps to strengthen resilience against phishing attacks and improve the responsiveness of the IT security infrastructure.

19.7   Technical Countermeasures Against Smishing

Given the ongoing threat posed by smishing attacks, the implementation of targeted technical defense strategies is becoming increasingly important. These measures aim to minimize the attack surface and protect users from deceptive or fraudulent activities associated with SMS-based phishing. In the context of IT security, particularly regarding the professional and personal use of smartphones, the following technical defense strategies play a crucial role.

19.7.1 Containerization via Mobile Device Management (MDM)

The implementation of container solutions within the MDM system ensures a clear separation between business and personal data on the mobile device. This prevents a smishing attack affecting the personal area from spreading to the corporate environment. Containerization creates separate areas for business and personal applications, thereby isolating data and applications. As a result, business information remains protected even if the personal area of the device is compromised.

This technology provides an effective security measure to ensure the confidentiality and integrity of business data on mobile devices.

19.7.2 Access Controls and Permissions

Defining and strictly enforcing access controls and permissions within the container ensures that only authorized applications and services can access business data. This measure guarantees that sensitive corporate information can only be retrieved by authorized individuals and processes. By precisely managing permissions, the risk of unauthorized access is minimized, thereby protecting the integrity and confidentiality of business data within the container.

19.7.3 Virtual Environment for Apps

The use of virtualization technologies enables business applications to run in a secure virtual environment within the container. This preventive measure makes it significantly more difficult for attackers to access business data. By isolating applications in a virtual environment, potential security vulnerabilities are minimized, as attacks are confined within the virtual environment and do not allow direct access to the entire system. This helps to maintain the integrity and confidentiality of business data.

19.7.4 Container-Level Encryption

The implementation of container encryption technologies ensures that even in the event of a successful smishing attack on the personal area, business data remains protected. This preventive measure ensures that even if the personal area is compromised, the encrypted business data remains inaccessible to the attacker. Container-level encryption thus provides an additional layer of security that preserves the confidentiality and integrity of sensitive business information.

19.7.5 Mobile App Reputation Services

Integrating mobile app reputation services into the MDM system helps to identify and block suspicious or malicious apps before they are installed on the device. Through continuous monitoring and analysis of app behavior and origin, these services enable proactive detection of potentially harmful applications. This helps to maintain the security of the mobile ecosystem by identifying dangerous apps early and preventing their installation on users' devices.

Having precisely outlined our technical baseline security concept as well as specific individual defense concepts, we will now turn to the presentation of organizational defense concepts before subsequently addressing individual and human defense strategies.

Organizational Basic Defense Concept

The holistic, organizational baseline defense concept comprises several key elements which, in combination, help to effectively protect the organization against social engineering attacks. These elements form a comprehensive security strategy that integrates both preventive and reactive measures. The following section provides a detailed explanation of the key elements of this concept.

Organizational Baseline Defense Concept

Designation
Establishment of a security team within a dedicated organizational structure.

Measure
Definition and establishment of a dedicated security team as an independent organizational unit with specific tasks and responsibilities in the areas of information security and data protection.

Application
Implementation of a security team as an independent organizational unit that addresses the individual and specific security aspects within the organization. This includes selecting qualified team members, developing internal roles and responsibilities, and designing, executing, and continuously optimizing specific security measures as part of holistic information security. The following areas must be taken into account:

- Risk management (risk assessment, treatment, communication, and monitoring and tracking of risks; [1]),
- Business continuity management and emergency management [2, 3],
- Incident response management [4–6],
- Vulnerability management.

Norm References

C. 5.2, C. 8.16 C. 5.29, C.30 ISO/EC 27001:2022, or ISO/IEC 27002:2022 [7, 8].
   ORP.1 IT-Grundschutz Compendium [9].

Designation

Establishment of knowledge management with security-specific policies and procedures.

Measure

Development and implementation of security-specific policies and procedures for integration into knowledge management.

   Creation of clearly defined guidelines for handling security-relevant knowledge, including classification, storage, access control, and the exchange of sensitive information.

   Implementation of review mechanisms and training to ensure that employees are familiar with the security-related knowledge management policies.

   Continuous updating and adaptation of policies in line with evolving security requirements and threats.

Application

Implementation of a knowledge management system specifically focused on security-relevant aspects. The developed policies and procedures are embedded to ensure structured and secure knowledge management within the organization.

   Implementation of mechanisms for regular review and updating of security-related policies to ensure they meet current threats and requirements.

Norm References

Section 7.5, 27001:2022, or ISO/IEC 27002:2022 [7, 8].
   ISMS.1 IT-Grundschutz Compendium [9].

Designation

Establishment and implementation of a detection and reporting process for recording and reporting information security incidents.

Measure

Definition of clear policies and processes to detect, analyze, document, and respond appropriately to security incidents.

   Establishment of reporting structures that enable rapid and effective communication of security incidents to minimize response time.

   Development of real-time response capabilities as well as digital forensics capabilities to minimize and isolate compromised areas and to reconstruct the digital attack path.

Application

Implementation of a detection and reporting process within the organization that enables employees to report suspicious activities or security incidents.

Integration of technologies for automated detection of security incidents to support the reporting process and improve efficiency in identifying threats.

Regular training and awareness programs for employees to ensure they are familiar with the detection and reporting process and can respond appropriately in the event of security incidents.

Review and update of the reporting process in line with changing security requirements and threats.

Norm References

C. 6.8, C. 5.24. ISO/EC 27001:2022, or ISO/IEC 27002:2022 [7, 8].
DER.2.1 IT-Grundschutz Compendium [9].

Designation

Establishment and implementation of reactive and corrective capabilities for real-time response and recovery processes.

Measure

Development and implementation of reactive and corrective capabilities for real-time response to security incidents, as well as corresponding recovery processes.

Creation of clear policies and procedures for real-time response to security incidents to ensure rapid identification and containment.

Establishment of expert teams and resources that are trained and available for immediate response to security incidents.

Implementation of recovery processes to restore normal operations as quickly and efficiently as possible after a security incident.

Regular training and simulations to improve the response capabilities of security teams.

Application

Establishment of a Security Operations Center (SOC) or a similar mechanism for monitoring security events and real-time response.

Implementation of technologies for automated detection of anomalies and threats to reduce response times.

Conducting regular emergency exercises to review and optimize the effectiveness of reactive and corrective capabilities.

Integration of feedback loops to conduct detailed post-incident analysis and improve processes.

Norm References

C. 6.8, C. 5.24. ISO/EC 27001:2022, or ISO/IEC 27002:2022 [7, 8].
DER.2.1 IT-Grundschutz Compendium [9].

Designation

Definition and integration of a security zone concept focusing on physical and environmental security perimeters.

Measure

Analysis and identification of critical physical and environmental security perimeters.

Definition and introduction of clear policies and procedures for establishing security zones based on the identified criteria, as well as implementation of access controls and monitoring systems at the physical security perimeters.

Development of mechanisms for detecting and responding to unauthorized physical access or environmental threats, along with regular training and awareness programs for employees to ensure compliance with security zone policies.

Application

Establishment of various security zones in physical environments such as data centers, server rooms, or other critical infrastructures. The different areas of a company are categorized accordingly. The so-called crown jewels are embedded in the highest security zone with the most comprehensive security measures. This ensures that an attacker located in a public zone (= security zone 1) must overcome significant security barriers before gaining access to the highest security zone (security zone 4).

Use of technologies such as access cards, biometric systems, and video surveillance to secure the physical security perimeters.

Integration of monitoring systems to respond to threats such as fires, water damage, or temperature deviations.

Conducting regular physical audits and inspections to ensure that the security zone concepts are effectively implemented.

Standards References

C. 7.1 ISO/EC 27001:2022 and ISO/IEC 27002:2022 [7, 8].

INF.1, INF.2 IT-Grundschutz Compendium [9].

Designation

Regulation of work in high-security areas and visitor management.

Measure

Implementation of clear policies and procedures for access and work in high-security areas, as well as the establishment of effective visitor management.

This also includes regulation of work with external service providers, clarification of visitor management policies, provision of special visitor badges, and regulation of visitor movement within the organization.

Additionally, work activities in high-security areas are carried out under supervision, while work in critical areas is subject to authorization.

Application

Implementation of security zones in physical environments such as data centers, server rooms, or other critical infrastructures.

Structured categorization of security zones from public areas to the highest security zones.

Ensuring that direct access from a lower security zone to the highest security zone is impossible, thereby providing a layered defense.

Use of physical barriers such as locked doors, airlocks, or security gates to control access to the various security zones.

Standards References

C. 7.6 ISO/EC 27001:2022 and ISO/IEC 27002:2022 [7, 8].

INF.1, INF.2 IT-Grundschutz Compendium [9].

Designation

Information Security Awareness, Training, and Education.

Measure

Development of a comprehensive training concept with various elements to accommodate different learning styles and preferences.

Integration of homogeneous training content tailored to specific target groups and needs.

Creation of diverse training environments, including in-person events, digital learning platforms, and gamification elements.

Implementation of exercises and training sessions to strengthen employees' defensive capabilities.

Use of realistic simulation scenarios that enable employees to practice emergency situations and respond appropriately.

Application

Regular delivery of training in various formats to ensure continuous education and knowledge development.

Adaptation of homogeneous training content to specific target groups, such as executives and finance/accounting staff, who are at increased risk, for example, from CEO fraud.

Integration of repeated training and exercises such as phishing and vishing campaigns to achieve long-term and sustainable improvement in security awareness.

Drawing on the design of pilot training, various simulation scenarios are constructed to cover a wide range of realistic attack situations. Even worst-case scenarios, such as plane crashes, are considered. The fundamental goal of such training sessions is not only to test the feasibility of defined protocols but also to optimize the individual skills of the participants. The aim is for responses to attacks to become conditioned behaviors, enabling employees to implement the necessary measures and defense mechanisms quickly, efficiently, and almost intuitively.

Specialized training for employees who are exposed to particularly high attack risks, in order to strengthen their resilience.

Standards References
Section 7.2, ISO/IEC 27001:2022 [7].
    C. 6.3 ISO/EC 27001:2022 and ISO/IEC 27002:2022 [7, 8].
    ORP. 3 IT-Grundschutz Compendium [9].
After outlining the organizational basic defense concept, we now turn to specific organizational defense concepts tailored to particular types of attacks.

References

1. ISO/IEC 27005:2011-06-01, Information technology—Security techniques—Information security risk management.
2. Deutsches Institut für Normung (DIN), Sicherheit und Resilienz – Business Continuity Management System – Anforderungen (ISO 22301:2019).
3. Bundesamt für Sicherheit in der Informationstechnik (BSI), Business Continuity Management, BSI-Standard 200-4, Reguvis Fachmedien GmbH, 2023.
4. International Organization for Standardisation, Electrotechnical Commission (ISO/IEC) 27035-3:2020-09, Informationstechnik – Informationssicherheit Vorfallmanagement – Teil 3: Leitlinien für IKT-Vorfallsreaktionsmaßnahmen.
5. International Organization for Standardisation, Electrotechnical Commission (ISO/IEC) 27035-2:2016-11, Informationstechnik – IT Sicherheitsverfahren – Informationssicherheit Störfallmanagement – Teil 2: Leitfaden zur Planung und Vorbereitung der Incident-Response, (ISO/IEC 27035:2011-09).
6. International Organization for Standardisation, Electrotechnical Commission (ISO/IEC) 27035-1:2016-11, Information technology – Security techniques – Information security incident management, Part 1: Principles of incident management (ISO/IEC 27035:2011-09).
7. Deutsches Institut für Normung (DIN), Informationssicherheit, Cybersicherheit und Datenschutz – Informationssicherheitsmanagementsysteme – Anforderungen (ISO/IEC 27001:2022).
8. Deutsches Institut für Normung (DIN), Informationssicherheit, Cybersicherheit und Schutz der Privatsphäre – Informationssicherheitsmaßnahmen (ISO/IEC 27002:2022).
9. Bundesamt für Sicherheit in der Informationstechnik (BSI), IT-Grundschutz-Kompendium, 2023.

Organizational Defense Techniques

21

21.1 Organizational Defense Tactics Against BEC and Phishing Types

In this chapter, we will address organizational defense tactics against various forms of deception, including vishing, phishing, smishing, and BEC. While these attack types differ in their specific manifestations, they share a fundamental tactical denominator: the use of electronic data transmission technologies to induce the target to perform actions that would normally be avoided. The interconnection of these attack types through this shared tactical element enables a coherent and comprehensive examination of defense tactics. By focusing on the underlying strategy, organization-wide defense measures can be designed more effectively. Our approach centers on developing effective defense measures that target this fundamental tactical element. By consolidating these threats, we enable a holistic view of defense tactics that significantly strengthen the security posture while providing a clear overview of protective measures against electronically based deception attempts.

In the context of organizational security, particularly regarding the attack types listed above, the following organizational defense strategies play a crucial role.

21.1.1 Design and Integration of a Verification Process (Vishing)

Implementing verification processes within organizations requires a structured and precise approach to ensure that sensitive information is disclosed only in response to legitimate requests. The verification process is intended to reliably confirm the caller's identity, especially for calls involving sensitive or confidential information. The following outlines the steps of this process in detail.

© The Author(s), under exclusive license to Springer-Verlag GmbH, DE, part of
Springer Nature 2025
E. Koza et al., *Social Engineering and Human Hacking*,
https://doi.org/10.1007/978-3-662-72084-4_21

Caller Identification

At the beginning of the call, the employee should identify the caller and verify the purported identity. It is important to ask for the caller's name, organization, and position.

Use of Authentication Methods

In addition to identification, an authentication method can be used to ensure the legitimacy of the caller. For example, this may involve requesting predetermined information that only legitimate users should know.

Callback Confirmation

If there are doubts about the authenticity of the caller, the employee should initiate a callback. It is important that the callback is made using an official, verified phone number to ensure that communication takes place with a legitimate party.

Additional Steps in Case of Uncertainty

If uncertainty about the caller's legitimacy persists, additional steps should be taken to confirm their identity. This may include contacting internal responsible parties or reviewing security protocols.

Documentation of the Verification Process

The entire verification process should be documented to ensure complete traceability. This includes the actions taken, the information verified, and the outcome of the verification.

In principle, the same process chain can be applied to the design and integration of verification processes for other types of phishing attacks. The meta-level of verification processes, which aims to confirm the legitimacy of requests and communications, remains consistent across many phishing scenarios. The specific details and measures may vary depending on the type of phishing, but the fundamental strategy of identification, verification, and response remains similar.

For example, similar verification processes could be developed for various forms of phishing such as spear phishing, clone phishing, or link manipulation. It is important to consider the specific characteristics and tactics of each phishing type in order to implement more effective verification measures.

The meta-level of verification also includes employee training, implementation of clear policies, automated verification tools, callback protocols, and a feedback process. These elements can serve as foundational building blocks that are modified and adapted as needed to meet the specific requirements of each phishing type.

The flexibility of this meta-level enables organizations to develop a consistent and effective defense strategy against a wide range of phishing attacks.

Below, we present two verification chains to help you better understand the process steps involved in request verification. For this purpose, we use two concrete types of phishing and vishing attacks.

Strict implementation of these verification processes helps ensure that sensitive information is disclosed only to authorized parties. By combining identification, authentication, and callback mechanisms, a robust security posture is established that protects the organization from the risks of vishing attacks.

21.2   Organizational Countermeasures Against Shoulder Surfing

Organizational countermeasures against shoulder surfing, especially in public areas, may include the following measures.

21.2.1 Telework Policies

Clear definition of guidelines governing the handling of sensitive information in public environments during telework. Employees are instructed to avoid confidential tasks and to take special precautions to ensure the security and integrity of transmitted data. These policies include precise instructions on the use of secure network connections, encrypted communication channels, and the avoidance of public computers or unsecured networks. Furthermore, employees should be informed about potential risks and made aware of how they can proactively contribute to maintaining the confidentiality of company information while teleworking.

Telework refers to a form of work in which employees perform their professional duties outside the traditional office environment. This can take various forms, including working from home, decentralized work, or virtual work from remote locations. Telework enables employees to work more flexibly and carry out their tasks from different locations, often using IT and digital communication tools. It can offer more flexible working arrangements in terms of both time and location, which can be particularly advantageous in situations such as global pandemics, mobility restrictions, or other special circumstances.

21.2.2 Privacy Screens for Monitors

Privacy screens (**Privacy Screens**) for monitors are devices used with computers to ensure that the content displayed on the screen is visible only to the person directly in front of the monitor.

These filters are designed to prevent unwanted viewing and so-called shoulder surfing by restricting the viewing angle and limiting the visibility of screen content from the side or other perspectives. The use of such privacy screens helps to maintain the confidentiality of information and protect sensitive data from prying eyes.

21.2.3 Training and Awareness

Employee training focused on raising awareness of the risks of shoulder surfing, particularly in environments such as public transportation or crowded public spaces. Training should aim to sharpen employees' awareness of potential threats and enable them to take appropriate protective measures. Especially in public areas, where the risk of shoulder surfing is increased, training should provide clear behavioral guidelines and protective measures.

The focus should also be on training, particularly through the simulation of attacks. The tool of "social engineering pentests," which was already introduced in the White Chapter, can be an effective support in this context.

21.2.4 Policies for Handling IT Assets

Establishing clear policies regarding the handling of IT devices and assets, especially in public areas. Employees should be encouraged to use their devices securely and to adequately protect sensitive information.

21.2.5 Clear-Screen Policies

Establishing clear policies for the clear-screen procedure to ensure that employees regularly clear their screens, especially in public areas or when unauthorized viewers may be present. These policies are intended to ensure that no sensitive information remains visible on screens, thereby minimizing the risk of unauthorized viewing. Employees should be made aware of the importance of consistently following these clear-screen policies to maintain the integrity and confidentiality of displayed information.

These organizational measures are intended to ensure that employees handle sensitive information consciously even in public areas and minimize the risks of shoulder surfing.

21.3   Organizational Countermeasures Against Dumpster Diving

Organizational countermeasures against dumpster diving include various measures aimed at protecting sensitive information from unauthorized access through the searching of waste containers. The following are some organizational countermeasures:

21.3.1   Policy for Secure Disposal of Removable Media

Defining clear policies and procedures for the secure disposal of company documents and materials includes the systematic establishment of structured protocols for handling removable media. As part of this process, employees are instructed to eliminate sensitive information using verifiable methods such as effective destruction techniques or redaction procedures prior to final disposal. These measures are intended to preserve the integrity of confidential company data and minimize potential risks of unauthorized disclosure.

The implementation of this policy is based on the standards of *DIN 66399* for secure disposal. DIN 66399 [1] defines specific classifications and requirements for the destruction of data carriers and thus documents best practices in the field of data security.

Incorporating this standard into the policy ensures compliant and effective implementation of security measures in the context of removable media disposal and helps to ensure the security of sensitive information in accordance with recognized standards.

21.3.2   Training and Awareness

Regular training and awareness programs for employees are intended to educate them about the potential risks of dumpster diving. Within this framework, employees receive clear instructions emphasizing the importance of proper disposal of sensitive information. It is recommended to inform staff about the dangers of dumpster diving and to train them on how to securely dispose of confidential information—both within company premises and in the context of working from home.

Employees should also be prepared to recognize the potential threat of dumpster diving in their daily work. Observations from physical social engineering pentests show that in larger companies and corporations, little attention is often paid to unknown individuals. This increases the risk that an external person could remove a data protection bin, typically found in office corridors, without being noticed, take it to an empty room or restroom, break it open, and extract sensitive paper data.

A security incident can be successfully staged without the bin ever being physically removed from the company building. Therefore, it is crucial to raise global employee awareness of the dangers of dumpster diving and to train them in appropriate security practices.

21.3.3   Use of Shredders

Providing shredders at strategic locations within the company, especially near office areas where confidential documents are regularly handled, serves to secure sensitive information. Employees are encouraged to promptly destroy papers that are no longer needed to ensure the confidentiality and integrity of business-critical data.

This measure is based on the strategic placement of shredders according to a risk-based analysis of work areas where sensitive information is processed. Targeted placement at strategic locations makes it easier for employees to access shredders and thus promotes timely and efficient disposal of documents that are no longer needed.

The recommendation for immediate destruction of unnecessary papers reflects a proactive approach to minimizing potential security gaps.

This call to action is based on the understanding that immediate measures to remove sensitive information minimize the risk of unintentional disclosure and thus contribute to the security of company data.

Integrating these preventive shredding measures into daily workflows helps to raise employee awareness of data protection issues and fosters a proactive approach to handling confidential documents.

21.3.4 Access Control for Waste Areas

Restricting access to the company's waste areas is essential for safeguarding confidential information. This restriction can be implemented through targeted security measures such as high-quality locks, access cards, or surveillance cameras. The objective is to prevent unauthorized access and thereby minimize potential security risks associated with the disposal of confidential documents.

Implementing such security precautions requires a targeted analysis of the waste areas and their potential vulnerabilities to unauthorized access. The selection of appropriate access control mechanisms, such as electronic access cards or biometric identification methods, helps ensure precise and effective access control.

The integration of surveillance cameras not only provides an additional layer of security but also enables comprehensive monitoring of access to waste areas. This supports the identification and tracking of individuals who may attempt to gain unauthorized access.

21.3.5 Use of Secure Containers

Providing secure waste containers that are closed and lockable is a fundamental measure to ensure the protection of sensitive information during the disposal process. This targeted security precaution makes it more difficult to search through waste containers, thereby reducing the likelihood of unauthorized disclosure of confidential data.

The use of closed and lockable waste containers creates a physical barrier against unauthorized access to discarded documents. This significantly increases the security of waste areas and greatly reduces the risk of information leaks.

The lockability of the containers ensures that only authorized personnel have access to the disposed materials.

The strategic placement of these secure containers in key waste areas of the company supports effective integration into daily operations. This enables seamless disposal of confidential documents without compromising the security of company data.

Overall, the use of closed and lockable secure containers contributes to the implementation of a comprehensive security strategy for handling sensitive information and minimizes potential security risks during the disposal process.

21.3.6 Labeling and Classification

Clearly labeling documents and materials to indicate their sensitivity is a fundamental security measure that enables employees to easily identify information requiring special protection prior to disposal. This precise labeling and classification provide transparency regarding the protection needs of company data and promote employee awareness in handling sensitive information.

Labeling is carried out using a clearly structured classification system that explicitly defines the sensitivity and confidentiality of documents. Through this visual marking, employees receive clear guidance on which protective measures must be taken before disposal. This helps minimize human error and raises awareness of the importance of security during disposal.

Implementing a standardized labeling and classification system also enables company-wide standardization in handling confidential information. This ensures consistent and effective enforcement of security policies.

Overall, clear labeling of documents and materials not only enhances security during the disposal process but also strengthens employees' security awareness, fostering a proactive approach to protecting confidential company data.

21.3.7 Contractor Management and Supplier Security

Implementing security standards for external service providers responsible for the disposal of company materials is a key component of effective contractor management. Contractually defined security requirements should be established to ensure that third parties implement appropriate protective measures.

These security standards for external service providers are designed to ensure that all parties involved in the disposal process adhere to uniform security policies. Contractors are required to implement appropriate technical, physical, and organizational measures in the course of their activities to ensure the confidentiality and integrity of disposed company materials.

Contractually defining security requirements enables clear communication of expectations regarding data security to external service providers.

This includes, for example, data encryption, secure transport methods, and secure disposal at the end of the material lifecycle.

Overall, integrating security standards into contractor management helps minimize the risk of security breaches related to the disposal of company materials. This not only enhances data security but also strengthens trust in the overall security of business operations.

In the context of information security, it is essential to emphasize that the term data carrier is not limited to physical paper documents. It also includes logical and electronic removable media, such as hard drives, computers, and USB sticks. Therefore, security policies and measures must address not only traditional paper documents but also digital and electronic storage media. Comprehensive consideration of these various types of data carriers is crucial to ensuring holistic protection of confidential information.

21.4   Organizational Countermeasures Against Tailgating

In the fight against unauthorized entry into secure areas through tailgating—that is, the unauthorized following of authorized individuals—effective organizational countermeasures are of critical importance. Implementing such measures helps ensure the physical security of access points and minimizes the risk of unauthorized entry. The following outlines several proven organizational tactics.

21.4.1 Deployment of Security Personnel

The presence of qualified security personnel at access points is an effective countermeasure against tailgating. Security staff should undergo specific training aimed at identifying suspicious behavior and taking appropriate counteractions. These security professionals play a crucial role in ensuring physical security by not only monitoring legitimate access but also intervening immediately in the event of unauthorized entry to prevent potential harm.

The competence of security personnel extends beyond the targeted verification of authorized access credentials.

By being able to recognize suspicious behavior, they actively contribute to preventing unauthorized entry. Their training also includes the application of appropriate security protocols to respond to potential security threats.

Moreover, qualified and vigilant security personnel serve as a deterrent, as their mere presence has a preventive effect. This creates a security-conscious environment that can discourage potential intruders from attempting unauthorized access.

The comprehensive role of security personnel at access points ensures not only a reactive defense against tailgating but also proactive support through preventive measures and continuous monitoring of the security situation.

21.4.2 Awareness, Education, and Training of Employees

It is essential to educate employees about the potential dangers of tailgating. Training sessions are designed to sharpen employees' awareness of the signs of tailgating and to teach them how to respond appropriately. Strict adherence to security policies is particularly important, as is the immediate reporting of suspicious individuals or incidents. The principle applies: "Personnel with special authorization require special awareness." Individuals with specific authorization to access highly protected areas bear an additional level of responsibility. Therefore, this group requires intensive training to ensure that their privileges cannot be exploited by unauthorized persons.

Training should specifically target the identification of tailgating situations and enable employees to proactively contribute to access security. This includes not only recognizing suspicious behavior but also understanding the importance of promptly reporting such incidents.

Additional awareness and training for specially authorized individuals ensure that they are aware of their responsibilities and can take the necessary steps to prevent unauthorized use of their credentials. This contributes to the integrity of the access control system and minimizes security risks posed by tailgating.

The combination of these organizational countermeasures creates a robust defense against tailgating and helps maintain the integrity of secure areas within organizations.

References

1. Deutsches Institut für Normung (DIN), DIN 66399-1:2012-10 Büro- und Datentechnik – Vernichten von Datenträgern – Teil 1: Grundlagen und Begriffe, pp. 1–8.

Human-based Basic Defense Concept

22

A human-based foundational defense concept against social engineering requires a multi-layered, holistic approach to definition, planning, and implementation [1].

22.1 Security and Error Culture

Various characteristics play a decisive role here, with the fundamental element lying in the understanding of leadership. The responsibilities of an organization's leadership in terms of security engineering are defined not only by the integration of sufficient resources and support, but above all by the insistence on creating an environment in which a security culture can flourish. This also includes an open error culture.

In a healthy security culture, mistakes are not seen as grounds for sanctions, but as opportunities to identify, analyze, and implement measures to close gaps and increase resilience. This requires exemplary behavior from leadership, which establishes a security culture that truly benefits the organization's security.

Implementing this paradigm requires long-term effort, as a people-oriented security culture takes time to be integrated, internalized, and ultimately lived. Psychological aspects are of central importance and should be given special consideration. Later on, for example, we will show how placebo and nocebo effects can influence your employees [2].

Once this paradigm has been successfully implemented, every employee becomes an active sensor, comparable to the military concept of "every soldier is a sensor." Employees act as indispensable detectives within the security concept by actively participating, proactively identifying security gaps, and constructively contributing to compliance with security measures.

This active participation leads to increased resilience at the operational level, in the first line of defense, since no purely technical or physical solution alone is

© The Author(s), under exclusive license to Springer-Verlag GmbH, DE, part of
Springer Nature 2025
E. Koza et al., *Social Engineering and Human Hacking*,
https://doi.org/10.1007/978-3-662-72084-4_22

capable of identifying individual suspects who may be roaming the company to plan acts of sabotage. The analogy of employees becoming sensors illustrates that they uncover infiltrations, vulnerabilities, and anomalies. It is comparable to a network of vigilant participants who can detect and report potential threats at an early stage.

In an empirical study examining the effectiveness of human detection capabilities compared to technological solutions in information security, researchers conducted a simulation procedure. Attack scenarios based on social engineering, spear phishing, and fake Facebook accounts were simulated. The aim was to assess the performance of human users and technical monitoring systems.

The results were remarkable. Of the simulated attacks, only 10% went undetected by users.

In contrast, technical sensors and early warning systems failed to trigger an alert in over 81% of the simulated attacks [3]. This underscores the critical role of human intuition and vigilance in identifying subtle attack methods based on social manipulation.

The conclusion drawn from this study highlights the necessity of a balanced security strategy that not only relies on technological solutions but also strengthens human-centered security. The realization that technological systems may struggle to detect certain manipulative social engineering attack methods emphasizes the importance of a holistic security culture.

This participatory approach not only strengthens the security culture but also creates a dynamic, learning organization that continuously improves. A culture of vigilance is established in which mistakes are not sanctioned but seen as opportunities for improvement. Through this type of involvement, a more resilient and robust organization emerges, one that proactively addresses the challenges of information security and can respond flexibly to changes in the threat landscape.

Overall, we consider the establishment and sustainable integration of a security culture to be an essential foundational defense concept against social engineering. The metaphorical use of the First Line of Defense highlights the role of employees as the first line of defense against security threats.

22.2   Security Training and Exercises

In our human-based foundational defense concept, we also focus on the comprehensive topic of awareness, training, and education [4]. This is not only about raising employee awareness, but about a holistic concept that addresses and implements the three central factors of "knowledge, motivation, and ability."

It is crucial not only to convey these aspects theoretically, but also to operationalize them through concrete exercises and training sessions. A compelling argument for this approach can be derived from the field of emergency drills. Why do the military, security agencies, and fire departments conduct regular exercises? The purpose is to prepare for potential scenarios.

Through repeated exercises, participants not only sharpen their knowledge, but also train their skills and strengthen their willingness to act appropriately in critical situations. The value of exercises is manifested in improved responsiveness, accelerated decision-making, and increased effectiveness in real emergency situations.

Additionally, security exercises provide a practical means to test theoretically developed procedures, defense concepts, communication plans, and alerting protocols for their feasibility. Each exercise reveals new insights that gradually lead to the optimization and actual practical implementation of emergency plans and behavioral protocols.

In addition to validating emergency plans, communication structures and responsibilities can also be specifically trained. Furthermore, repeated security exercises serve to train and optimize responses, particularly the speed of operational processes.

This approach is not only aimed at ensuring that employees are already familiar with the situation in the event of an incident, but also enables confident and active participation. Through these exercises, employees have the opportunity to test their own abilities and, over time, gain confidence, especially when it comes to effectively implementing practical countermeasures. As a result, they do not appear passive, but rather active and self-assured in dealing with potential security threats.

Let us now examine our argumentation in more detail using a practical example. The implementation of vishing training as part of a comprehensive security training program offers several significant advantages, which are based on the previously explained arguments regarding the value of exercises and training.

First, vishing training enables targeted sensitization of employees to a frequently overlooked threat, namely the danger posed by telephone attacks. Focused training empowers employees to recognize potential attacks and respond appropriately, thereby increasing overall security competence.

Second, such training sessions contribute to strengthening the security culture within the company. Employees who have undergone vishing training not only develop an awareness of potential threats, but also become active contributors to collective security resilience.

Third, vishing training allows employees to practice dealing with social engineering tactics used in voice phishing attacks. This knowledge enables employees to recognize skillfully executed manipulations and take appropriate countermeasures.

Fourth, vishing training strengthens employees' ability to act as a human firewall. This human component in the security strategy helps not only to close technological security gaps, but also to minimize human vulnerabilities.

Fifth, vishing training helps reduce security risks by putting defined verification chains to the test in practice. This ensures that both organizational and technical verification processes are evaluated and optimized. Sixth, such training provides both operational staff and those in tactical and strategic roles with a certain level of confidence, thus contributing to the so-called placebo effect.

Overall, vishing training promotes cross-cultural preparedness for real-world scenarios by providing realistic simulations of attack scenarios.

These training sessions not only optimize employees' responsiveness, but also make it possible to review and improve the effectiveness of countermeasures and behavioral protocols.

By integrating vishing training into the training and education program, not only is awareness of voice phishing heightened, but employees' practical skills are also strengthened, enabling them to act appropriately in critical situations.

22.3 Humans as Pillars of Information Security

Information security is a collective endeavor that requires the commitment and participation of all stakeholders: from management to operational units. While information security has traditionally been viewed as a multidisciplinary field, the role of humans as central actors in this security paradigm is increasingly being recognized. Human-centered security does not address the "human factor" as a vulnerability, but rather regards employees as a crucial pillar [5] of information security. Below, we outline why, as a security professional, you should not only understand this perspective but also truly put it into practice [6].

Human behavior in relation to information security is significantly influenced by psychological factors. Considering the placebo and nocebo effects opens up interesting perspectives. The placebo effect refers to a positive change in a person due to expectations, even when no active therapeutic intervention is present. In the context of information security, this means that positive expectations and beliefs among employees can influence their security perceptions and actions.

In contrast, the nocebo effect describes a negative change in condition due to negative expectations, even when no actual threat exists. This effect can occur when employees are confronted with excessively negative scenarios and threats.

In the context of information security, there is thus a risk that employees may adopt a defensive or anxious attitude as a result of an excessive emphasis on risks and threats. This can lead to several problematic consequences.

First, employees may feel overwhelmed by the volume of information about threats and believe they cannot manage all potential risks, which could lead to anxiety and panic.

Second, employees may lose interest in secure behavior if they feel that their efforts toward information security are irrelevant in the face of seemingly insurmountable threats.

Third, the nocebo effect [2] can impair behavioral intention, as employees may be less motivated to exhibit security-conscious behavior due to possible negative expectations. Overall, the nocebo effect can lead employees to feel powerless in the face of threats and to regard their actions regarding information security as irrelevant. Therefore, it is essential to develop strategies to reduce the nocebo effect and reinforce a positive outlook.

This can be achieved by emphasizing positive aspects, empowerment and training, the use of gamification, and positive communication.

By highlighting positive expectations and beliefs, employees can be encouraged to take independent action in information security. Belief in the effectiveness of security measures, combined with a positive security environment, can have a significant impact on employees' actual behavior.

First, positive expectations and beliefs can help employees understand their role as active pillars of information security. If they are convinced that their security knowledge and skills make a decisive contribution to the organization's security, they are more likely to be motivated.

Second, the placebo effect fosters a positive security culture by recognizing employees as valuable participants in strengthening information security. Positive expectations can increase the willingness to engage in security initiatives and influence the perception of security measures as meaningful and effective [2].

Third, positive beliefs can help employees see themselves as confident and capable actors in information security. The belief that their efforts actually contribute to risk reduction and the strengthening of information security leads to a higher behavioral intention to demonstrate security-conscious behavior.

Overall, the placebo effect enables the creation of an environment in which employees perceive their security efforts as effective and meaningful. This can lead to long-term engagement, active participation in security activities, and a positive shift in security awareness. Therefore, integrating the placebo effect into security training and strategies is a meaningful measure to strengthen the role of humans as pillars of information security.

However, promoting security-compliant behavior requires consideration of the dogmatic triangle of "knowledge," "motivation," and "ability" [7].

Knowledge of security practices forms the foundation upon which security professionals can build. However, imparting knowledge alone is not sufficient. Employees' beliefs and attitudes—their "motivation"—are crucial. This is where the placebo effect comes into play. By positively emphasizing security practices, positive expectations can be created that influence behavior [2].

The combination of the placebo effect with knowledge, skills, and behavioral intention underscores the importance of viewing employees as pillars of information security. Positive communication, empowerment through training, and gamification are effective strategies for promoting security-conscious behavior. Positive communication highlights the positive aspects of security-compliant behavior and thus strengthens employees' beliefs.

Training and empowerment enable employees to develop and apply their skills. Gamification uses playful elements to increase employee engagement and achieve long-term learning effects.

After presenting the global basic defense concept with a focus on the "human factor," the following chapters of this book introduce individual practices, tools, and methods against specific types of social engineering attacks. These are intended to help you protect yourself effectively against social engineering attacks, both personally and professionally. It should be emphasized that an active and sustainable defense strategy must be continuously "trained."

References

1. Rohani Rohan, Suree Funilkul, Debajyoti Pal, Wichian Chutimaskul, Understanding of Human Factors in Cybersecurity: A Systematic Literature Review, in: International Conference on Computational Performance Evaluation (ComPE), Shillong, Indien, 2021, pp. 133–140.
2. Erfan Koza, Placebo- versus Nocebo-Effekt. Die Psychologie hinter der Security Awareness, unter: https://www.csoonline.com/de/a/die-psychologie-hinter-der-security-awareness,3681104 (Accessed: 06.01.2024).
3. Ryan Heartfield, George Loukas, Detecting semantic social engineering attacks with the weakest link: Implementation and empirical evaluation of a human-as-a-security-sensor framework, in Computers & Security, Vol. 76, 2018, pp. 101–127.
4. Hussain Aldawood and Geoffrey Skinner, Educating and Raising Awareness on Cyber Security Social Engineering: A Literature Review, IEEE International Conference on Teaching, Assessment, and Learning for Engineering (TALE), Wollongong, NSW, Australien, 2018, pp. 62–68.
5. Esmeralda Kadena, Marsidi Gupi, Human Factors in Cybersecurity: Risks and impacts, Vol. 2. No 2. 2021.
6. Alessandro Pollini, Tiziana C. Callari, Alessandra Tedeschi, Daniele Ruscio, Luca Save, Franco Chiarugi & Davide Guerri, Leveraging human factors in cybersecurity: an integrated methodological approach. Cogn Tech Work 24, 2022, pp. 371–390.
7. Daniel Montaño, Danuta, Kasprzyk, Theory of Reasoned Action, Theory of Planned Behavior, and the Integrated Behavioral Model, im Buch: Health Behavior: Theory, Research, and Practice, 2008.

Human-based Defense Tactics

23

In this chapter, we invite you on an enlightening journey, offering you the opportunity to educate yourself or perhaps gain a deeper understanding of your own behavior. The aim of this presentation is to identify red flags, recognize anomalies, learn about possible defense mechanisms, and thus respond appropriately to potential attack vectors.

By immersing yourself in the world of detection and response, you will be empowered to understand potential threats at an early stage and take effective action.

23.1 Anti-Social Engineering Mindset

To protect yourself both personally and professionally from social engineering—that is, manipulation—it is first useful to define the term manipulation:

Manipulation can generally be understood as the intentional influence or control of the behavior, opinions, or emotions of others, often for one's own benefit or to the detriment of the manipulated person. This influence can occur in various ways and contexts, whether in interpersonal relationships, politics, advertising, or information security. It is important to note that not all forms of influence are negative. In many cases, people attempt to influence others to bring about positive change. For example, in behavioral psychology and medical psychology, the consistent application of positive manipulation is well established. This is particularly the case when encouraging patients to abandon harmful behaviors such as smoking or overeating in favor of healthier habits.

However, the term "manipulation" is often used when influence is exerted in an unethical or deceptive manner, to the detriment of the manipulated individual. To protect against manipulation, it is helpful to cultivate an anti-manipulation mindset. But why a mindset?

The concept of a "mindset" refers to the fundamental beliefs, attitudes, and thought patterns that a person holds regarding their abilities, intelligence, qualities, and potential. Mindset shapes how people approach challenges, deal with success and failure, and behave in various situations.

So why not work on developing an anti-manipulation mindset or, to stay within the context, an anti-social engineering mindset? Our approach is not only to address the symptoms (e.g., recognizing red flags in a phishing email) but also to tackle the root cause. The goal is to understand what makes us susceptible to manipulation and why.

23.1.1 Types of Mindsets

There are two main types of mindsets, as defined by psychologist Carol Dweck (2009) [1]:

Fixed Mindset
Individuals with a fixed mindset believe that their abilities and intelligence are set. They tend to think they are either "good" or "bad" at something and view change as difficult to achieve. This mindset can lead people to avoid challenges in order not to question their existing abilities.

Growth Mindset
In contrast, people with a growth mindset believe that their abilities and intelligence can be improved through effort, learning, and perseverance. They see challenges as opportunities for personal growth, while failure is viewed as a chance to learn. Individuals with a growth mindset are willing to take on new challenges, as they see effort as a path to success.

Mindset not only influences an individual's perception of their own abilities, but also affects interactions with others, responses to setbacks, and the pursuit of goals. It plays a crucial role in various areas of life, such as education, career, sports, and personal development.

It is important to emphasize that mindset is not static and can change over time. Through experience, conscious effort, and self-reflection, people can influence their mindset and develop a growth mindset, which can have a positive impact on their abilities and performance.

If we want to develop an anti-social engineering mindset, it is helpful to first engage with the essential aspects of social engineering manipulation.

23.1.2 Personality Traits

A human hacker will attempt to influence our behavior to their advantage by exposing us to various external stimuli. These stimuli can be conveyed in different ways:

Verbal: through oral communication or presentations
Nonverbal: through facial expressions, gestures, and body language
Paraverbal: relating to how the spoken word is emphasized and its tone of voice (intonation)
Written: for example, via analog/digital letters, notices, flyers, newspapers

Regardless of the type of communication channel, what matters is the reaction that this stimulus elicits in us. To be able to anticipate this, the human hacker needs information about their target (see Sect. 6.4 in the White Chapter).

However, there are also stimuli that work universally. We often believe that each of us is unique and individual, and to some extent, that is certainly true. Nevertheless, typologies of people and personality traits show that we also exhibit behaviors that can be similar to those of others. How can this perspective be explained in more detail?

The universal effectiveness of certain stimuli can be explained by evolutionary and neurocognitive mechanisms.

Throughout evolution, certain behaviors and responses have developed that were advantageous for survival and reproduction. These can serve as the basis for universally effective stimuli.

An example of this is the innate response to faces. Even newborns show a preference for facial stimuli. This makes evolutionary sense, as the ability to recognize faces and interpret emotional expressions is crucial for social interaction and bonding. A social engineer or human hacker could exploit this universal principle by using specific facial cues to evoke trust or sympathy.

Furthermore, research in psychology shows that people tend to behave similarly in certain situations. For instance, there are socially accepted behavioral norms across different cultures. A skilled social engineer could use this knowledge to target behaviors that are considered positive or desirable within a particular social group.

The categorization of personality traits and behaviors into typologies makes it possible to identify certain patterns. Even though every person is an individual, similarities and commonalities in behavior can exist due to personality traits.

Psychological models that describe personality dimensions play a role here. One example is the Five-Factor Model (Big Five Model), which identifies personality traits such as openness, conscientiousness, extraversion, agreeableness, and neuroticism.

In summary, evolutionary mechanisms, social norms, and psychological models illustrate why certain stimuli and behaviors can function universally. This understanding is crucial for explaining social dynamics and the potential influencing factors in social engineering.

There are various models for typologization. Some of these are listed below, with the caveat that this list is not exhaustive and the order is arbitrary. Depending on the target audience and context, specific models can be included to support the learning process. These models provide a foundation for understanding different behavioral patterns and personality traits and for placing them in the context of social engineering.

Myers-Briggs Type Indicator (MBTI)
The Myers-Briggs Type Indicator (MBTI) is a widely used personality assessment tool based on four dichotomous dimensions: extraversion vs. introversion, sensing vs. intuition, thinking vs. feeling, and judging vs. perceiving [2]. The combination of these dimensions results in 16 different personality types.

Big Five Personality Traits
The Big Five Model (also known as the OCEAN model) is based on five fundamental personality traits: openness, conscientiousness, extraversion, agreeableness, and neuroticism. Compared to other models, these traits offer a broader and more comprehensive view of personality [3].

DISC Model
The DISC (or DISG) model divides personality into four main types: dominance (D), influence (I), steadiness (S), and conscientiousness (C). It is frequently used in professional settings for team management and communication [4].

Enneagram
The Enneagram is a symbol with nine points, each representing a different personality type. Each type is described by a specific set of characteristics and allows for a deeper analysis of individual personality structure [5].

Personality Models According to Carl Gustav Jung
Carl Jung [6], a pioneer in psychology, introduced fundamental concepts such as extraversion and introversion, which were later incorporated into models like the MBTI.

His groundbreaking ideas have had a far-reaching impact on the development of various personality models and contribute to a deeper understanding of human personality.

These models offer different approaches to categorizing and describing personality traits. Each model has its own advantages and disadvantages, and their application can vary depending on the context—be it personal development, professional environments, teamwork, or other social settings.

However, the effectiveness and applicability of personality models vary. As a result, there is no general consensus on which model should be considered superior. The choice of an appropriate model depends heavily on the specific requirements of the application context.

If we acknowledge that people exhibit comparable behaviors, it logically follows for the social engineer that topics such as "typology," "understanding people," "behavioral psychology," and similar aspects—including the previously mentioned OSINT (Sect. 6.5 of the White Chapter)—must be part of the essential toolkit for conducting professional social engineering attacks. At the same time, it becomes clear that we must also master this knowledge and these skills in order to develop effective defense strategies against the efforts of human hackers.

23.1.3 Emotional Stimulus-Response Chain in Practice

Do you recall our discussion of the emotional stimulus-response chain in Sect. 4.7 in the White Chapter? We now know that stimuli can be perceived consciously or subconsciously through any of our senses.

These stimuli trigger associations in our memory, even if we believe we are consciously perceiving the stimulus for the first time. It should be noted in advance that every perceived stimulus is also linked to an emotion during interpretation in our brain.

The model of the emotional stimulus-response chain not only provides an explanation or guide for the social engineer on how to skillfully use stimuli to influence the behavior of their targets, but also offers a solution for successfully protecting oneself against social engineering manipulations and, more generally, against manipulation (Fig. 23.1).

Consider the following thought experiment: You are exposed to a stimulus that, through a conditioned reflex, triggers an emotional reaction in you. Depending on the nature of the stimulus, this can lead to stress, causing stress hormones to be released and narrowing your perception. In this emotional state, you then make a decision and respond.

However, it is clear that the first reaction under stress is not always appropriate or suitable. Attackers exploit this fact. Beyond social engineering manipulations,

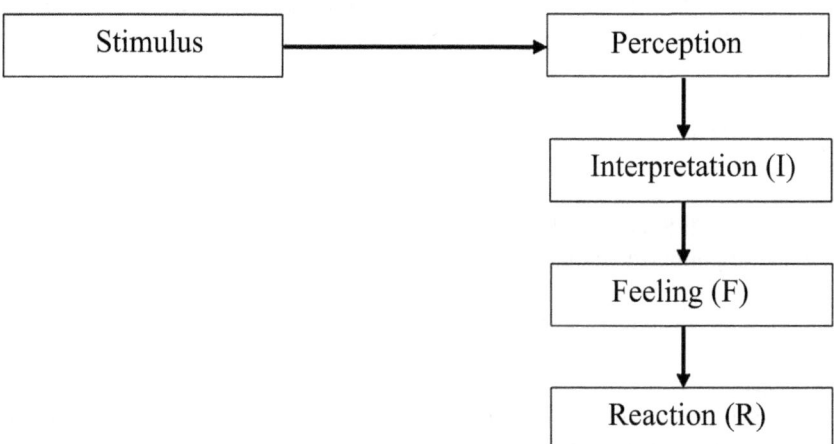

Fig. 23.1 Emotional stimulus-response chain

it can also happen in conversations and negotiations that your counterpart, either consciously or unconsciously, tries to throw you off your objective, rational footing in order to steer the conversation in their favor.

In such situations, we tend to respond to the stimulus—such as a verbal attack—in ways that are often shaped and familiar from our past experiences, including those from childhood (mindset).

Let us now take it a step further and look at this from the attacker's perspective:

One tactic used by social engineers or human hackers is to put their target into a state of high "emotional arousal" in order to hinder, if not completely block, objective, rational, and analytical thinking.

External stimuli that trigger stress in us lead to the production of so-called stress hormones in our brain, including adrenaline, noradrenaline, and cortisol. These hormones affect not only our physical responses, such as preparing the cardiovascular system for fight or flight, but also our perception. As stress levels rise, our field of perception narrows, which can result in tunnel vision, where we perceive our environment as if looking through a tunnel. Tunnel vision is a crucial tool for a social engineer, as it allows them to direct the focus precisely to the perspective that supports their attack and deceives their victims. In this way, they steer our attention and perception toward what they want us to see.

What does tunnel vision look like in practice? Here are some real-world examples:

Attack Type 1: Vishing
Attacker:

Hello, this is Thomas from **IT.** We're having **problems** with an important **security update,** and unfortunately, I can't install it remotely on your system, so we'll need to do this together quickly.

As long as this update isn't **installed on your PC,** there's a **serious security vulnerability** in the entire system, and I need to fix this **problem** now, **before it's too late.**

Target Person
Okay, sure. But can we please do this quickly now?

Attack Type 2: Spear Phishing
The blue-highlighted text passages are used by the social engineer to trigger emotions and appeal to our personal human traits. In this process, two fundamental emotions are specifically targeted (Fig. 23.2).

Curiosity
Targeted stimuli or information are used to arouse the target's curiosity, prompting them to take further action.

Subject: -IMPORTANT INFORMATION-

Dear Mr. Müller,

We would like to inform you that a **WDR** report was **published** yesterday in which we as a company/association etc. were unfortunately given an **unpleasant supporting role**.

Link to the media library: www.mediathek.com

It goes without saying that all **accusations** against our company are unfounded and **legal action** has already been taken.

I would ask you all, should you be approached by the press or other persons in this regard, to absolutely refuse to comment.

Please do not allow yourself to be **unsettled**, we will continue as usual.

Yours sincerely

Name of the management

Signature

Fig. 23.2 Spear phishing link

Fear/Malicious Joy

The social engineer aims to induce fear or provoke malicious joy. These emotions are intended to prompt the target to click on a provided link. To relieve the experienced fear or indulge in malicious joy, all that is required is to click the provided link.

To act more securely in the realm of human hacking and prevent manipulation, it is necessary to protect oneself from emotional reactions triggered by conditioned reflexes, so as not to be externally controlled.

It is not advisable to simply switch off this reflex, as it has accompanied humanity since the dawn of time and protects us from danger—for example, by prompting us to flee or defend ourselves from saber-toothed tigers.

This vital survival reflex is still present today, even though the dangers have changed and now more often take the form of supervisors, unpleasant neighbors, or irate customers.

Nevertheless, there are two effective strategies for successful self-protection:

a) *Know your strengths, weaknesses, and personal traits, as well as the triggers that could prompt you to act under external influence.*

b) *Train yourself to consciously recognize the triggered emotional stimulus-response chain and counter it with an opposing strategy.*

We can practice and achieve this conscious awareness using the strategies outlined below.

23.1.4 Strategy 1: Recognizing and Responding to Stressors

In the context of the section on the typology of personality models in Sect. 23.1.2 of the Yellow Chapter, this approach proves promising for protection against manipulation. Awareness of individual strengths, weaknesses, personal motives, and dominant character traits can serve as an early warning system against social engineering. The key lies in self-reflection, which requires regular alignment between self-perception and external perception. Equally important is the ability to observe actively and to listen attentively, as well as the capacity to minimize one's own **ego**. The significance of this approach lies in the improved ability to recognize risk situations in communication at an early stage and to respond appropriately, based on a deeper self-understanding. By knowing one's individual, pronounced characteristics, potential vulnerabilities to social engineering manipulations can be identified.

In general, many of our traits are to be regarded as positive, as they are often fundamental to (surviving) life in society. However, under stress, there is a risk that positive traits may turn into negative ones. It is evident that in relaxed situations, both we and others would evaluate our traits positively, whereas under stress, negative tendencies can quickly emerge.

Examples of Overcompensation Include
Frugality
Proactively managing financial resources under normal circumstances demonstrates a person's frugality. Under stress, however, there is a tendency to intensify financial restraint, which can potentially be perceived as stinginess.

Determination
In times of stress, highly determined individuals tend to intensify their ambitions excessively. This intensification can reach a point where they overwhelm others in their team or environment.

Dominance
Dominant personalities may tend to act more authoritatively and exert increased control under stress. This tendency can reach a point where they are perceived as excessively domineering.

Steadiness
Individuals who are usually characterized by calmness and composure may, under stress, tend to withdraw or react in a passive-aggressive manner instead of expressing their opinions openly.

Conscientiousness
Under stress, people with high conscientiousness may tend to act in an overly perfectionistic manner and raise their standards. This behavior can lead to increased stress for themselves and those around them, while also impairing their ability to make quick decisions.

Overcompensations can occur to varying degrees and are often situation-dependent. **Stress** affects different individuals in different ways, even if they share similar personality traits. The previous examples illustrate how certain personality traits can be overcompensated in stressful situations. General tendencies and individual reactions to stress can be influenced by numerous factors. The ability to adapt one's behavior in different situations is inherent to humans, provided they do not operate on "autopilot" but act mindfully and with self-reflection. This is where the anti-social-engineering mindset comes into play.

In striving to consciously perceive our personal traits and behaviors as part of our social engineering early warning system, self-reflection is of crucial importance. It is sufficient to look inward and consider what triggers a state of heightened emotional reactivity in us—in other words, which stimuli elicit a conditioned reflex.

For example, if we react to pressure or stress by avoiding or evading, this can be an important insight. It enables us to determine what is essential about this stimulus (stressor) and why it triggers stress in us in the first place.

A thorough analysis of the nature of the stimulus often reveals that, regardless of the situation and context, it is frequently the same stimuli to which we react. In this way, we identify our individual stressors.

A stressor is an external or internal situation that causes or triggers stress. Stressors can arise in various areas of life, including work, relationships, finances, health, or other personal challenges. These factors can differ from person to person, as everyone responds differently to certain situations or circumstances.

To better cope with stressors, it is important to develop effective coping strategies. This may include self-care, social support, time management, problem-solving skills, and the ability to adapt to change.

Dealing with stress often requires a combination of different strategies tailored to the specific demands and causes of the individual stressor.

Individuals who are aware of their stressors have the opportunity, with appropriate training, to recognize them in communication in a timely manner and not be caught off guard by them.

23.1.5 Strategy 2: Mindfulness through Pausing

The second strategy is primarily concerned with **mindfulness.** Here, the focus is on consciously perceiving the feeling of heightened emotional reactivity and the conditioned reflex. This involves a deeper awareness of the emotion triggered by the stimulus just experienced.

The goal is to resist the initial impulse and develop a counter-strategy. Such a counter-strategy can, for example, be structured as follows:

Example
Imagine you are walking through a pedestrian zone and spot a friend about 50 meters ahead, with whom you have not had contact for three weeks. At your last meeting, this friend borrowed €200 from you to buy a pair of shoes, but has not repaid the money to this day. Just as you raise your arm to greet him, take a deep breath, and try to catch his attention from afar, he suddenly turns into a side street and disappears.

Let us now examine together how this cognitive process unfolds in your brain:

Perception of the Stimulus
You perceive the stimulus through your senses, triggered by your friend's behavior.

Cognitive Processing
The perceived stimulus is compared in your brain's "library of knowledge and experience" with your expectations, memories, and prior experiences. The situation is thus interpreted and given meaning.

Emotional Reaction
As a result of this comparison, a feeling arises—presumably a negative one in this example.

Behavioral Response
Only after this emotional evaluation does your response to the experience occur.

Through mindfulness and appropriate training, it is possible to consciously recognize that the conditioned reflex has occurred and that an external action has triggered an emotional response. This enables you to initiate the counter-strategy, interrupt the initial impulse to act, pause, and consciously reflect on the situation you have experienced. In this context, the question arises as to what exactly was perceived in this example and to what extent we can be sure that our perception is not flawed or clouded. The answer to this question is: **mindfulness through pausing** (Fig. 23.3).

Here, we deliberately choose to pause for a moment in order to allow one or, ideally, several alternative interpretations to emerge. On this basis, we develop our strategy for defending against social manipulation (social engineering).

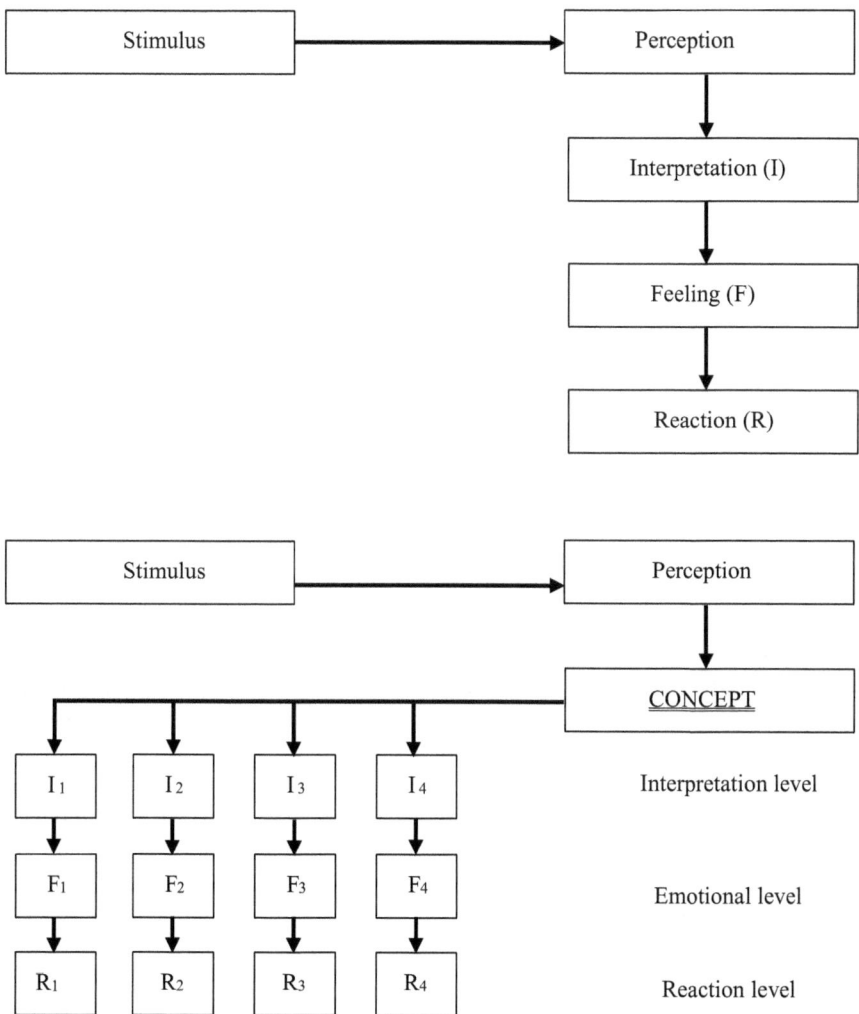

Fig. 23.3 Emotional stimulus-response chain with alternatives

In the present example, alternative interpretations could be considered as follows:

first interpretation (I_1): He disappears and does not return my money,
feeling (F_1): negative,
presumed reaction (R_1): negative,
second interpretation (I_2): Maybe it wasn't him at all?
feeling (F_2): uncertainty,
presumed reaction (R_2): caution and restraint,

third interpretation (I₃): Maybe he didn't see me at all?
feeling (F3): neutral to positive feeling,
presumed reaction (R3): expectant openness,
fourth interpretation (I4): Perhaps there is an ATM in the side street?
feeling (F4): hope or curiosity,
presumed reaction (R4): inquiry about possible ATMs.

By opening up different interpretive possibilities, we broaden our perspectives and create space for alternative responses that are not solely shaped by the initial negative interpretation. This supports a flexible and situation-appropriate social engineering defense strategy.

Those who consciously perceive the conditioned reflex of heightened emotional reactivity resist the first interpretation and thus the initial impulse to act. In this process, the person leaves their "autopilot" mode, regains control over their reactions, and becomes able to make more conscious decisions. Through this awareness, the person avoids potential manipulation attempts.

23.1.6 Strategy 3: Reflection

In the process of training to resist the conditioned reflex, various exercises and reflection methods are available to help identify one's own stressors in interactions with others. Below are some approaches suitable for this type of self-training:

Self-reflection
Regular self-reflection makes it possible to analyze past stressful situations and identify the specific elements of the interaction that may have triggered the stress.

Keeping a Journal
Keeping a journal about interpersonal relationships provides an opportunity to record stressful situations and describe the associated feelings and thoughts.

Seeking Feedback
Obtaining feedback from trusted friends, family members, or colleagues allows for external perspectives to identify patterns or stressors that may not be apparent to oneself.

Emotional Intelligence
Engaging with the concept of emotional intelligence fosters an understanding of one's own emotions, which in turn helps to better recognize stressors.

Stress Management Techniques
Learning various stress management techniques such as breathing exercises, meditation, neuroathletics, or mindfulness helps to reduce stress and improve overall well-being.

Visualizing Scenarios
Consciously visualizing different social scenarios enables the anticipation of potential stressors and the development of coping strategies.

Professional Self-analysis
Reflecting on one's own behavior in professional situations helps to identify certain patterns or relationships that may repeatedly cause stress.

Strengthening Self-Awareness
Developing strong self-awareness by reflecting on strengths, weaknesses, values, and beliefs supports a deeper understanding of one's own identity and helps to better comprehend reactions in interpersonal situations.

Improving Communication
Reflecting on communication habits helps clarify how thoughts and feelings are expressed and enables the identification of potential misunderstandings or conflicts.

Setting Boundaries
Considering whether there are difficulties in setting clear boundaries allows for the identification of stressors that may arise from the violation of personal limits.

Observing Habits
Observing recurring behavioral patterns in interpersonal situations helps to identify habits that could lead to conflicts and to develop strategies for modification.

Exploring Causes Delving deeper to explore the underlying causes of stressors opens up the possibility of identifying past experiences or unconscious beliefs that may trigger certain reactions.

Utilizing Feedback Constructively using feedback from others, especially regarding interpersonal skills, serves as an opportunity for self-reflection.

Implementing a training process to strengthen the ability to resist conditioned reflexes requires a structured approach.

Here are some guidelines and introductory steps for conducting such training:

Introduction
Raise awareness. Begin with an introduction to the importance of mindfulness in interpersonal contexts. Emphasize the role of conditioned reflexes and how they operate in social interactions.
Clarify objectives. Define clear goals for the training. Do you want to strengthen your capacity for self-reflection, identify specific stressors, or develop alternative response strategies?

Training Phases

Initiate self-reflection. Encourage self-reflection by prompting yourself to think about past stressful situations. Specify the analysis of elements that may have triggered the stress.

Introduce journaling. Internalize the importance of keeping a journal for interpersonal relationships. You should record situations in which you felt stressed, along with your feelings and thoughts about them.

Highlight feedback mechanisms. Clarify the role of external feedback. Ask your peers or trusted individuals for feedback on your behavior in social situations.

Understand emotional intelligence. Engage with the concept of emotional intelligence. Identifying and understanding your own emotions are key elements in better recognizing stressors.

Practice stress management techniques. Choose an appropriate mix of stress management techniques such as breathing exercises, meditation, and mindfulness.

Visualize scenarios. Practice exercises in which you mentally rehearse social scenarios and pay attention to your reactions. The goal is to anticipate potential stressors and develop coping strategies.

Encourage professional self-analysis. Motivate yourself to reflect on professional situations and identify patterns or relationships that may have repeatedly caused stress.

Foster self-awareness. Strengthen your self-awareness by addressing your own strengths, weaknesses, values, and beliefs. A deeper understanding of your identity helps to comprehend reactions in interpersonal situations.

Address communication and boundaries. Reflect on communication habits and the ability to set clear boundaries. Determine how these factors can influence stress in social interactions.

Explore habits and causes. Pay attention to recurring behavioral patterns in social situations and encourage yourself to explore the underlying causes of stressors.

Integrate feedback. Recognize the importance of constructive use of feedback. This provides opportunities for self-reflection, especially regarding interpersonal skills.

Conclusion

Summary and outlook. Conclude the training with a summary of the insights gained and an outlook on the ongoing development of the skills learned. Encourage yourself to maintain continuous self-reflection and mindfulness in dealing with social stressors.

Before we continue our journey with further strategies, we would also like to share the following: In this section, we deepen our understanding and expand our toolkit to overcome the conditioned reflex in the context of social interactions. Through targeted methods and exercises, we will further sharpen your abilities in self-reflection and stress management.

However, self-reflection is a powerful process that is often associated with enlightenment and personal growth. It is important to understand, though, that this path can also involve **uncomfortable phases**. In fact, nothing can be more painful than genuine self-knowledge, which confronts us with the unvarnished facets of our own personality.

Enlightening Phase
Self-reflection enables deep insights into our behavior, motives, and interpersonal relationships. In this enlightening phase, we recognize our strengths, weaknesses, and values more clearly. This understanding can serve as a catalyst for personal growth and empower us to make more conscious decisions.

The Challenges of Self-Knowledge
However, self-knowledge is often accompanied by a phase of discomfort. Recognizing habits we might have preferred to ignore and confronting aspects of our personality that we perceive as less positive can be painful. It takes courage to face our own shadow sides.

Overcoming Resistance
Self-reflection can trigger resistance and inner conflict. It is important to understand that these challenges are part of the process. The path to self-knowledge is not a linear journey, but a cyclical process of growth and learning. The discomfort that accompanies self-knowledge is often a precursor to personal transformation.

The Value of Discomfort
Although it may initially be painful to acknowledge discomfort, there is also great opportunity in doing so. The willingness to face our weaknesses enables us to work on them and continue to develop. It opens the door to deeper self-acceptance and a more authentic way of life.

Self-reflection, even when accompanied by temporary discomfort, is a key to personal growth. By overcoming challenges and embracing the enlightenment that comes from self-knowledge, we can establish a deeper connection with ourselves and lead a more fulfilling life. As a side effect, we can also defend ourselves more effectively against social engineering.

23.1.7 Strategy 4: Identifying Social Triggers

Given the focus on social manipulation in this book on social engineering, this section is of particular importance. The aim is to identify the specific social triggers that can cause stress on an individual level. In quiet moments, readers should reflect inwardly to recognize social situations or behaviors of others that could potentially trigger stress, looking for recurring patterns in the process.

Mentally reviewing past situations and recording thoughts and feelings can help enable deeper personal reflection. In the context of social triggers, the following points may be relevant:

Lack of Recognition
The feeling of not being adequately recognized or appreciated can cause stress.

Conflicts and Disputes
Conflicts on a professional or personal level can trigger stress, as they disrupt the need for harmony.

Injustice
Witnessing or experiencing actions perceived as unjust can provoke stress.

Lack of Communication
Unclear or ineffective communication can create uncertainty and stress.

Lack of Autonomy
The feeling that personal freedom of choice is restricted can be burdensome.

Negative Evaluation or Criticism
Criticism or negative evaluations can trigger stress or insecurity.

Uncertainty About Expectations
The absence of clear expectations or unclear roles in social interactions can cause uncertainty.

Social Rejection or Isolation
Feelings of rejection or social isolation can provoke strong emotional reactions and stress.

Violation of Personal Boundaries
Overstepping personal boundaries can cause stress.

Lack of Cooperation
Difficulties in collaborating with others, whether in a professional or personal context, can trigger stress.

The exercises presented in this chapter should be understood as an ongoing process that is crucial for personal growth, the development of healthy interpersonal relationships, and the cultivation of an effective anti-social-engineering mindset.

Implementing these exercises requires time, patience, and above all, honesty with oneself. Seeking professional support, whether through coaching or counseling, can help to delve deeper into personal stressors and develop concrete coping strategies.

This approach is essential for unlocking the full potential of self-reflection and effecting lasting changes in thinking and behavior.

23.1.8 Strategy 5: Practice Saying "No"

Social engineers are often able to identify potential vulnerabilities in their targets, whether through OSINT or by gradually approaching the intended victim.

Sometimes, social engineers get lucky if their attack scenario catches the victim off guard or if the chosen approach simply fits the context.

Despite self-reflection, personal development, and continuous training of the anti-social-engineering mindset, there are certain traits and behaviors that are difficult or even impossible to change.

A particularly successful approach in social engineering is exploiting helpfulness. Helpfulness is an important social trait. However, this book does not aim to encourage readers to suppress their helpfulness just to protect themselves from manipulation. The mindset can also be supportive here. If you know that you find it difficult to refuse a request for help, you can ask yourself whether the person is truly in need and whether you are the right person to provide assistance.

Consider whether you can provide help that enables self-help.

Another aspect is practicing the ability to say no.

You can use simple everyday situations to practice saying no. Learn from positive experiences that saying no does not necessarily have negative consequences. Train yourself to set clear boundaries by, for example, politely but firmly declining sales pitches for products you are not interested in. Respond to fundraisers with attention, listen to their arguments, and learn to say no appropriately in such situations—a useful skill, especially in the context of potential social manipulation.

When practicing saying no, it is essential to consciously experience how any potentially negative feelings develop when you say no. Encourage yourself to observe and examine how your feelings change as you use this skill more frequently.

Consciously reflect on the actual consequences that saying no has had for you.

Reflect on whether the anticipated negative outcomes actually occurred, or whether your well-being and self-confidence have improved as a result of setting clear boundaries. This reflective approach is crucial for personal development and for strengthening your ability to say no appropriately.

It is evident not only with our muscles but also with our brains that training through repetition plays a crucial role.

Each of us is equipped with individual programs and routines that cannot be changed at the push of a button—especially not under stress.

Neuroplasticity, the brain's ability to adapt and change, is a key aspect to consider. Established neural pathways and thought patterns can be modified through continuous training. However, this modification requires time and perseverance.

In stressful situations, we often revert to automated patterns of thinking and behavior that are deeply embedded in our neural networks. Therefore, it is crucial to initiate a change in these patterns through targeted mental training.

Various methods, such as cognitive exercises, mindfulness training, or mental coaching, can help create new neural connections and overcome existing patterns. A conscious approach to neuroplasticity enables the development of new ways of thinking and acting, even under stress.

23.1.9 Strategy 6: Continuity Through Training

The effectiveness of the approaches described above is often linked to regular training and repetition. Through continuous practice, acquired skills can remain active and effective, even over extended periods.

The practice of regular training and exercises not only initiates change but also anchors new ways of thinking and behavior patterns in the brain. Just as physical fitness requires ongoing care and effort, so too does mental agility. Integrating newly acquired knowledge into daily life and applying it regularly enables sustainable change.

Findings from neuroplasticity thus underscore the importance of systematic and repeated training to foster mental flexibility and adaptability. This is especially relevant in the context of social engineering, as it concerns resistance to manipulation and the development of a strong anti-social-engineering mindset.

23.1.10 Strategy 7: Understanding Reciprocity

In addition to widespread helpfulness, social engineers can draw on other universally applicable approaches, with the psychological principle of reciprocity (Sect. 4.14 in the White Chapter) playing a particularly prominent role.

Reciprocity, as the principle of mutual exchange, describes the tendency of people to respond to actions or gestures they receive in a similar manner. When someone does us a favor, we feel obliged to return the favor. This principle is deeply rooted in culture and plays a crucial role in social relationships, as it promotes the exchange of resources, assistance, and support.

In the context of social engineering, an attacker can exploit reciprocity, for example by offering gifts or favors.

Small actions can make the victim feel obliged to reciprocate. The attacker may share information to build trust and prompt the victim to disclose information in return. Cooperative behavior can trigger reciprocity by encouraging the victim to act cooperatively as well.

To protect yourself against such attacks, it is necessary to maintain a healthy skepticism toward unknown individuals or requests.

Unexpected gifts, favors, or information should be critically examined. Kindness is important, but skepticism helps guard against potential risks. It is essential to set clear personal and professional boundaries and to be prepared to say "no" if something seems questionable.

Verifying information from unknown sources before responding is also an effective protective measure. When claims are made about an organization, independent verification is especially important.

23.1.11 Strategy 8: Avoiding the Halo Effect

The halo effect describes the tendency for positive evaluations or impressions in one area to lead to a generally positive perception of a person. This means that people tend to infer additional, as yet unknown, positive traits from known positive characteristics of a person.

For example, a person's physical attractiveness may lead to other qualities, such as intelligence or social skills, being rated positively, even though there is no direct connection.

A possible attack vector for a social engineer is to deliberately exploit the halo effect to gain trust and cooperation. This can be achieved by feigning expertise in a particular field or claiming to hold a high position, thereby automatically generating trust. By displaying positive emotions such as friendliness and helpfulness, the social engineer can transfer these to other aspects of their personality or intentions.

A professional outward appearance further reinforces the halo effect, as people tend to infer other positive qualities from attractiveness or professionalism. By pretending to share common interests or values, the social engineer can establish a connection and use the halo effect to create positive associations.

To protect yourself against such attacks, it is important to question positive impressions and verify verifiable facts. Checking background information and references of supposed experts is crucial. Setting clear personal and professional boundaries and not being deceived by appearances or friendly behavior are also critical protective measures.

This underscores the importance of mindfulness, critical thinking, and awareness that the halo effect can be used by social engineers to create a trustworthy façade. Regular training and reinforcement of acquired knowledge help ensure that this awareness remains active and effective, even over longer periods.

To protect against the halo effect in the context of social engineering, the following measures can be taken:

Questioning Impressions
It is essential to question positive impressions and not automatically infer all other qualities of a person from known positive traits. Consciously challenging assumptions helps to make more realistic assessments.

Verification of Background Information
Verify the background information and references of individuals who present themselves as experts or authorities. This is particularly important to ensure that positive associations are based on verifiable facts.

Set Clear Personal and Professional Boundaries
It is advisable to set clear boundaries in personal and professional relationships. Be prepared to say "no" if something does not seem right, and do not be misled by appearances or friendly behavior.

Mindfulness and Critical Thinking
Cultivate mindfulness and critical thinking in social interactions. This includes consciously examining emotions, thoughts, and assumptions to protect yourself from unconscious influences.

Self-Reflection
Regularly reflect on your own thought patterns and assumptions. Being aware of personal biases and tendencies helps to recognize the halo effect and actively counteract it.

Question Your Own Beliefs and Values
Take time to review your own beliefs and values. Conscious self-reflection enables you to better resist external influences.

By applying these measures, organizations and individuals can develop effective strategies to defend against the potentially misleading effects of the halo effect and ensure a higher level of security in social interactions.

Having presented the basic defense concepts as well as individual strategies for countering social engineering attacks, we now turn to the specific types of attacks. Here, we present effective human-centered lines of defense to help you activate your human firewall in a targeted manner for each type of attack.

23.2 Human-Based Defense Tactics Against BEC and Types of Phishing

Identifying BEC, CEO fraud, and phishing emails requires a fundamental level of caution when handling emails and other communication channels. When analyzing an email, it is advisable to calmly consider the following questions:

Anomaly Detection 1: Red Flag "Pressure – Urgency – Deviation"
Does the content of the email, especially through its wording, attempt to suggest a need for action, possibly even an urgent and imperative one? Does the email use certain phrases to create pressure, such as:

"If you do not act now/do XY, then …"?

Anomaly Detection 2: Red Flag "Link Compulsion"

Does the email contain links or attached files that you are "required" to open?

Hover your mouse pointer over the link – **without clicking on it.** *This procedure is also known as hovering or mouseover.*

The term hovering or mouseover comes from English and means to float or hover. In the context of computers and user interfaces, hovering refers to placing the mouse pointer over an element, such as a link, without clicking it. This action often triggers a specific response, such as displaying a tooltip with additional information or, in the case of links, showing the target address in the browser's status bar. In relation to phishing emails, the term is used to indicate that by hovering the mouse pointer over a link without clicking it, a different website may be revealed than what the visible link text suggests. This can be an indication of fraudulent intent.

Anomaly Detection 3: Red Flag "Input Compulsion"

Are you being asked to disclose confidential information such as PINs, TANs, passwords, or bank details, or to perform sensitive actions, such as making transfers?

Anomaly Detection 4: Red Flag "Error Deviation"

Does the email contain spelling mistakes or linguistic inconsistencies?

For example, there could be an inappropriate level of formality (too distant and formal/too casual) or an impersonal salutation such as "Dear Customer …".

Anomaly Detection 5: Red Flag "Time Deviation"

Is the time the email was received unusual?

Anomaly Detection 6: Red Flag "Sender Deviation"

What email address is actually behind the sender's name? Is it consistent with the context of the email and the sender's name?

In fraudulent emails, often only a sender name is displayed in the standard view of an email instead of the actual email address—just as is the case with contacts you have already saved in your email program under a specific name.

Example

At first, you only see "Amazon Customer Service" as the sender's name. However, if you click on the name in the email program's header or display more details, you will see that the name "Amazon Customer Service" actually hides the email address "oix902bjk@gmail.com". This inconsistency is a strong indication that the email is fraudulent.

It can be helpful to copy and paste the sender's address into a Word document. You will notice that the email identifier or alias "Amazon Customer Service" is resolved, and the paste function usually reveals the actual sender address: "oix902bjk@gmail.com".

It is also important to note that this line of reasoning must not be applied in reverse. This means that an apparently plausible sender address such as "kunden-service@amazon.de" is not, by itself, a guarantee that an email is not a phishing attempt.

The attacker could still have used email spoofing or registered a domain that closely resembles the original domain:

e.g.
"service@beispielunternehmen-gmbh.de"
instead of
service@beispielunternehmen.de.

Anomaly Detection 7: Red Flag "Procedure Deviation"

Is there an attempt to bypass standard processes, established procedures, or even required approvals?

For example, a customer might try to request personal data via email instead of using the designated customer portal. Similarly, a bank employee might ask you to log in to an online banking portal via a specific link, rather than using the familiar login page you normally access through your browser.

Anomaly Detection 8: Red Flag "Context Anomaly"

Are there inconsistencies in the context of the email, or does the content deviate from the norm?

Or does the message content significantly differ from standard or expected parameters?

An example of a contextual inconsistency in an email would be receiving an alleged invoice from a company with which you have no business relationship. In this case, the context of the email does not make sense, as there has been no prior transaction or interaction with the named company.

An example of content deviating from the norm would be receiving an email from your bank urgently requesting confidential information, even though your bank typically does not make such requests by email. Here, the content deviates from the bank's usual procedures and may indicate fraudulent intent.

If something about an email gives you a bad gut feeling, even if it is not covered by the points listed above, it is important to trust your instincts. Even if you cannot pinpoint exactly what seems off about an email, you should still trust your intuition and proceed with caution.

Once you have classified an email as potentially suspicious, you can take the following steps:

Defense Strategy 1: Pause

As a general rule: Avoid taking any action or disclosing information, even if the email tries to create a sense of urgency. Security is the top priority. Take a moment, breathe deeply, and do not let yourself be influenced by emotional pressure tactics. Remember the emotional stimulus-response chain and try to use the pause to consider possible interpretations and actions. Avoid impulsive reactions and take your time to make rational decisions.

Defense Strategy 2: Wait for the Results of the Clarification Phase

Instead, it is advisable to first verify the authenticity of the email and the sender through another channel before taking any action. Avoid clicking on links, opening attachments, or disclosing information until you are sure that the sender exists and the email actually originated from them. Keep in mind that even with an email that appears legitimate, caution is warranted, and sensitive information should not be disclosed if there is any doubt.

Here are some concrete suggestions on how you can verify authenticity:

Verification Tactic 1: Callback Method

If the sender is already known to you, try to reach them through another communication channel you are familiar with, such as by phone.

Verification Tactic 2: Point-of-Contact Method

If, for example, the sender claims to be a new employee of a customer, a business partner, your bank, or your company's IT department, you could first get in touch again with your previous contact person in the organization.

Verification Tactic 3: Manual Method

If no other contact person is available, try reaching out to the company via its official contact point. You can do this by manually searching for the sender's company using a search engine and contacting the company using the contact details provided there. Refer to the received email and the sender when making your inquiry.

Good to know: Email spoofing only works in one direction. This means that if an attacker uses email spoofing to simulate the email address of a known sender, your reply will be sent to the spoofed email address, i.e., to the actual owner of the manipulated address.

Example

Attacker (A) sends a spear-phishing email to the target (B), pretending to be person (C) by using email spoofing.

If person (B) replies to this email, the reply will be sent to the actual email address of person (C).

However, this only works with spoofing.

If an attacker (A) sends a spear-phishing email and uses email spoofing to impersonate a trusted person (C), and the victim (B) replies to this email, the reply will actually be sent to the real email address of person C. This is because email spoofing fakes the sender's identity in this specific situation. However, it should be noted that this only applies in the case of spoofing.

Counterexample

If the attacker (A) has registered their own domain and does not use technical spoofing but instead uses layout spoofing, replies will also go to the attacker, since they own the email address.

Therefore, it is crucial not only to pay attention to the spoofing status, but also to perform other checks to ensure the legitimacy of an email.

Reassurance Tactic 4: IT Method

If you receive an email classified as suspicious in a business context, it is advisable to contact the IT department immediately and report the suspicious email. Especially if you receive file attachments, you should submit them to IT for inspection and only release the file for further processing after the IT department has confirmed its correctness and authenticity. It is essential to always act with the mindset that "prevention is better than cure."

Reassurance Tactic 5: Security Question Method

To avoid redundancy, we refer at this point to Sect. 19.1.5 of the Yellow Chapter, where we introduced the verification chain using security questions.

All tactics and strategies for identifying and defending against phishing types mentioned in this section can be seamlessly applied to the attack type vishing. The principles of vigilance, critical scrutiny, and caution apply equally when confronted with suspicious phone calls. Be sure to question unexpected calls, verify information, and, in case of uncertainty, ask additional security questions to protect yourself from potential vishing attacks.

23.3   Human-based Defense Tactics Against Shoulder Surfing

Detecting or identifying shoulder surfing requires attention and sensitivity to unusual behavior in your surroundings. Detection becomes even more difficult when attackers operate from a distance and use technical aids such as high-resolution cameras. Attackers also have the ability to move, which further complicates identification, as they essentially represent a "moving target." Nevertheless, there are some signs that may indicate possible shoulder surfing attacks:

Anomaly Detection 1: Red Flag "Behavioral Irregularity"

Observe people in your vicinity. Pay attention to individuals who remain in your immediate area longer than usual without an obvious reason.

You can also draw on insights from proxemics for this purpose.

Proxemics refers to the study of spatial distance between individuals in various social contexts and how these distances can vary culturally and individually. The term was coined by anthropologist Edward T. Hall [7] and helps to understand how people perceive and use the space around them.

In relation to shoulder surfing and the initiation of such activities, proxemics can be specified as follows:

Intimate Zone (0–45 cm) In this zone, which is normally reserved for very close relationships, unwanted intrusion by a stranger would be considered extremely conspicuous. If someone tries to enter this intimate zone to read information from a screen, it violates not only proxemics but also personal privacy.

Personal Zone (45 cm–1.2 m) Within this distance, normal social interactions can already take place. However, if a person comes unreasonably close in a situation that does not require closer interaction, this could indicate an attempt to view your screen area.

Social Zone (1.2–3.6 m) Even at a social distance, conspicuous behavior can occur. If someone in a public space deliberately moves close to another person to observe their activities, this is perceived as disruptive not only through proxemics but also according to normal social expectations.

Proxemics thus provides a framework for understanding appropriate behavior in different spatial contexts. Deviations from these expectations can serve as warning signs for possible shoulder surfing activities.

Anomaly Detection 2: Red Flag "Repetitive Irregularity"
If you feel that someone repeatedly stares at your screen or your inputs, this could be an indication of shoulder surfing—especially if this person shows no apparent interest in other activities in the area.

Anomaly Detection 3: Red Flag "Gaze Irregularity"
Individuals engaging in shoulder surfing tend to deliberately direct their gaze toward the screen or input keyboard. Watch for suspicious head movements or unnatural body posture.

Anomaly Detection 4: Red Flag "Movement Irregularity"
If you notice that someone reacts quickly to your movements, especially when you are entering sensitive information, this may indicate that they are trying to observe your inputs.

Anomaly Detection 5: Red Flag "Interest Irregularity"
Individuals who show disproportionate interest in your screen content or keyboard inputs may be attempting to intercept information.

In addition to the possibility of anomaly detection, there are also defense strategies that can be defined as follows:

Defense Strategy 1: Developing a Security Mindset
It is crucial to continuously work on developing security awareness. Especially in public environments, one should be aware of the potential risk of becoming a

victim of shoulder surfing. Awareness of your surroundings and vigilance toward possible threats are key aspects of this mindset. It is advisable to familiarize yourself with the basics and steps of the OODA loop from Sect. 8.1 of the White Chapter. This enables you to stay one step ahead of attackers both cognitively and physically.

Defense Strategy 2: Conscious Stress Management
Awareness of your own stress level plays a central role in protecting against shoulder surfing. By actively paying attention to how stress can affect perception, you can better assess when you are particularly susceptible to distractions or inattentive behavior. Conscious reflection on stress helps to increase the level of security.

Another important aspect is the effective management of work-related stress or high workload. Here, the ability to regulate stress plays a central role.

It is now also known that stress can cloud or even impair perception. Impaired perception increases the risk of security threats, especially in public environments. Therefore, it is crucial to take measures to manage stress effectively. Resilience training can help to better cope with stress and develop inner stability.

At the same time, identifying and eliminating the causes of stress is an effective strategy for establishing a sustainable approach in the sense of an anti-social engineering mindset in the long term. A balanced combination of both approaches could prove particularly effective.

This dual strategy integrates psychological aspects, which, when combined with organizational and technical aspects, can provide comprehensive protection against shoulder surfing.

23.4   Human-Based Defense Tactics Against Tailgating

Let us begin this section with a striking statement:

> *Smoking can put your information security at risk.*

Imagine you are enjoying a short smoking break outside your building. Suddenly, an attractive and seemingly friendly person joins you—apparently harmless. Yet here lies an underestimated threat to information security: tailgating. The seemingly innocuous cigarette break could invite uninvited guests to seek unauthorized access to sensitive areas. Smoking not only poses a health risk, but can also endanger the security of your information. In the following section, we will take a closer look at this seemingly trivial threat and discuss ways to protect yourself against it. Detecting or identifying tailgating is a challenge. Below, we list some signs that may indicate possible tailgating attacks:

Anomaly Detection 1: Red Flag "Accompanying Anomaly"
The sudden appearance of an unknown person attempting to accompany you or another authorized employee may indicate tailgating. This accompaniment is usually nonverbal, as verbal communication could potentially reveal the attacker's true identity.

Anomaly Detection 2: Red Flag "Attempted Courtesy Entry"
Tailgaters may try to exploit the behavior of authorized employees by posing as colleagues or delivery personnel. Unauthorized "courtesy entries" should serve as a warning sign.

Anomaly Detection 3: Red Flag "Unexpected Pressure"
Unauthorized individuals may attempt to exert pressure, such as time pressure, to persuade an authorized employee to escort them through security checkpoints. An exemplary scenario might look as follows:

An unauthorized person poses as a member of a TÜV inspection team and claims to need to perform urgent maintenance on the air conditioning system due to reported critical error messages. To increase the pressure, the intruder points out possible severe consequences such as building damage and significant financial losses. Arguing that immediate action is essential, he tries to persuade the employee to escort him through the access control points without the usual security checks.

Anomaly Detection 4: Red Flag "Responsibility Trap"
In this sophisticated scenario, two tailgaters work as a team to gain access to a building. Tailgater 1 disguises himself as a Deutsche Telekom service technician and claims to have an appointment to service the communications equipment. The responsible security staff deny entry due to missing verification. At this point, Tailgater 2 appears, dressed like the in-house security staff (If you are wondering how he is able to imitate the in-house staff: The answer is very simple—through OSINT).

Tailgater 2 calls out from a distance, claiming to be expecting the supposed Telekom technician, and explains that there was merely an internal oversight in registering the appointment. Tailgater 2 further states:

I will accompany the Telekom colleague through the building—no problem.

The story is convincing, leading the security staff to relent and allowing Tailgater 1 to enter the building together with Tailgater 2 without hindrance.

This illustrates the effective strategy of shifting responsibility by security personnel. In this sophisticated scenario, two tailgaters work as a team to gain access to a building. Tailgater 1 disguises himself as a Deutsche Telekom service technician and claims to have an appointment to service the communications equipment. Due to missing verification, entry is denied. Here, the clever tactic of shifting responsibility by the security staff becomes apparent. Tailgater 2 assumes the role of an internal colleague and builds trust by claiming to have been expecting him and pointing to an internal oversight. The security staff give in by transferring the responsibility for the decision to the supposed internal colleague. By skillfully redirecting responsibility, the vigilance of the security staff is bypassed and the tailgaters are able to successfully gain access to the building.

Defense Strategy: "Zero-Trust Strategy"
A memorable social engineering maxim that has proven especially effective in this context:

> *Any employee can be a tailgater, but not every tailgater is an employee.*

The zero-trust philosophy in dealing with tailgating is based on a fundamental distrust of everyone, regardless of their apparent trustworthiness. This strategy, which aims to minimize unauthorized access, can also be extended to human interactions:

Pause and Verify
Employees should always pause if unknown individuals follow them or attempt to enter secure areas together with them. The basic principle is: everyone must authenticate themselves before trust is granted.

Take Time for Verification
The zero-trust approach requires thorough verification of identity, regardless of claimed appointments or tasks. Take the time to ensure that the person is indeed who they claim to be.

Trust No One Unconditionally
Anyone requesting access to sensitive areas must provide identification and should not be regarded as trustworthy by default. Trust is not automatically granted based on uniforms, badges, or other external features. This is especially relevant for partner companies such as cleaning services or similar firms, whose personnel deployment is characterized by volatility and high turnover rates.

Adopt a Pessimistic Perspective
Employees should be aware that tailgaters can use various tactics to gain trust. Emphasize the idea that every employee can potentially act as a sensor, and encourage a healthy degree of skepticism.

Training for Zero-Trust Behavior
Implement training programs that promote zero-trust behavior and prepare employees to recognize unauthorized access attempts.

Raise awareness of the fact that not everyone seeking access has the best intentions.

Fostering a Culture of Healthy Distrust

A culture of healthy distrust does not mean creating a negative work environment, but rather encouraging employees to proactively verify and question in order to ensure security.

Fostering a culture of healthy distrust is central to strengthening physical security in an organizational context. This culture involves proactive analysis of situations and the identification of potential irregularities by employees. By encouraging critical questioning of unknown individuals or suspicious activities, employees actively contribute to security without creating a negative work environment. Questioning should be seen as a strength, and employees should be encouraged to actively inquire in situations with intuitive or perceived irregularities. This culture is based on the principle of shared responsibility, making employees aware that their involvement is crucial to the security of the entire organization. Training and awareness are essential elements to sensitize employees to the importance of their role in physical security and to equip them with the skills to recognize suspicious activities and respond appropriately. This approach not only enhances security but also creates a positive and collaborative atmosphere within the company.

References

1. Carol Dweck, Selbstbild: Wie unser Denken Erfolge oder Niederlagen bewirkt, 2009.
2. Isabell Briggs Myers, Peter, B. Myers Gifts, Differing: Understanding Personality Type—The original book behind the Myers-Briggs Type Indicator (MBTI) test, Davies-Black, Neue Ausgabe der 2. Edition, 2010.
3. Robert R. McCrae, Paul T. Costa Ir., Personality in Adulthood. A Five-Factor Theory Perspective, The Guilford Press, 2. Auflage, 2003.
4. William Moulton Marston, Emotions of Normal People, Read & Co. Science, (Original 1928), 2014.
5. Wolfgang W. Liebelt, Enneas: Das Enneagramm Gurdjieffs, BoD, Books on Demand, 2017.
6. Carl Gustav Jung, Psychologische Typen, 1921, im Archiv 2020: https://archive.org/details/Psychologische_Typen (Accessed: 03.01.2024).
7. Edward T. Hall, 1976, Beyond Culture, unter: https://monoskop.org/images/6/60/Hall_Edward_T_Beyond_Culture.pdf (Accessed: 03.01.2024).

Part IV
Red Chapter: Design an Attack

Scenario-based Red Teaming

24

By gamifying the learning process, especially when it comes to understanding an attacker's mindset, an efficient and effective approach is chosen. By getting to know the adversary better, one can take targeted action against them and develop protective mechanisms to fend off potential attacks. The playful approach makes it possible to convey complex topics in an illustrative way and to achieve a deep engagement with the content.

Now we come to our actual game concept.

We playfully take on the role of an attacker in order to target a fictional company using manipulation techniques and social engineering methods we have previously learned. Our goal is to penetrate the company, infiltrate it, and ultimately compromise it by leaving behind a so-called ransom note. In doing so, we deliberately employ specific tactics and strategies to exploit the company's vulnerabilities and gain access to sensitive information or systems.

A ransom note (also known as a blackmail letter) is a message or notification sent by cybercriminals to their victims after compromising their systems or data. Typically, this message is used to inform the victim about the successful encryption or theft of their data and to demand a ransom payment in order to release the data or restore the system. The ransom note usually contains instructions and information on how the victim can pay the demanded ransom, often in the form of cryptocurrencies such as Bitcoin. The note may also include threats, such as permanent loss of access to the data or public disclosure of stolen information if the ransom is not paid.

To bring our playful idea to life, we have developed the red-teaming game "Design an Attack" for you. "Design an Attack" enables you to better understand and directly apply what you have learned so far. You will take on the exciting role of the attacker and have the opportunity to experience the motto "know your enemy" firsthand. In the process, you will learn how your potential adversaries think, act, and operate.

© The Author(s), under exclusive license to Springer-Verlag GmbH, DE, part of
Springer Nature 2025
E. Koza et al., *Social Engineering and Human Hacking*,
https://doi.org/10.1007/978-3-662-72084-4_24

The game offers you valuable insights into how the opposing side operates and helps you further deepen your knowledge and skills. By immersing yourself in the attacker's mindset, you gain valuable insights that will help you strengthen your defense strategies and better protect your systems.

"Design an Attack" is a simple way to expand your understanding in a playful manner and improve your skills in the field of information security.

However, before you can really get started, we will guide you through a trial run so that you can familiarize yourself with the game rules. Once you have successfully completed this trial run, you will receive your own individual scenario and can immediately dive in.

24.1 Test Scenario

The following game objectives should be achieved:

Combine the given information and cards. Proceed as follows in a two-stage attack wave:

Read the employee profiles and try to obtain secret authentication information (username + password) via a specific and non-dangerous communication channel.

After obtaining this information, attempt to gain physical access to the company in the second attack wave in order to upload and activate the malicious code undetected.

The results presentation thus offers you a valuable opportunity to be creative and free. This is the moment when you bring together your insights, learning outcomes, or experiences. There are, of course, no limits to artistic design or individual expression.

Now we come to our first game concept.

Our fictional company, which we as attackers aim to compromise using a combination of technical and human-centered techniques, is called *Victory Line GmbH*. The following diagram illustrates the organizational chart of Victory Line (Fig. 24.1) and at the same time represents the crime scene.

The organizational chart initially provides us with valuable insights into the composition of the physical and spatial units as well as the security barriers implemented in the company. On closer inspection, we are even able to identify vulnerable points, i.e., weaknesses, in order to plan possible on-site sabotage. But let us proceed step by step and address things in order.

Victory Line GmbH *is a cloud service provider.*

A cloud service provider is a company that delivers cloud computing services. Cloud computing enables companies and individuals to use resources such as computing power, storage, applications, and services over the internet instead of operating them locally on their own computers or servers.

A cloud service provider supplies the necessary infrastructure, platforms, and software to enable customers to access cloud services.

Cloud service providers are attractive targets for cyberattacks for the following reasons: they manage valuable data, have a large number of customers,

Organization chart of the Victory Line company:

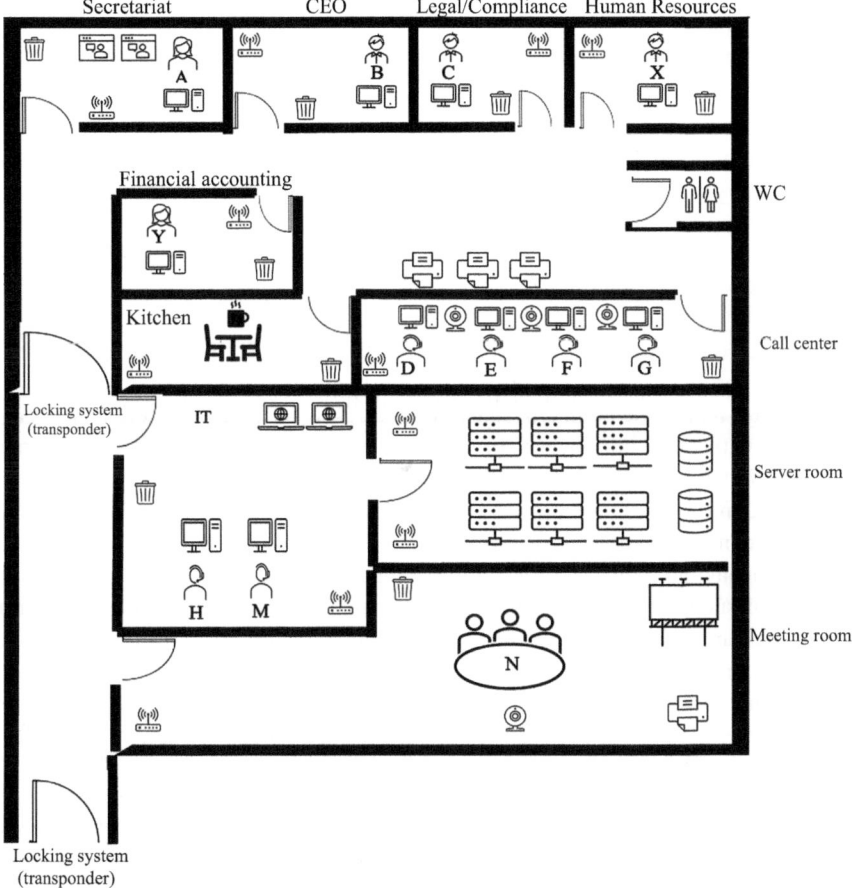

Fig. 24.1 Organizational chart Victory Line

offer potential access to many companies, possess extensive infrastructure and resources, and operate complex systems with potential vulnerabilities. Compromising a cloud service provider can therefore have direct consequences for multiple companies. For this reason, cloud service providers are increasingly becoming the primary target of attacks, as the potential impact is significant due to the large number of affected customers. In addition, higher ransom demands can be made, since the consequences would be felt by several companies at once. As a result, cloud service providers are increasingly at the center of, for example, ransomware attacks.

Our fictional cloud service provider thus plays a significant role for a total of 75 companies in the logistics sector. Among these customers are 25 A-level clients and 50 B-level clients, who benefit from Victory Line's logical and physical infrastructure to varying degrees. With a team of 11 employees, Victory Line generates annual revenue of €3 million (Table 24.1).

After gathering background information about the target company—including its industry, the number of employees in various departments, the security measures in the physical premises, and the access methods—we turn our attention to Ms. A, whom we as attackers need to infiltrate. With this information, we can proceed in a targeted manner and tailor our attack strategy to the vulnerabilities and potential entry points associated with this individual.

A precise understanding of her role, activities, and connections within the company enables us to define our attack objectives accurately and deploy effective tactics.

To achieve this, we identified Ms. A as our target individual and created a comprehensive profile of her. This profile provides detailed information about Ms. A, her position within the company, her tasks and responsibilities, as well as her relationships with other employees. In addition, we collected information about her personal preferences, hobbies, and interests to gain a complete picture of her.

By creating this detailed profile (Tab. 24.2), we are able to develop attack techniques and manipulation strategies specifically tailored to Ms. A. We can analyze her behaviors, vulnerabilities, and potential points of attack to maximize our chances of successful infiltration and compromise. By engaging intensively with Ms. A, we can better understand her mindset and behavioral patterns and adapt our attacks accordingly.

It is important to emphasize that this approach is used exclusively for educational purposes and within the context of a simulated scenario. The ethical aspects and legal boundaries of the "Design-an-Attack" concept must always be observed to ensure that the privacy and rights of the individuals involved are respected.

As the game progresses, we now receive the so-called attack cards, which specify which manipulation techniques, social engineering methods, and attack vectors must be used to design the attack on *Ms. A and Victory Line*.

The attack cards provide us with a structured guide for developing targeted tactics and strategies. They give us concrete instructions and help us plan and execute the attack precisely. Each attack card represents a specific technique, method, or

Tab. 24.1 Victory Line company profile

Number of employees	11
Business unit	Cloud computing provider
Annual revenue	€3 million
Number of customers	25 A-level clients and 50 B-level clients
Segment	Logistics sector as primary target group

Tab. 24.2 Victory Line profile of Ms. A

Name	A
Area of activity	Organization
Role	Executive Assistant
Responsibilities	Back office—organization Ad hoc requests Visitor management and Single Point of Contact (SPOC)
Specific IT expertise	None
Age	36
Education/Training	Commercial apprenticeship
Access rights (physical)	Everywhere
Access rights (IT)	Terminal PC in the secretariat
Permissions	For the applications released for A by IT (Outlook, MS Office, HR and Legal)
General information	A is very familiar with the individual applications and software provided to her by the IT department. She is responsible for organizational processes and acts as assistant to the management, handling scheduling, presentations, preparation for acquisitions, and managing visitors. Employees regard A as the heart and soul of the office and try to discuss both private and professional matters with her. A is active on social media channels and regularly posts about private and professional situations, sharing pleasant and sometimes informative anecdotes. For example, she recently posted about meeting the company's best client, Ms. K from "LoGO," in a private setting. Ms. K is also tagged in the photos. According to her Instagram account, she is 40 years old, works as a secretary for "LoGO," and serves as the SPOC (Single Point of Contact) for her organization. However, as Ms. K has recently been experiencing increasing health problems, she is being supported internally at LoGO by Mr. Q and Ms. W. Note: A specific area within the company "Victory Line" is not monitored.

attack vector that we can use to manipulate the target individual, obtain information, or exploit vulnerabilities in the system.

By following the attack cards, we ensure that we proceed systematically and do not overlook any important aspects of the attack. They serve as a guide to structure the process and steps of the attack and to ensure that we act effectively.

At the outset, we specifically identify the emotional and personal characteristics of the target individual **Ms. A** on the **Principle Card** that we wish to leverage for our attack.

Our goal is to combine and analyze the specific characteristics of the target individual—in this scenario, **helpfulness**—together with the detailed information from the profile (Fig. 24.2) in order to develop an effective approach. We take into

Fig. 24.2 Principle Card
"helpful"

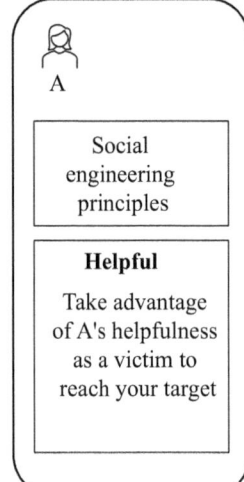

account her emotions, personal preferences, fears, or interests to find an attack strategy that targets her individual reactions and behaviors.

By focusing on the emotional and personal **level (Profile + Principle Card)** of the target individual, we can specifically address her motivations and needs. This enables us to establish a connection with her and gain the trust necessary for a successful attack.

Now the **Attack Cards** come into play, which specify the attack techniques and vectors that we may and must use to carry out the attack. Here are some examples of the available Attack Cards (Fig. 24.3).

Finally, we only need to determine which attack types we must use. This information is provided by the **Attack Type Cards**. These cards offer clear guidance on which specific attack types to employ and recommend appropriate procedures. By following the Attack Type Cards, we ensure that our attacks are defined and planned according to specified types and vectors (Fig. 24.4).

*A rootkit is a type of software designed to gain unauthorized and often covert access to an IT system. It consists of a collection of programs or scripts intended to integrate deeply into the operating system and obtain privileged access to all system functions. Rootkits are frequently used by malicious software such as viruses, trojans, or malware to operate undetected on a computer or network.

24.2 Trial Run

To make your approach simpler and more efficient, you will receive a universal game guide to help you better understand the game **Design an Attack—Red Teaming**:

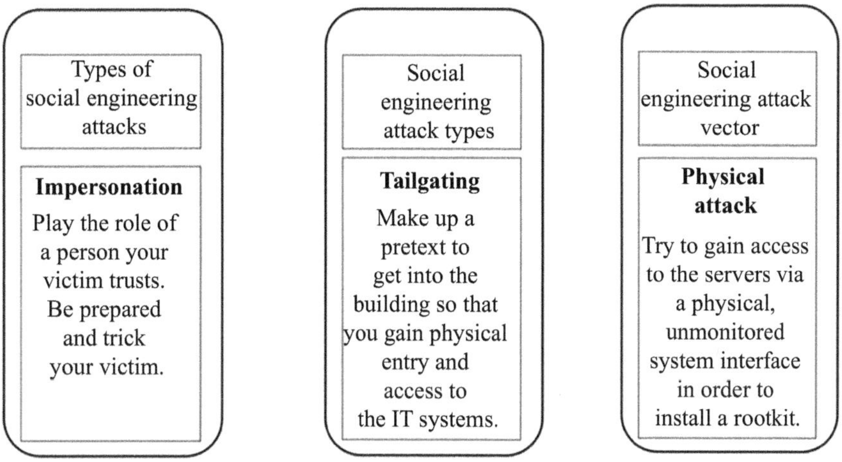

Types of social engineering attacks	Social engineering attack types	Social engineering attack vector
Impersonation Play the role of a person your victim trusts. Be prepared and trick your victim.	**Tailgating** Make up a pretext to get into the building so that you gain physical entry and access to the IT systems.	**Physical attack** Try to gain access to the servers via a physical, unmonitored system interface in order to install a rootkit.

Fig. 24.3 Attack Cards "Impersonation," "Tailgating," "Physical Attack"

Fig. 24.4 Attack Type Card "external attacker"

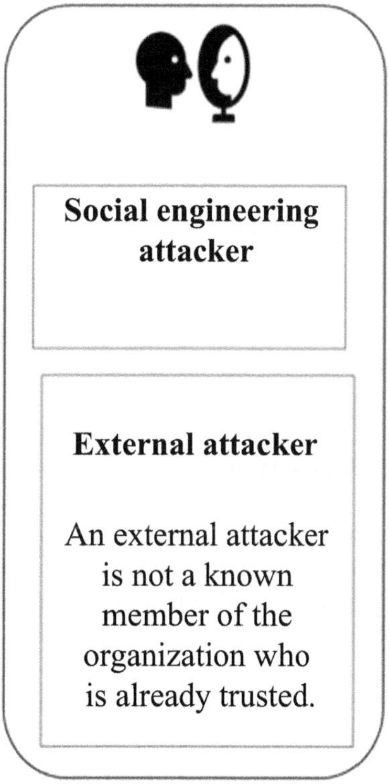

Social engineering attacker

External attacker

An external attacker is not a known member of the organization who is already trusted.

1. **There is no right or wrong. The focus is on the plausibility and feasibility of your scenario.** Therefore, study the organizational chart of Victory Line GmbH in detail to more precisely define the physical vulnerabilities and susceptible areas. Through thorough analysis, you can identify potential weaknesses and determine targeted physical attack objectives.
2. Read the **profile of Ms. A** carefully and try to connect the profile information with Ms. A's personal characteristics. Use this information to develop a better understanding of her motivations, preferences, or weaknesses.
3. The profile description provides valuable information that you may have obtained through the use of **OSINT and SOCMINT**. Use this information to specifically address the target individual and anticipate their reactions. You may also make your own assumptions if needed for your attack concept.
4. Link the information you have gathered with the **Attack Cards** and the **Attack Type Cards.** Consider whether there are meaningful ways to combine the cards to develop an effective attack plan.
5. **Take what you have learned into account.** Consider whether you can incorporate a deception mechanism, perception killer, a time factor, and one or more cover stories into your attack plan to increase your chances of success.
6. Work with the required level of granularity and delve into the details. Focus on the information available to you and develop your attack plan based on this. The more precise and detailed your approach, the greater your chances of success.

By following this guide, you will be well equipped to plan and execute your attack. However, always remember that the use of attack techniques and methods must comply with ethical principles and legal requirements.

To give you a better understanding of the game, we would now like to present a possible solution path before you dive into the game yourself. This solution serves as an example and is intended to help you better understand the various game mechanics and elements.

Please note, however, that there are many different approaches and solutions, and you are encouraged to develop your own (realistic) strategy and be creative. Let us now explore a possible solution path together before you embark on your own journey into the game.

Solution Approach
At the outset, we conduct a thorough physical vulnerability analysis, closely examining the physical and environmental perimeters. The focus is placed on potential weaknesses and security gaps in the physical infrastructure. We carefully analyze the individual units and their interactions to identify possible vulnerabilities and assess the company's physical security. This detailed analysis enables us to gain a comprehensive understanding of the physical weaknesses and, based on this, to derive further appropriate steps for attack planning. In the initial preparation phase and during the vulnerability analysis, we identify a total of four vulnerable (V) points that we can exploit (Fig. 24.5 and 24.6).

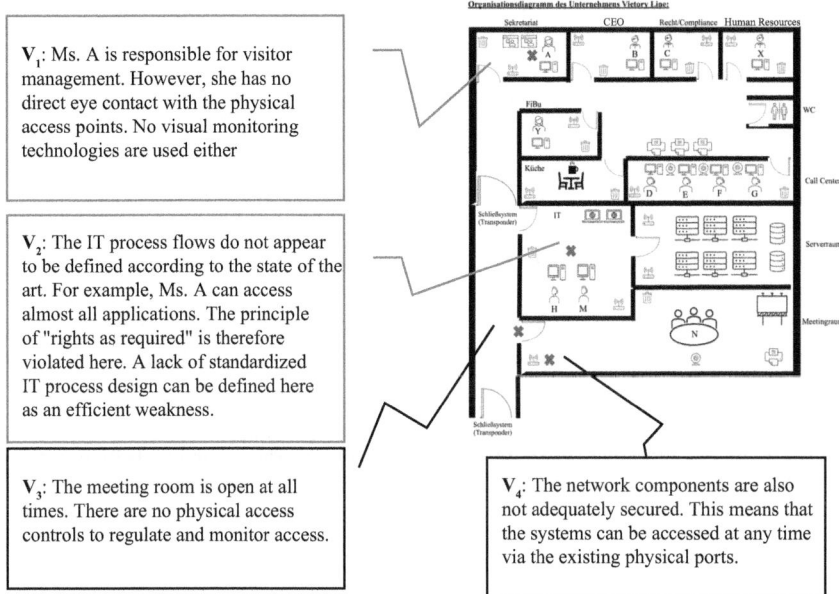

Fig. 24.5   Solution Approach V_1–V_4

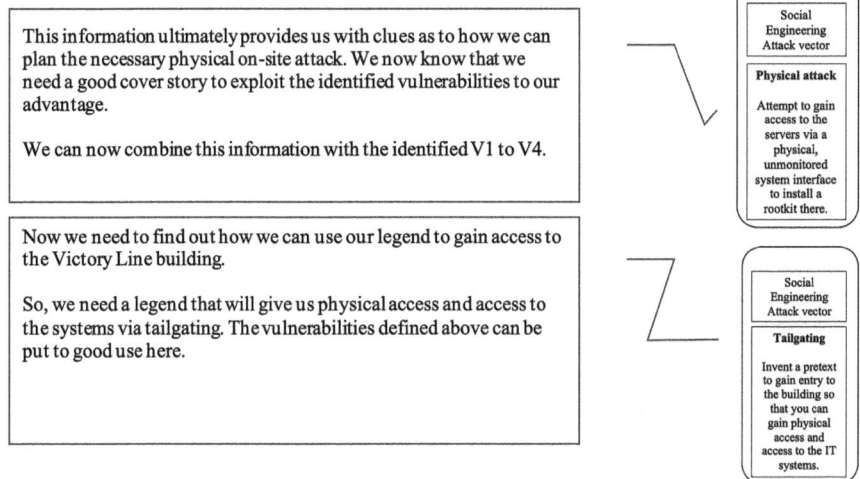

Fig. 24.6   Solution Approach "Physical Attack and Tailgating"

Next, we attempt to link the profile information with the human characteristics of Ms. A. By making this connection, we may be able to gather additional information relevant to carrying out the attack. Furthermore, it is also possible to combine this information with the remaining "Impersonation" card. By skillfully linking the profile information and personal traits of Ms. A with the contents of the remaining attack card, new avenues open up for further refining our attack plan (Fig. 24.7).

Through further in-depth research, the linked individuals, including **Ms. K,** are analyzed in greater detail. The websites of both companies are also thoroughly examined to obtain additional information about the respective areas of activity of the two individuals.

The results of this research phase reveal a close connection between **Ms. A and Ms. K**. The organizational units involved are in direct communication and can be defined as a Single Point of Contact (SPOC).

This means that the two individuals work closely together and serve as a central interface between the companies. It also becomes apparent that **Ms. K** is currently supported internally by two other employees.

Ms. Q and Mr. W are listed as deputies for **Ms. K**.

Based on the information obtained, we, as an external attacker (our assigned attack type), devise the following attack scenario:

We employ the social engineering method of **impersonation to obtain Ms. K's access credentials.** The attack is carried out as follows:

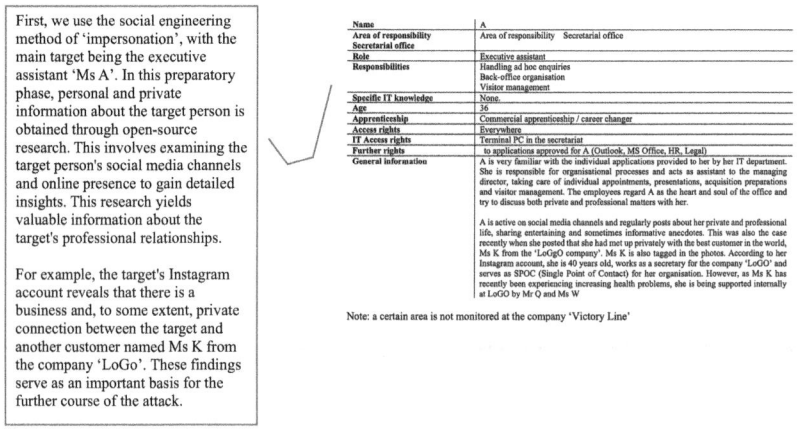

Fig. 24.7   Solution Approach Employee Profile

i) Ms. A is called at the phone number listed on the website of the company Victory Line GmbH.

ii) The timing of the call is set to **a Tuesday in December at 8:05 a.m.**

iii) We pose as **Mr. W** from the company "LoGO." In this case, the "Impersonation" method is embedded and executed as part of a vishing attack (Figs. 24.8, 24.9, 24.10, 24.11, 24.12, 24.13, and 24.14).

iv) Mr. W thanks her for the quick assistance and calls Ms. A a **lifesaver in an emergency.**

With this, we have successfully completed our first attack objective using the social engineering method of impersonation, namely to obtain the login credentials of Ms. K.

In the next step, we observe the premises of Victory Line to identify both regular and irregular physical access points. As attackers, our only option for physical entry into the building is through the main entrance door.

The attack method used here is "tailgating." Since the entrance door is secured with an electronic locking system, we must first gain legitimate access to the building under a plausible pretext. For this purpose, we disguise ourselves as a **DHL courier.**

📅 Tuesday in December

🕐 08:05

Good morning dear Ms. A. This is Mr. W from the company "LoGO". I'm standing in for Mrs. K at short notice today.

Good morning Mr. W, what has happened and how can I help you?

You'll notice that we've even chosen the right time of year and time of day for our legend. Because a good social engineer leaves nothing to chance. A very good one even checks every step.

Abb. 24.8 Dialogue between Ms. A and Mr. W—Part 1

Abb. 24.9 Dialogue between Ms. A and Mr. W—Part 2

From the job description in Ms. A's profile, we learn that she is also responsible for visitor management. Therefore, we initially assume that we can specifically exploit Ms. A in our upcoming attack.

Our attack plan is based on combining the "tailgating" attack method with the "physical attack" vector and is carried out as follows:

i) *The supposed DHL courier rings the central entrance doorbell at the Victory Line company at 2:00 p.m. on a Friday.*

ii) Ms. A answers the request.

iii) The pretext given is the delivery of a package for the Victory Line company.

Abb. 24.10 Dialogue between Ms. A and Mr. W—Part 3

We deliberately include the time factor here. The time factor is intended to represent an additional subliminal pressure here - but this essentially has an indirect effect on Ms. A, because the actual time pressure to complete the work affects Mr. W only.
Nonetheless, this indirect time factor creates a feeling of stress, which is also perceived subconsciously by Ms A. Our second perception killer "stress" is now also on its way.

Abb. 24.11 Dialogue between Ms. A and Mr. W—Part 4

Abb. 24.12 Dialogue between Ms. A and Mr. W—Part 5

iv) **Ms. A** opens the entrance door using the electronic locking system.

 v) The attacker thus gains access to the office premises of Victory Line. Upon entering, the attacker notices that the meeting room is accessible to everyone without any additional access controls.

vi) To avoid drawing unnecessary attention, the attacker first goes to Ms. A. In doing so, he must overcome the second access barrier. He rings again, and the request is once more directed to Ms. A, who is expecting the DHL courier. Ms. A grants the attacker entry. The attacker enters Ms. A's office and hands her the supposed package.

vii) The package is presented as a personal item for management, "Attn: Mr. B." A personal signature from Ms. A is not required due to the new procedures introduced during the Covid-19 pandemic.

viii) Ms. A accepts the package and then says goodbye to the DHL courier.

The success of a cyber attack rarely depends on a single vulnerability. Rather, it requires a careful concatenation of several vulnerabilities in order to successfully carry out an attack. This insight is also evident here: it is the interplay of various vulnerabilities that ultimately leads to a successful human-based cyber attack. Our ingredients for this: Ms. A can be described as the good soul of the office, which means that she enjoys a respected position (informally) internally among the employees. This means that the employees in the IT department are also willing to meet Ms A's requirements quickly. This informal relationship with our defined V4 leads us to success.

Note: If we later want to define the so-called kill chains for this scenario, we should use precisely these weak points **(V1 to V4)** to define and implement defensive measures.

Abb. 24.13   Dialogue between Ms. A and Mr. M

This clearly shows that we as attackers have incorporated strategic dynamism and flexibility into our attack. It is precisely this dynamic and agile approach that is the key to the success of a professional human hacker. Such a hacker has a well-founded main strategy as well as several alternative strategies. In addition, he always has one or more suitable exit strategies ready to end the conversation inconspicuously and conclude the attack without suspicion.

Abb. 24.14 Dialogue between Ms. A and Mr. W—Part 6

ix) As he leaves, the courier asks Ms. A to remain seated, as he already knows the way. "It's not a maze, Ms. A, I just have to go straight out. I'll find my way. Thank you very much for your help in accepting the package."

x) On his way out, the attacker is able to enter the meeting room unnoticed and without the employees' awareness.

xi) In the meeting room, there is a network device that is also unattended and freely accessible.

xii) With physical access to the network component (unattended physical ports of the network devices), the attacker connects to the internal IT network of Victory Line without being noticed.

xiii) To do this, he uses Ms. K's login credentials via the authentication interface and verifies and authorizes himself as an external end user at the system level.

xiv) He then uploads the malware and installs the "user-mode rootkit." Once integrated into the system, the rootkit uses "stealth" techniques to conceal its presence. As a result, antivirus programs only receive falsified information during scans, with any relevant details and indicators of the rootkit filtered out. After successful installation, the rootkit sets up an additional piece of malware, a "backdoor," to enable future remote access to the computer.

xv) Through the integrated backdoor program, another piece of malware, "ransomware," is installed, which arbitrarily encrypts data records, rendering them inaccessible for regular use.

xvi) And finally, our ransom note appears (Fig. 24.15).

From: RabitHole (RabitHole)
To: herr.b@victory-line.de
Cc:
Bcc:
Subject: You have been hacked.

Dear Mr B,

We deeply regret to inform you that your sensitive files have been encrypted and are now in our possession. In order to regain access to your important information, we are demanding a ransom of €545,000.

We have opted for payment in Bitcoin, as this is a secure and anonymous method that allows us to process the transaction discreetly. Please ensure that the amount is transferred to the Bitcoin account below within 48 hours:

Bitcoin address: 1A1zP1eP5QGefi2DMPTfffTL$$Lmv7DivlNa

Please note that we will irrevocably delete the data after the deadline if payment is not made on time. We would like to point out that any attempts to cooperate with law enforcement agencies or contact IT security companies will lead to further complications.

We strongly recommend that you take this demand seriously and comply with it within the specified deadline to prevent permanent loss of your data. If you have any questions or difficulties with payment, we are not available to offer support or negotiate.

Please note that we expect your full cooperation and discretion. Any unauthorised disclosure of this communication or the information involved will result in serious consequences.

We hope for a smooth and swift resolution of this matter.

Kind regards

Your unknown sender 'RabitHole'

Fig. 24.15 Ransom note

24.3 Design an Attack

Now that we have provided you with a detailed insight into working through a fictional scenario, it is your turn to get involved and independently design the next attack scenario. You are now invited to apply your skills and creativity to develop your own scenario. Take this opportunity to further deepen your knowledge and strengthen your capabilities in attack simulation. We look forward to your ideas and wish you every success in designing the next scenario (Fig. 24.16, Table 24.3, and 24.4).

Procedure
i) Put yourself in the position of the attacker (attacker type).
ii) Combine the specified human behaviors with the two given attack methods and attack vectors. Proceed as follows:

a) Read the employee profile and attempt to carry out the attack using the specified attack type. Use the **Attack Card Baiting.** Important note: Ensure that the attack can be executed technically.
b) After executing the attack, initiate an anonymous email and demand a specific ransom amount.
c) Your demand should include the threat that, if the ransom is not paid, you will disclose the incident to the press.

Human Behavior M is assigned a dedicated human behavior (Fig. 24.17).

Scenario:

Please design a dedicated attack scenario in which the following features are integrated and described:

Organizational chart of the Victory Line company:

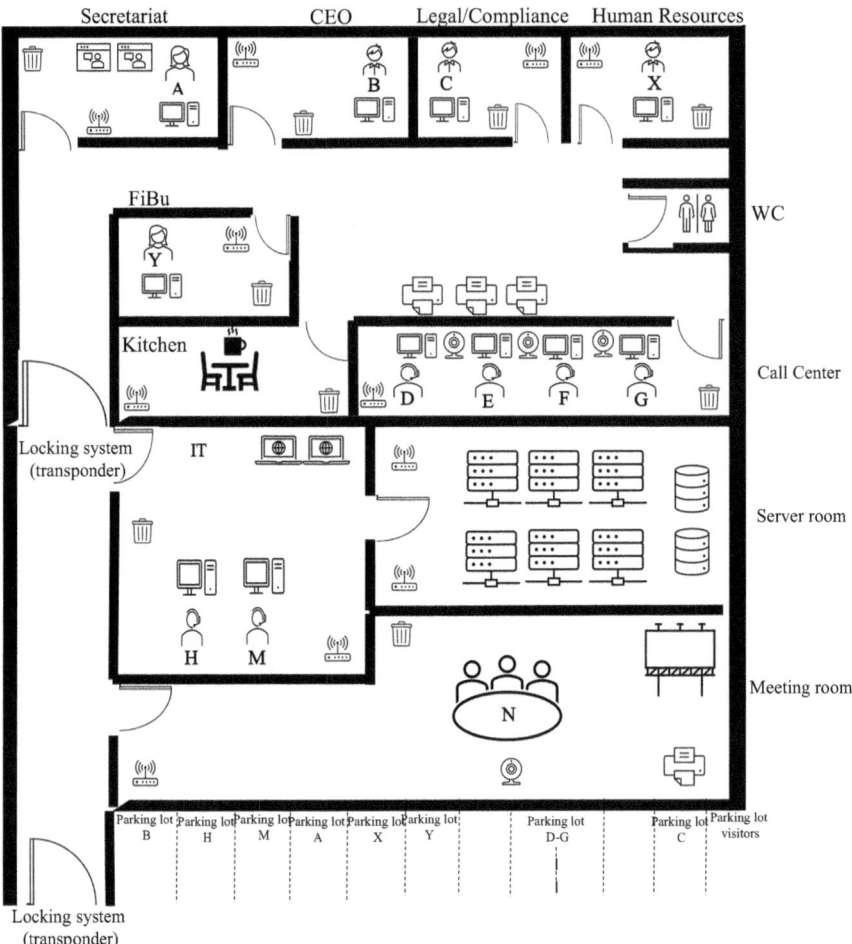

Fig. 24.16 Organizational chart "Design an Attack"

Table 24.3 Fictional company profile

Number of employees	11
Business unit	Cloud computing provider
Annual revenue	€3 million
Number of customers	25 A-customers and 50 B-customers
Segment	Logistics sector as primary target group

Table 24.4 Profile of Mr. H

Name	H
Department	IT department
Role	IT admin
Responsibilities	System administration Software maintenance and configuration Identity Access Management Network Access Control IT support (levels 1 to 3) Data center operations
Specific IT expertise	Yes
Age	45
Education/training	IT specialist
Physical access rights	Everywhere
System access rights	System and application level (everywhere)
Data access rights	System and application level (everywhere)
General information	H is very familiar with the individual applications and IT systems provided to the employees of Victory Line by the IT department. In addition, H is also responsible for data center operations and administers both the logical software components and the hardware components of Victory Line. H is also responsible for IT incident management processes and acts at the 1st, 2nd, and 3rd levels of support processes. He receives incidents via the hotline, initiates immediate response, and, if necessary, also handles on-site support processes to administer customer systems. Although H and M have the same areas of responsibility and workload, H earns significantly less than M. This creates a persistently dissatisfying situation for H. After an internal discussion with management, Mr. B, his request for a salary increase is denied. H considers this behavior unfair. Since H and M have a good collegial relationship, H tries to discuss his perspective with M. M does not agree with H's view and claims that he contributes much more than H, which greatly annoys H. Through his observations, H notices that Victory Line has gained more than 20 A-customers in the past two years, increasing its revenue by 40%. H is becoming increasingly dissatisfied at work, particularly with his supervisor Mr. B and his long-time colleague Mr. M. He perceives a significant discrepancy in his career progression, especially when comparing himself to Mr. M. During the design and integration of the IT system landscape, the two administrators decided against decentralized system logging. As a result, system logs and individual system commands (e.g., System Event Manager) are stored and retained centrally.

Attack Methods To exploit M as a vulnerability, you must use the two specified scenarios (attack types as social engineering methods) in a two-stage attack vector (physical attack) (Fig. 24.18).

Fig. 24.17 Principle Card
"Curiosity"

M

Social
engineering
principles

Curiosity

Exploit M's
curiosity as a
victim to reach
your target

Social
engineering
attack types

Baiting

Baiting involves
preparing a USB stick
so that it infects the
computer with malware
when it is used. Place
the storage medium
in a prominent location.

Social
engineering
attack vector

**Internal
attacks**

Try to compromise
information and data
via the "internal
attacks" vector on
the intranet by
infiltrating the
system with a Trojan*.

Fig. 24.18 Attack Cards "Baiting" and "Insider Attacks"

*The Trojan, also known as the Trojan horse, derives its name from Greek mythology. It refers to an application or a hidden malicious function that masquerades as a useful program. In addition to the well-known features that serve as a disguise, there are functions that are executed without the user's knowledge. The Trojan horse does not spread by itself but is installed by the user. This type of malware can only be detected by Trojan scanners, as the hidden programs are embedded in the code. Many Trojans hide behind seemingly attractive software offers, leading users to unwittingly download the software from an unknown source.

Attacker Type

Below is the Attack Type Card for the insider attacker (Fig. 24.19).

The following game objectives should be achieved:

Combine the specified information and cards. In a single attack wave, proceed as follows:

a) Read the employee profiles and attempt to place the pre-prepared USB stick in such a way, using a specific and non-threatening contact method, that it will be found by the target.

Fig. 24.19 Attack Type Card
"Insider Attacker"

Social engineering attacker

Internal attacker

An internal attacker
is a known member of
the organization who
is already trusted.

b) Keep in mind that small nuances—such as the appearance of the USB stick, the timing of the attack, and the type of attack method—must be carefully planned and executed.

c) When reconstructing the attack, there must be no evidence that can be traced back to you as the attacker. Therefore, consider how you will cover your physical and logical tracks.

Part V
Green Chapter: The Art of Holistic Defense

Hell is Other People... **25**

The famous statement, "Hell is other people," originates from Jean-Paul Sartre and appears in his play "No Exit" ("Huis clos"). In this work, published in 1944, Sartre presents a bleak vision of hell, characterized not by physical torment, but by relentless surveillance, judgment, and confrontation with other people.

In "No Exit," three characters are placed in a windowless room after death, where they realize that they are not being tortured by demons, but that they themselves are each other's tormentors and judges. Hell consists in the fact that the characters are forced to remain in each other's company forever, without the possibility of escape or privacy.

Sartre's statement emphasizes the difficulties and torments that can arise from social relationships and the constant presence of others. Hell is not created by external forces, but by interpersonal dynamics and conflicts. Each character is both victim and perpetrator, and the inescapability of social interactions is depicted as agonizing.

This philosophical perspective can be applied in our context to underscore the importance of the methods, strategies, and tactics we present. By outlining ways to protect oneself from social manipulation, we simultaneously offer a response to the potential "hell" that can arise from interpersonal relationships. Our work aims to enable positive change within the social fabric and to prevent a "hell" of manipulation and deception.

By promoting a culture of healthy skepticism and awareness of various social manipulation strategies, the techniques presented enable individuals to critically examine their interpersonal relationships. This critical awareness not only contributes to increased security, but also fosters self-knowledge and a better understanding of one's own actions and reactions in social situations.

Self-reflection, mindfulness, and conscious pause become key components not only for protecting oneself from potential attacks, but also for possibly leading a more pleasant life. As people learn to question their emotions, thoughts, and

E. Koza et al., *Social Engineering and Human Hacking*, https://doi.org/10.1007/978-3-662-72084-4_25

actions, they can establish a deeper connection with themselves and with others, and largely free themselves from the negative influences of social manipulation.

Someone who consciously engages with the techniques of self-reflection is not only able to recognize and avoid potentially dangerous situations, but is also better equipped to build authentic and meaningful relationships. The ability for self-reflection not only enhances security, but also leads to a more fulfilling life by fostering deeper self-acceptance and a more mindful approach to others.

The defense strategies we present emphasize not only the importance of verbal communication, but also that of nonverbal and paraverbal communication, as well as interpersonal dynamics. In a social context where every action, every word, and every gesture can be considered communication, it becomes clear that the approaches presented are based not only on avoiding attacks, but also on communicating consciously and effectively.

The principle, "One cannot not communicate," formulated by Paul Watzlawick, highlights that every form of behavior conveys a message, even silence. In the context of our protective measures, this means that awareness of one's own communication and the ability to interpret the signals of others are essential not only for protecting oneself from manipulation, but also for building authentic and clear relationships.

By integrating communication skills into defense strategies, individuals can not only recognize potential dangers, but also actively contribute to fostering positive social interactions. Conscious and clear communication thus becomes an additional means of protection against manipulation, while at the same time laying the foundation for successful interpersonal communication.

CISOs and ISOs Must Be Able to Communicate…   **26**

CISOs (Chief Information Security Officers) and ISOs (Information Security Officers) play a critical role in a company's security architecture [1]. Their communication skills are of paramount importance, as they require not only technical and organizational expertise but also the ability to effectively convey complex security concepts and communicate with various stakeholders.

Internal communication requires the ability to present complex security concepts in a way that is understandable to different target groups within the company. This may include the executive board, IT teams, employees, and other departments. The ability to translate security-related details into clear language is essential for the successful and practical implementation of security strategies.

Communication with the executive board requires a clear presentation of the security strategy in the context of corporate objectives. CISOs must be able to present security risks and measures in financial and business terms in order to secure the board's support and resources.

External communication with partners, regulatory authorities, or the public is also important. CISOs must be able to effectively explain security practices and measures to build trust among customers, partners, and the public.

In the event of security incidents, CISOs and ISOs must be able to implement a clear and comprehensive communication strategy. This includes collaborating with PR teams, legal departments, and other relevant parties to protect the company's reputation.

The ability to develop and conduct training and awareness programs is also crucial. CISOs must be able to convey the importance of security to employees at all levels and implement awareness-raising initiatives.

To ensure the successful implementation of security concepts, it is essential for CISOs and ISOs to act not only as technology experts but also as effective communicators. They face the challenge of not only explaining the technical aspects of security policies but also conveying a broader perspective. This includes the

E. Koza et al., *Social Engineering and Human Hacking*,
https://doi.org/10.1007/978-3-662-72084-4_26

impact on employees' daily work, fostering a security-conscious culture, and promoting collective responsibility for security issues.

Persuasion plays a key role in this context. CISOs must master the art of persuasion by not only arguing logically and professionally, but also addressing the emotional aspects of employees, such as their fears. For example: What happens to me if I make a mistake? Or what happens if I report an error? Will I face consequences?

Various communication and negotiation strategies are employed here, aimed at fostering understanding and involving employees in the security process.

Transforming security concepts into tangible actions therefore requires clear and precise communication. CISOs should be able to translate complex technical concepts into messages that are easily understood. These messages must not only emphasize the necessity of security measures but also highlight the benefits for employees.

The implementation of security concepts should not be seen as a mere directive, but as a dialogue between CISOs and employees. Open channels of communication allow employees to voice concerns, ask questions, and actively participate in the security process. This fosters a culture of mutual understanding and collaboration.

At this point, the methods we have presented make a significant contribution to developing a more effective communication strategy. By fostering empathy for employees and understanding how social engineering works, those responsible can purposefully initiate and guide communication within the organization. This enables a holistic preparation of the organization for upcoming threat scenarios.

Ultimately, the goal is to create a security culture in which employees are not merely recipients of instructions, but active participants in shaping the security of their work environment. CISOs play a decisive role in establishing this culture and must continuously develop their communication skills to meet the dynamic demands of digital security.

References

1. Erfan Koza, Information Security Awareness and Training as a Holistic Key Factor—How Can a Human Firewall Take on a Complementary Role in Information Security? In: *13th International Conference on Applied Human Factors and Ergonomics (AHFE 2022), Human Factors in Cybersecurity*, Vol. 53, New York, USA, S. 49–57.

Key to Success 1: "Security Culture"

27

The implementation and maintenance of a robust security culture within an organization is essential for effective protection against cyber threats. Technical safeguards can be deployed almost immediately to secure the system.

In contrast, strengthening the human firewall—which relies on awareness, training, and culture—requires continuous and long-term investment.

A concrete example in this context is the use of an intrusion detection system (IDS) or the installation of a security door. These technological measures can be put into operation quickly and contribute immediately to the organization's security. By contrast, raising employee awareness and providing security training, fostering understanding, and developing effective defense mechanisms against threats require a longer-term perspective.

Activating the technical firewall happens instantly—whereas activating the human firewall takes time, continuity, and training.

The analogy between technical measures, such as the rapid activation of a firewall, and the development of a human firewall highlights the difference in the time required for effectiveness to begin.

Have you ever wondered why Coca-Cola continues to invest millions in marketing and advertising, even though the "Coca-Cola" brand enjoys unparalleled recognition and is known virtually everywhere in the world?

The answer lies in the volatility of the circumstances and environments in which Coca-Cola operates. This market volatility results from emerging competitors, changes in competitors' strategies, shifting consumer behavior, and other factors. Coca-Cola's marketing strategy ultimately aims to further consolidate its already established market position through continuity and repetition. The guiding principle is: Once anchored in long-term memory, it is essential to remain present there.

The same analogy applies to volatility in information security. Attack types, attack vectors, and the tactics of human hackers change, AI is used for OSINT,

E. Koza et al., *Social Engineering and Human Hacking*, https://doi.org/10.1007/978-3-662-72084-4_27

or new business processes emerge—such as the sudden shift to remote work due to the COVID-19 pandemic—and virtual meetings become increasingly relevant. Just as people and hackers adapt their strategies to new circumstances, the constantly evolving threat landscape requires continuous adaptation of security measures.

Therefore, the security situation in the world of information security is continuously shaped by adjustments to new challenges and developments. This approach underscores the importance of continuity in information security in order to remain effectively prepared for evolving threats over the long term.

It is therefore important to recognize that developing a sustainable security culture is time-intensive and requires ongoing investment. Unlike technical and organizational approaches, which can deliver short-term results, integrating security practices among employees is an individual and collective process that can take months or even years.

Continuity, as well as training and education initiatives, play a crucial role in consolidating a security culture. Emphasizing continuity ensures that security awareness and practices are not only temporary but are sustainably embedded within the organizational structure. This understanding is central to establishing the necessary foundations for an effective security culture that can dynamically adapt to changing threat scenarios.

Key to Success 2: Holism

28

When examining the digital battlefield between system defenders and attackers, it becomes clear that we are operating within a sociotechnical system in the context of an organization, where all elements of the triangulation converge. It would therefore be misleading to believe that an isolated technical security strategy is sufficient to adequately protect our networks, applications, and data.

Rather, the key to success lies in the ability to align these layers and to develop a defense concept capable of implementing all three aspects both in depth and breadth.

The effective design of such a defense concept requires a holistic approach in which all security aspects are coordinated. The alignment of IT security, organizational security, and human security practices not only ensures comprehensive and integrated protection, but also establishes an adequate line of defense. A successful triangulation, in which technical, organizational, and human aspects interact harmoniously, thus forms the foundation for effective threat mitigation.

A well-orchestrated ensemble of various defense mechanisms ensures that your organization is adequately prepared against diverse attack vectors.

This approach reflects the understanding that securing our digital resources depends not only on technical solutions, but also on the thoughtful integration of organizational processes and human defense practices. By purposefully coordinating these elements, we create a resilient line of defense against the multifaceted challenges in the field of information security.

© The Author(s), under exclusive license to Springer-Verlag GmbH, DE, part of
Springer Nature 2025
E. Koza et al., *Social Engineering and Human Hacking*,
https://doi.org/10.1007/978-3-662-72084-4_28

A Day in the Life of a Hacker

29

Design an Attack, or in other words, "a day in the life of a hacker," offers a fascinating perspective that provides deep insights into the mindset and methods of attackers. The principle of designing an attack by putting oneself in the position of the attacker is fundamental to developing sustainable defense strategies in the field of information security.

The ability to adopt a hacker's perspective enables security professionals and experts, as well as ordinary system users and operators, to identify and understand vulnerabilities and potential attack vectors from the attacker's point of view. This approach goes beyond traditional security concepts and requires a thorough understanding of the methods, motivations, and techniques employed by hackers.

By putting oneself in the attacker's position, one can better comprehend how a potential attacker thinks and acts. This makes it possible to better understand security practices, detect possible anomalies more quickly, and develop preventive measures to fend off potential attacks.

Exploring a day in the life of a hacker in this book, as defined by our gamification approach, provides valuable insights into the different phases of an attack, from information gathering and planning to execution. This understanding is crucial for developing appropriate countermeasures and strengthening lines of defense.

Overall, the principle of "Design an Attack" makes it clear that effective defense against cyberattacks requires a proactive and holistic understanding of attack methods. By putting themselves in the attacker's shoes, users and security experts lay a solid foundation for developing and implementing robust security strategies that can withstand ever-evolving threats.

E. Koza et al., *Social Engineering and Human Hacking*,
https://doi.org/10.1007/978-3-662-72084-4_29

Conclusion of the Book

30

In this comprehensive overview of the world of "Social Engineering and Human Hacking," we have not only analyzed the tactics and techniques, but also gained deeper insight into the connection between people and security. The guiding principle that information security cannot be achieved without considering the holistic triangulation of human, technical, and organizational factors represents a key aspect.

The diversity of attack techniques examined, based on findings from communication and linguistics, psychology, security engineering, economics, and other disciplines, provides a holistic foundation for understanding social engineering.

This book not only invites readers to protect themselves against the dangers of social engineering, but also to use the knowledge gained as tools for improving interpersonal relationships. It opens doors to a deeper understanding of the pitfalls, offers countermeasures, and at the same time inspires more conscious and enriching communication.

The journey through the complexity of "Social Engineering and Human Hacking" concludes not only with an expanded understanding of digital security, but also with a richer set of tools for deepening interpersonal relationships. May this book not only open your eyes to the complexity of digital threats, but also open doors to deeper and more fulfilling human interaction.

In conclusion, we would like to share the following with you and also ask for your support: As you may have noticed, we have attempted to illustrate the sometimes theory-heavy topics with vivid and practical examples. If we have succeeded, our examples possess, in accordance with Klafki, an exemplary, contemporary, and forward-looking significance. With their help, we aim to highlight various dimensions and facets of social engineering and human hacking.

In this context, we would also like to emphasize that knowledge can only be considered good and meaningful when it is shared. Therefore, as authors, we would like to build this bridge to you so that we can continue to learn from each

E. Koza et al., *Social Engineering and Human Hacking*, https://doi.org/10.1007/978-3-662-72084-4_30

other. Using the following email address, you have the opportunity to a) send us your gamification results and request feedback if you are interested, and b) take the opportunity to share your opinions and suggestions for improvement with us, and perhaps also tell us your own story on the topic of social engineering. For knowledge is enriched through exchange.

We look forward to your feedback and wish you much success.

E-mail: socialengineeringfeedback@gmail.com